NAMING THE MIND

HOW PSYCHOLOGY FOUND ITS LANGUAGE

KURT DANZIGER

SAGE Publications
London • Thousand Oaks • New Delhi

SAGE Publications Ltd
6 Bonhill Street
London EC2A 4PU

SAGE Publications Inc.
2455 Teller Road
Thousand Oaks, California 91320

SAGE Publications India Pvt Ltd
32, M-Block Market
Greater Kailash – I
New Delhi 110 048

British Library Cataloguing in Publication data

A catalogue record for this book is available
from the British Library.

ISBN 0 8039 7762-X
ISBN 0 8039 7763-8 (pbk)

Library of Congress catalog record available

Typeset by Mayhew Typesetting, Rhayader, Powys

CONTENTS

ACKNOWLEDGEMENTS

This book includes three paragraphs from my chapter, 'The practice of psychological discourse', in K.J. Gergen and C.F. Graumann (eds), *Historical Dimensions of Psychological Discourse*, Cambridge University Press, 1996; and five paragraphs from my chapter, 'The historical formation of selves', in R.D. Ashmore and L. Jussim (eds), *Self and Identity: Fundamental Issues*, Oxford University Press, 1997. These sources are gratefully acknowledged.

1

NAMING THE MIND

Alternative psychologies

Many years ago, before Kuhnian paradigms had ever been heard of, I spent two years teaching Psychology at an Indonesian university. When I arrived to take up my duties, I discovered that a course on Psychology was already being taught by one of my Indonesian colleagues. But whereas my subject matter was identified on the timetable as *Psychologi*, his was identified by the Indonesian equivalent, *ilmu djiwa*, 'djiwa' meaning 'soul' or 'psyche', and 'ilmu' being a science or an '-ology' of some kind. So there was a literal local equivalent of 'psychology', but I was not the one scheduled to teach it. I soon found out why. What my colleague was teaching was not Western psychology, but something based on an extensive local literature that had roots in Hindu philosophy with Javanese additions and reinterpretations. So the students had a choice of two psychologies, one Western and one Eastern.

At the time, that struck me as odd. After all, if both my Indonesian colleague and I were dealing with psychological reality, there ought to be some points of contact, even convergence, between our domains. Certainly, our ways of approaching this reality were very different, but that difference might perhaps be used constructively, if we could combine the strong features of both approaches. So I rashly suggested to my colleague that we consider offering joint seminars in which each of us would explain our approach to the same set of psychological topics, followed by an analysis of our differences. Very politely, he agreed to my proposal, and we sat down to discuss the topics we would cover in such a seminar. That is where the problems began. There seemed to be virtually no topics that were identified as such both in his and in my psychology.

For instance, I wanted to discuss the topic of motivation and was interested in hearing what theories my colleague might offer about how motives operated and developed. But he said that would be quite difficult for him, because from his point of view motivation was not really a topic. The phenomena that I quite spontaneously grouped together as 'motivational' seemed to him to be no more than a heterogeneous collection of things that had nothing interesting in common.

This simply was not a domain he could recognize as a good candidate for a unifying theory. Of course, some of my examples of 'motivational' phenomena would remind him of issues that he did consider important, and he could talk about those; but then, unfortunately, he would no longer be discussing 'motivation'. He would be forced to change the topic. He had a few topics he could suggest – how about devoting a seminar to each of them? That took me aback, for his topics were not only unfamiliar to me, I found his description of them hard to follow. They did not seem to me to constitute natural domains, and the questions to which they led seemed to be based on assumptions I could not share. Then he pointed out that I too was making a few assumptions which he found equally difficult to accept. In drawing up our list of topics and in formulating our questions about them we were both taking a lot for granted, but agreement on what was to be taken for granted proved quite elusive. It became obvious that if we were to have a joint seminar it would quickly turn into a discussion of philosophical, not psychological, issues. That was not what I had had in mind.

Perhaps motivation was a bad topic to begin with. I tried other topics: intelligence, learning, and so on. But the result was the same. My colleague would not recognize any of them as domains clearly marked off from other domains. He granted that each of them had some common features, but he regarded these features as trivial or as artificial and arbitrary. Grouping psychological phenomena in this way seemed to him to be, not only unnatural, but a sure way of avoiding all the interesting questions. Similarly, I could do nothing with the topics he proposed; in many cases I failed to see the *point* of asking the questions he wanted to ask. Regretfully, we reached an impasse. The seminar series never happened. If there is a way of planning and publicizing such a series without an agreed list of topics and issues, it eluded us.

Now, I must emphasize that my Indonesian colleague's stand was not idiosyncratic. He represented a coherent set of ideas embodied in a significant tradition of texts and practices. The latter included various forms of meditational and ascetic practice that could be employed to produce specific psychological phenomena as reliably – and perhaps more reliably – as many of our psychological experiments. The concepts of *ilmu djiwa* embraced these phenomena among others. This *other* Psychology could not be dismissed as armchair speculation; it was surely a discipline in the double sense of the term, as a body of systematic knowledge and of strictly regulated practices. Yet neither the organization of its knowledge nor the practices it favoured had much in common with their counterparts in Western psychology.

Being confronted with my own discipline's exotic *Doppelgänger* was an unsettling experience. It was clearly possible to carve up the field of psychological phenomena in very different ways and still end up with a set of concepts that seemed quite natural, given the appropriate cultural context. Moreover, these different sets of concepts could each make perfect practical sense, if one was allowed to choose one's practices. What did that imply for the objectivity of the categories with which Western psychology operated? Did my list of seminar topics represent a 'true' reflection of how Nature had divided up the psychological realm? In that case, my colleague's alternative would seem to be a grossly distorted reflection, at best. He certainly did not think so, and neither did his students. To be honest, neither of us had any empirical justification for making the distinctions we did, or perhaps we both had. We could both point to certain practical results, but they were results we had produced on the basis of the preconceptions we were committed to. We knew how to identify whatever presented itself in experience because we each had a conceptual apparatus in place that enabled us to do this. The apparatus itself, however, seemed to be empirically incorrigible.

My experience in Indonesia was not unique. Some time later, I came across a book, entitled *Mencius on the Mind*, by the well known literary and linguistic scholar, I.A. Richards (1932). In 1930 Richards had spent some time at the University of 'Peking' (as it was then known in the West) and had been made aware of the psychological content of some of the old Chinese texts. In particular, some writings of the philosopher Meng Tzu, quaintly westernized as 'Mencius', seemed to present a coherent body of psychological concepts. What intrigued Richards was the fact that these concepts had no modern equivalents. For instance, there were terms which he ended up translating as 'mind' and as 'will', yet he is quite clear about the fact that they do not represent what we mean by those terms. Another term seemed to mean both 'feelings' and 'propensities', which to us are quite different. So here was an alternative psychology that divided up its subject matter in a completely different way from our own.

That led to some serious questioning of the basis for the psychological distinctions we tend to accept without question:

> Chinese thinking often gives no attention to distinctions which for Western minds are so traditional and so firmly established in thought and language, that we neither question them nor even become aware of them *as distinctions*. We receive and use them as though they belonged unconditionally to the constitution of things (or of thought). We forget that these distinctions have been made and maintained as part of one tradition of thinking; and that another tradition of thinking might neither find use for them nor (being committed to other courses) be able to admit them. (Richards, 1932: 3–4)

Such considerations led Richards (1932: 81) to note that 'Western psychology has unduly refrained from examining and criticizing its own basic hypotheses'. The distinctions embodied in these hypotheses are based on convention, not on undistorted observation, for we can only 'see' what our 'framework of conceptions' allows us to see.[1] It is difficult to escape such reflections when confronted with alternative frameworks for organizing psychological knowledge and experience. Certainly, while teaching in Indonesia, I could never forget that mine was only one *possible* psychology.

The other possible psychologies which Richards and I had encountered were both embodied in written texts, a feature that encouraged direct comparison with Western psychology. But there is no textually inscribed psychology, Western or otherwise, that has lost its links with the psychology embodied in ordinary language. Those who produce texts with a psychological content have to take most of their terms from the ordinary discourse that goes on around them. Were they not to do so, they would have nothing meaningful to communicate to those to whom their texts are addressed. Whatever the gloss put on a term within a certain literary tradition, there is a fund of commonly accepted meaning on which it must rely in order to be comprehensible. Ordinary languages may therefore embody different psychologies as much as written texts.

This insight has informed studies in a field known as 'ethnopsychology'. Questions have been raised about the way in which members of other cultures, irrespective of literacy, conceptualize matters that to us appear to be psychological in character. At the simplest level, one can ask how their definition of psychological terms differs from ours. In this vein Wober (1974), working in Uganda, obtained reactions to a local word which dictionaries translate as 'intelligence'. He found that one feature which was negatively linked to intelligence was speed, an interesting finding in light of the fact that a major American modification of intelligence testing makes speed all-important. He also noted that African words indicating mental ability had been reported as referring to caution and prudence, or even knowledge of etiquette, rather than intelligence in the modern Western sense.

Probing more deeply, Smith (1981) noted that the relationship between self and experience was represented quite differently in Maori culture than in the West. Instead of attributing experiences to a central 'self', they were seen as originating in specific 'organs of experience', identified by names that were untranslatable because we lack such a notion altogether. Conversely, when describing the folk psychology of Marquesans, Kirkpatrick (1985: 94) noted that they did not distinguish a domain that would correspond to our 'cognition'.

More generally, ethnopsychological studies have produced a mass of converging evidence on the non-universality of some basic distinctions that form the conceptual skeleton for our own conventions of psychological classification. One of these distinctions – amounting to an opposition – is that between what belongs inside the individual and what belongs to a social sphere entirely outside the individual. Such a distinction is implied, not only in the concept of 'social stimulation', but in the notion of 'personality' as a set of individual attributes that exist separately from any social situation and can be described by abstracting from such situations. Yet, against the background of a great deal of evidence from non-Western societies (Markus and Kitayama, 1991; Kitayama and Markus, 1994), this way of posing the individual–society relationship appears as culturally specific. More usually, descriptions of persons and their characteristics are not separated from descriptions of social situations (e.g. Shweder and Bourne, 1984). In contrast to our psychological vocabulary of intra-personal essences, we find lexicons of interpersonal terms whose meaning cannot be conveyed without elaborate explanation (e.g. Rosaldo, 1980; White, 1985, 1994).[2]

Another taken for granted distinction that underlies our classification of psychological phenomena is that between the rational and the irrational, the cognitive and the affective. Separating a category of events labelled 'emotions' from another category of events identified as 'cognitions' expresses this distinction. However, this does not correspond to the way in which emotion words are used in everyday life, either in our own or in other cultures (Averill, 1985; Lutz, 1988). Rather, such words are used to talk about particularly meaningful, culturally defined, situations and problems. That is why there is so much variation in the vocabulary of emotions across cultures (Heelas, 1986; Russell, 1991). Moreover, because each emotion word embodies a cognitive scenario, it cannot be assumed that such words reflect universal psychological states that do not vary from one culture to another (Wierzbicka, 1995).

In short, there is a substantial body of cross-cultural evidence which throws doubt on the universal validity of many of the categories with which the discipline of Psychology has been operating. Contrary to common belief, these categories do not occupy some rarefied place *above* culture but are embedded in a particular professional sub-culture. There is a certain arrogance in taking it for granted that, alone among a myriad alternative ways of speaking about individual action and experience, the language of twentieth-century American Psychology accurately reflects the natural and universal structure of the phenomena we call 'psychological'. If such arrogance is to be avoided, a closer examination of this language has to be undertaken.

The categories of Psychology

Do the categories that are currently popular among us, categories like cognition, emotion, learning, motivation, personality, attitude, intelligence etc., represent natural kinds? Are we the people who happen to have hit on a nomological net that genuinely reflects the natural, the objective, divisions among classes of psychological events? Perhaps. But if we are, it is not because of our superior methods of empirical investigation. For the categories in question were not invented as a consequence of empirical investigation – they were there before anyone used them to identify the objects of empirical studies. Psychologists did not invent the concept of 'emotion', for example, to account for certain empirical findings; they obtained certain empirical findings because of their desire to investigate a set of events which their culture had taught them to distinguish as 'emotional'.

The objects of a science are usually taken to refer to some distinct aspect of a reality that is thought to exist independently of the science whose objects they are. When we claim that psychological science adds to our knowledge of attitudes, motives, personalities and so on, we assume that psychological reality divides up along the lines indicated by this received network of categories. A sensation is not an attitude and a motive is not a memory, though of course there may be relationships between them. Similarly, psychological theory commonly builds hypotheses *about* the structure of attitudes or the laws of learning, but does not question that 'attitude' and 'learning' describe distinct kinds that each require their own theoretical constructs. In other words, psychological theory operates on the basis of some pre-understanding of that which it is a theory of.

Traditionally, psychologists have felt justified in ignoring this problem by adopting a kind of conventionalism. On this account, the naming of psychological categories is really quite arbitrary. Psychological measuring devices yield certain products to which names are attached. Most of the time, terms in common use are employed for this purpose, but in the last analysis it is solely the operation of measurement that defines the scientific meaning of the term. Whether this scientific meaning corresponds to the everyday meaning of the term is an empirical matter, to be resolved by establishing the 'external validity' of the procedure.

The trouble with this way of disposing of the matter is that it conflates the *sense* of a term with its *reference*. Saying that intelligence is what intelligence tests measure, for example, establishes a particular reference for the term 'intelligence' but does not establish its sense. The act of categorizing a phenomenon always involves two decisions. First, we decide that there really is a phenomenon of sufficient distinctness and stability to warrant giving it a name. The phenomenon will now give whatever name we choose a reference. But the name should also be the *right* name. So we now have to decide which of the myriad names at our disposal is the appropriate one to use. In making *that* decision we have opted for the particular sense that our term is to have. Sense and reference are independent. In psychological research it sometimes happens that after a phenomenon has already been named it turns out to be irreproducible. In that case, there are serious doubts about whether this is a real phenomenon after all, and therefore we may be left with a term without a reference in the world outside the printed page. But such a term would still have sense. The term 'unicorn' has some sense, even though there are no unicorns. Similarly, the term 'intelligence' would have some sense, even if it turned out that there was nothing in human individuals that corresponded to this term. Conversely, there might be something out there, but it could turn out that 'intelligence' was quite the wrong word for it. In that case, there would be a reference but our sense of what it was would have been mistaken.[3]

What gives a particular sense to a term is the discourse of which it is a part. My Indonesian colleague understood the sense of terms like 'intelligence' and 'motivation' because he was familiar with certain psychological texts from the West, and he knew how these terms were used in those texts. Without studying that literature he would not have known what to make of such terms. Similarly, to get an adequate sense of *his* terms, I would have had to acquaint myself with his psychological literature. No amount of mere pointing to non-textual phenomena could have done the job for either of us. To get at the sense of such category labels we would need, not only positive examples, but also some appreciation of how each category was embedded in relationships of distinction, opposition, super- and subordination, etc. to other categories. And that could only be gathered from a discourse that embraced them all. To understand what made an example exemplary, looking would not be enough – we would again have to enter into a world of discourse in which the questionable category occurred. The distinction then is one between a discourse which provides terms with their sense and something outside this to which terms can refer. That something outside may or may not be another discourse. Pointing to the reference of a class term cannot provide its sense, unless we are told, or already know, what features of the referent make it a member of the class. For this we have to rely on a discursive interpretation of what we observe.

We can only communicate (and probably only make) empirical observations by applying a network of pre-existing categories. Every empirical description is an account that has been organized in terms of certain general categories. These categories define what it is that is being observed. For an observation to be psychologically relevant and interesting it has to be couched in terms of psychological categories. The report that the pencil in someone's hand made contact with a piece of paper at a certain distance from the top of the page does not count as an empirical observation in personality psychology. The report that someone received a certain score on the Taylor manifest Anxiety Scale does. It is not enough to make any kind of observation in science – one has to make relevant observations. And one cannot make psychologically relevant observations without the use of psychological categories. We have to have some agreed-upon notions of what it is we are investigating before we can make empirical additions to the sum total of our shared knowledge. This is not to say that our preconceptions are necessarily incorrigible, but the more we take them for granted, the less aware we are of their very existence, the less corrigible they are likely to prove in practice.

And that kind of incorrigibility could well rob us of the fruits of our empirical research. Our empiricist tradition has accustomed us to constantly correct our *explicit* theories about classes of psychological events in the light of empirical evidence. But post-empiricist philosophy alerts us to another kind of theory, i.e. the presuppositions about our subject matter that are implied in the categories we use to define the objects of our research and to express our empirical findings. If we render these presuppositions practically incorrigible because we never examine them we set very narrow limits to the progress of our science.

For psychology the problem is particularly serious because even after a century of specialized usage most of its terms remain heavily dependent on shared understandings in the general culture. Psychology may have developed certain theories *about* motivation, *about* personality, *about* attitudes, and so on, but the network of categories that assigns a distinct reality to motivation, to personality, to attitudes etc. has been taken over from a much broader language community of which psychologists are a part. Most psychologists want to preserve the relevance of their work for life outside the laboratory. To do this they have to demonstrate correlations between their scientific categories and phenomena defined in terms of common categories of everyday life. But that entails taking on board much of the traditional meaning of the everyday category.

Although psychologists are conventionalists in the definition of their theoretical concepts, they act like naive naturalists with respect to the domains that their theories are meant to explain. They tend to proceed as though everyday psychological categories represented natural kinds, as though the distinctions expressed in their basic categories accurately reflected the natural divisions among psychological phenomena.[4] Psychological discussions typically assume that there really is a distinct kind of entity out there that corresponds exactly to what we refer to as an attitude, say, and it is naturally different in kind from other sorts of entities out there for which we have different category names, like motives or emotions. Of course, our naturalists are always convinced that it is the categories which became popular in the twentieth century, and not any old-fashioned set of categories, that exactly represent the natural kinds into which the subject matter of psychology is divided. But, as we saw in the previous section, the existence of alternative psychologies encourages some scepticism about such implications.

Psychologists have devoted a great deal of care to making their theoretical concepts clear and explicit. But much of this effort has been rendered futile by their complaisance about the way in which psychological phenomena are categorized. The meaning of these categories carries an enormous load of unexamined and unquestioned assumptions and preconceptions. By the time explicit psychological theories are formulated, most of the theoretical work has already happened – it is embedded in the categories used to describe and classify psychological phenomena. To excavate this hidden level of theory, to make it visible, we need an analysis of the discourse from which psychological categories derive their sense.[5] But it is difficult to undertake such an analysis without recognizing a crucial feature of this discourse, namely, that it is a historical formation. All psychological categories have changed their meaning through history, and so has the discourse of which they were a part. To gain an understanding of the categories in common use at the moment, we need to see them in historical perspective. When we go back to the origin of these categories we usually find that what later became hidden and taken for granted is still out in the open and questionable. We also discover some of the reasons why a new category was introduced and by whom. These are the kinds of task to which this book is devoted.

Historiography

Looking at psychological categories and concepts with a historical perspective runs directly counter to one of the most deeply embedded features of modern psychology: its *ahistoricism*. History is only permitted into psychological discourse in the form of individual development, and even in that form it is commonly segregated as a field separate from the rest of the discipline. As for history in the usual sense, it is not regarded as having any significance for current psychological investigation or its products.

The most obvious reason for this is based on Psychology's wishful identification with the natural sciences.[6] Psychological research is supposed to be concerned with natural, not historical, objects, and its methods are considered to be those of natural science, not those of history. Psychology is committed to investigating processes like cognition, perception and motivation, as historically invariant phenomena of nature, not as historically determined social phenomena. Accordingly, it has strongly favoured the experimental approach of natural science and rejected the textual and archival methods of history. This means that historical studies have as little relevance for current work in the discipline of Psychology as the history of physics has for current work in that science. In both cases, the low status of history is based on an implicit belief in scientific progress. If the historical course of science represents the cumulative improvement of knowledge, then the past simply consists of that which has been superseded. The main reason for bothering with it at all is to celebrate progress, to congratulate ourselves for having arrived at the truth which the cleverest of our ancestors could only guess at.

One feature of this kind of historiography is its acceptance without question of currently entrenched divisions between psychological domains. It is assumed that those divisions truly reflect the actual structure of a timeless human nature. Thus, even though pre-twentieth-century writers may not have organized their reflections around topics like 'intelligence', 'personality' and 'motivation', they are presented as having had theories about such topics. If changes in such categories are recognized at all, it is their present-day form that is held to define their true nature, so that older work is interesting only insofar as it 'anticipates' what we now know to be true.[7] In that case, all we can learn from history is an old lesson in smugness: we can see further than our ancestors because we stand 'on the shoulders of giants'. If this is to be the approach to historical studies one would be justified in doubting their value, for their only function with respect to current practice would be one of celebration.

The older historiography was an expression of a positivistic philosophy that recognized only two kinds of factor in the development of a science: empirical phenomena and explicit theories that would account for these phenomena. What was not recognized was the factor which has been emphasized here, namely, the organization of both phenomena and theories by a framework of categories that incorporate taken for granted assumptions about the subject matter under investigation.

The French historian of biology, Georges Canguilhem, was perhaps the first to make this recognition the basis of his work. One of the topics whose history Canguilhem investigated was that of the reflex (Canguilhem, 1955). But what is a reflex? Clearly, it is not a theory. There have been many theories *about* reflexes, but the reflex itself is not a theory. Is it a phenomenon, then? That is how positivist historiography has always treated it. But, when Descartes speculated about the bodily mechanics of animal reactions, was he dealing with the same phenomena that Sherrington observed in his Cambridge laboratory two and a half centuries later? Clearly not. What then might connect the two? Canguilhem's solution was to point to the existence of a third kind of entity, neither phenomenon nor theory, which he referred to as a concept. The reflex was a concept, a way of grouping observations and giving them a particular significance. In the history of science we need to focus on changes in concepts if we want to get beyond superficialities. As it happens, Canguilhem's historical analysis of the *concept* of the reflex led him to conclude that Descartes could not be regarded as its originator and to show exactly when and why this particular origin myth made its appearance.[8] Other topics to which Canguilhem turned his attention were those of biological regulation (1988) and normality (1989). Again, his historical inquiry was concerned with concepts that 'provide[s] us with the initial understanding of a phenomenon that allows us to formulate in a scientifically useful way the question of how to explain it' (Gutting, 1990).

What Canguilhem referred to as a 'concept' is very close to the 'categories' that form the topic of the present volume.[9] An example of such a category is that of 'stimulation', whose earlier history is discussed in Chapter 4. As in the case of the reflex, we can ask, what is a stimulus? One can have theories *about* how stimuli act, but a stimulus is not a theory, nor is it a raw phenomenon. It is a phenomenon interpreted in a certain way, a phenomenon under a particular description, namely, as a stimulus. Any phenomenon classified as a stimulus could also be described in terms of some other category. The possibility of describing something as a stimulus did not always exist. This category makes its historical entry at a certain point, and in the course of its subsequent history it underwent many changes (Danziger, 1992b). A part of that history is traced in Chapter 4.

Ignoring the fact that scientific categories have a history makes it possible to avoid fundamental questions. One way in which this operates is through the history of specialisms. Producing a history of 'motivational psychology', for example, is an excellent way of side-stepping the historicity of the category of motivation itself. The real existence, independently of any discourse, of natural divisions between motivational and other phenomena is assumed from the outset, and all that remains is the reconstruction of some historical material to fit in with this division. As Markus (1987) has suggested, this kind of history should be regarded as a way of cementing consensus among working scientists who can afford neither the disruptive effects of persistent controversy about fundamental issues nor the demoralizing effects of scepticism about the intellectual constructions on which their work is based.

In the past, this positivistic historiography led a comfortable co-existence with another trend, derived from the so-called history of ideas. In this approach, the modern development of psychological specialisms is seen against the background of historically permanent categorical parameters that have always directed psychological reflection into a limited number of channels – eighteen, according to R.I. Watson (1971), a prominent representative of this approach in the historiography of psychology. Such channels are defined by a pair of opposites: functionalism versus structuralism, physicalism versus mentalism, monism versus dualism, etc. These polarities have never changed, from Homer to B.F. Skinner; what change historically are the dominant norms that prescribe the position to be taken up with respect to the eternal bipolar categories. This scheme is merely an extreme example of a once popular approach which effectively disposed of the history of psychological categories by denying that they had a history.[10]

Ahistoricism formed the common basis of this approach and the history of specialisms with which it co-existed. Where the latter simply ignored the possibility that current psychological categories might be historical ephemera, those inspired by the history of ideas elevated such categories to the status of eternal givens. In both cases, history is replaced by essentialism. Categories currently fashionable in American psychology are taken as expressions of some timeless defining feature of human nature. Inevitably, such an approach falls victim to a gross parochialism that elevates local and ephemeral concerns to the status of eternal verities.

By contrast, this book starts with the assumption that the essence of psychological categories (insofar as they have one) lies in their status as historically constructed objects. There are no 'perennial problems' driving the history of psychology through the ages (cf. Skinner, 1988a). At different times and in different places psychologically significant categories have been constructed and reconstructed in attempts to deal with different problems and to answer a variety of questions, many of them not essentially psychological at all.[11] Identification with the natural sciences by no means guarantees that psychology's categories are exempt from the flux of history. Even the categories of physics are historical constructions, as some philosophers have observed:

> Whether it be space, time, the starry heavens, the forces which move bodies, or some other object of science, we would look in vain for some shared or common meaning which might apply to any of these objects throughout their respective histories and which as such, like a red line traversing the changes in meanings and slowly broadening itself, might serve as the common and continual ground for all the scientific theories devoted to any such object. It was hard enough for mankind to grasp that the same time does not tick off in all parts of the world. It may be even more difficult to grasp that when we investigate some scientific object, both today and as it existed in the past, we are not necessarily speaking about one and the *same* thing. (Hübner, 1983: 123)

Writing history is not the same thing as exploring *historicity*. As the above examples from the historiography of psychology show, it is quite possible to write history in an utterly ahistorical way. Individuals and their ideas follow one another in an extended sequence, but the ideas are just variations on a finite set of constant themes and the individuals all take positions with respect to the same set of questions. The exploration of historicity, however, involves looking for the radical shaping of themes, questions, and even individuals, by particular historical circumstances. This book is much more concerned with historicity, specifically the historicity of psychological categories, than with the writing of history.

But how does one explore the historicity of categories? This is where language comes in. Categories of scientific discourse have *names* that identify and objectify them and situate them in a network of semantic relationships with other categories. Could one then explore the history of categories by tracing the history of their names? About twenty years ago Raymond Williams (1976) tried to do something along these lines in a book he called *Keywords*. He looked at terms that were of fundamental importance in social and political debate, terms like 'democracy' and 'society'. Some of the terms were psychological, 'behaviour' and 'personality', for example. In the case of 'behaviour' he noted how the twentieth-century change in the meaning of the word had been in the direction of supplying a morally neutral description of human actions. Williams' explorations constituted an interesting pioneering effort, but they had their limitations (Farr, 1989; Skinner, 1988b).

First of all, there are problems with the identification of word and concept that is implied in Williams' approach. Is it not possible that there was an appreciation of the concept of democracy, for example, before people had the word? Ultimately, the answer to such a question depends on one's views about the role of language. But it is better to address that question after, rather than before, gathering evidence on the historical development of psychological categories.[12] Over large parts of the present study the problem of word and concept hardly arises. This is because, for the most part, we will be concerned with a special case, namely, the use of categories in a disciplinary context. The effect of that context is to produce a converging standardization of both language and concept. Moreover, in studying the *emergence* of categories, changes in the meaning of terms provide the best clues we have, for, as one well-known historian has observed, 'the surest sign that a group or society has entered into the self-conscious possession of a new concept is that a corresponding vocabulary will be developed, a vocabulary which can then be used to pick out and discuss the concept with consistency' (Skinner, 1988b: 120).

The 'keywords' approach also harbours the potential danger that, by taking single words as its focus, it will promote an excessively atomizing account of conceptual history. It is therefore important not to lose sight of the fact that single terms are always embedded in a network of semantic relationships from which they derive their meaning and significance. In such a network, changes in the meaning of one term are not independent of changes in the meaning of others, and the significance of each term depends on the position it occupies in a larger whole that is best thought of as a *discursive formation*. By this I mean a language that constitutes an integrated world of meanings in which each term articulates with other terms so as to form a coherent framework for representing a kind of knowledge that is regarded as true and a kind of practice regarded as legitimate.[13]

The history of categories as elements in discursive formations obviously cannot be written in terms of the history of individual personages. A language has its own history; it is the work of many hands and it informs the thought and practice of large groups. Again, there is a difference between the kind of history that has usually been favoured by historians of psychology and the kind of history pursued here. Understandably, when psychologists turn to the history of their subject, they often do so with a psychologist's bias in favour of accounts centred on individuals. Their professional training is likely to exaggerate an already strong cultural tendency to interpret social and historical events in terms of the actions, thoughts and personalities of individuals. Like much of social psychology, this tendency is often based on an implicit metaphysical individualism that reduces all social phenomena to the behaviour of individuals.[14] The very notion of history as a history of discursive formations is foreign to this approach. It is much more in tune with more recent historiographic trends like the 'linguistic turn' in the history of science (Golinski, 1990).

Rejection of metaphysical individualism does not mean that all reference to individual historical actors must be avoided. A history of psychological language written in this way would probably look a lot like an etymological dictionary. In fact, this was one of the limitations of Williams' 'Keywords' approach. It was able to describe historical changes but could only speculate about reasons. To get to the reasons for change one has to relate texts to historical actors. But this does not mean explaining the text in terms of the personal life of its author. Authors enter the picture only as historical agents. Through their texts authors intervene in and become part of an ongoing historical process. Their texts may *do* something, but the historical significance of what they do does not depend on the private intentions of the author so much as on the state of the discursive field of which the text is a part. A well-known intellectual historian has expressed this as follows:

> When we ask about an author's 'intention', moreover, we are seeking evidence, not about his state of mind while writing a particular work, but about certain objective characteristics of his text, and especially about its relationship to a given complex of other texts. We are asking questions, in short, about the positional characteristics of a text in its field. (Ringer, 1990: 271)

In the following chapters there will be many references to individual contributions considered as elements in discursive formations, not as elements in personal biographies.

Overview of the book

It is hardly possible to present anything like a comprehensive history of psychological language within the confines of a single volume. In fact, such an undertaking would be highly problematical, even in the absence of any limitations of time and space. For to write the history of psychological language one would first have to know how to define the boundaries of such a topic. That would require a clear understanding of what was meant by 'psychological'. How is psychological language distinguished from other language, and how are psychological categories distinguished from other categories? Many different answers to such questions are imaginable, and two or three centuries ago the questions would not even have been intelligible. Clearly, 'psychological' is itself an example of a psychological category with a history that needs investigation. Because it did not always exist, we have to fall back on modern conceptions of 'the psychological' for the criteria that will enable us to distinguish between relevant and irrelevant material from the past. But that is a dangerous undertaking. It commits us to the worst kind of 'presentism', where the past is summarily reinterpreted in terms of the categories of the present, so that history comes to look like a catalogue of 'errors' and 'anticipations'.

The only part of the history of psychology that has a relatively unproblematical subject matter is the part that is defined by the modern discipline of Psychology (Smith, 1988). Once the texts and institutional structures of that discipline appear on the scene we have a clearly identifiable field with relatively sharp boundaries. This field is characterized by certain categories of discourse whose history can be investigated in a relatively straightforward way. That is the main focus of the present book. However, this does not mean that no attention need be paid to developments prior to the advent of a discipline of Psychology. As has already been indicated, restricting oneself to the use of categories in scientific Psychology is a recipe for avoiding fundamental issues. To understand the nature of these categories one has to know where they came from. In particular, one has to understand the problems that their construction was expected to deal with and what assumptions, taken over from an older tradition, they embody.

For example, in considering the category of 'intelligence' in Chapter 5 considerable space is devoted to the emergence of the modern understanding of this category in the nineteenth century. Two sources of this understanding present themselves, evolutionary biology and a rationalized system of universal education. Chapter 5 traces the dependence of the twentieth-century psychological meaning of 'intelligence' on these twin roots.

There were other nineteenth-century developments which provided essential components in the conceptual equipment of twentieth-century psychology. Some of the more important ones are considered in Chapter 4, which is devoted to the historical appearance of fundamental psycho-physiological concepts, like those of stimulation, the reflex, and psycho-physical energy. A common feature of nineteenth-century physiological discourse was the gradual imposition of a dualistic structure on categories that previously had not implied a sharp distinction between the mental and the physical. Modern Psychology had to come to terms with that.

The continuities between twentieth-century psychological discourse and earlier forms of discourse become more remote and more doubtful the further back we go in time. While there are still many points of contact in the nineteenth century, the trail becomes ever more uncertain beyond that. Prior to the late seventeenth century, the categories available for analysing human experience and conduct were so different from modern psychological categories that one can no longer claim to be tracing the history of the latter when dealing with these earlier periods. As our aim here is not to construct psychology as a historically permanent entity but to explore the historicity of psychological categories, there is no reason to begin these explorations much before the year 1700.

Nevertheless, I have included a brief overview of some historically much older material in Chapter 2. For the most part, this concentrates on Aristotelian conceptions, because these were historically so important for Western speculations about the life and experience of the human individual. But this sketch deals with a subject matter that I consider to be different from the rest of the book. It is included merely as a historical counterpoint, to illustrate, by way of contrast, the radical novelty of modern conceptions. Readers who are already convinced of this may wish to skip this chapter and begin with Chapter 3.

In that chapter I briefly review some of the earlier developments that provided a conceptual basis for a modern network of psychological categories. For the most part, these developments date from the eighteenth century. It is only then that there is clear evidence of systematic reflection about subjects that are unambiguously psychological in nature. Much of this reflection took place in Germany, where the term 'psychology' began to be used in a recognizably modern sense at this time. However, it was British empiricist philosophy that provided much of the stimulus for this development (Dessoir, 1902; Sommer, 1892). For this reason, and more particularly because the historical continuity between this philosophy and twentieth-century American psychology is so pronounced, it is the traditional British version of mental philosophy that forms the focus of Chapter 3. Among the concepts singled out for attention are those of emotion, motive, consciousness and the self.

Unlike the categories considered in later chapters, these concepts were not the creation of the modern science of Psychology, though eventually they came to form part of the subject matter of that science. This illustrates the dual origin of the categories with which the discipline of Psychology operates. Many of them, including 'behaviour', 'learning' and 'motivation', did not exist as categories of psychological reflection before the twentieth century and are constructs whose history is entirely tied up with that of the discipline.[15] But other categories, like 'emotion', 'consciousness' and 'self', are older and date from the eighteenth century or even a little before that. They are the products of a historical process of reconstructing human subjectivity in psychological terms, a process that was particularly in evidence in certain parts of post-mediaeval Europe. Without this development there could be no modern discipline of Psychology. The subject matter of that discipline depends on a culturally embedded tendency to experience much of human life in psychological terms. Such a layered conception of the emergence of modern Psychology is suggested by the extensive historical work of Graham Richards (1987, 1989, 1992), who has documented the earlier development of a language that permits the representation of specifically psychological objects. Subsequently, those objects became the targets of disciplined investigation and intervention, a practice which effectively reconstituted them. In the present volume I have adopted Richards' proposal to distinguish references to Psychology as a discipline from references to its subject matter by using upper case 'P' for the former and lower case 'p' for the latter.[16]

Chapters 5 to 9 represent the core of this book and are devoted to an examination of a number of categories whose origin is intimately tied up with the history of American Psychology. In view of the multiple origins of the discipline of Psychology (Danziger, 1990a) this requires some explanation. It is certainly true that there were fundamental differences between psychological discourse in America and in Continental Europe – not to speak of non-Western psychologies. Until the second half of the twentieth century there was not one but several disciplinary languages of psychology, and each of them had its own historical trajectory. In the aftermath of World War II, however, the language of American Psychology was adopted virtually everywhere, a situation that has only begun to change relatively recently. Therefore, that language occupies a specially significant place in the history of the discipline. It represents the most appropriate point of entry for a conceptual history, though it is to be hoped that comparative studies of other psychological languages will be undertaken in the future.

There is of course a certain distortion in referring to *the* American language, as though there were only one. It is true that American Psychology always had its dissidents who wanted to speak a language other than the official one. But a striking feature of the discipline in its American incarnation was the impressive degree of uniformity achieved in its discourse, at least for a time. If one were to give a name to this hegemonic form of discourse one would have to call it 'behavioural'. This does not mean that most American psychologists were behaviourists, a judgement about their explicit theoretical commitments. Whatever those commitments might have been, most of them were quite ready to use the specialized terms of their discipline in a manner that conceded many of the assumptions of behaviourism and made them invisible. This process is dissected in subsequent chapters, especially Chapters 6 and 9.

The fact that American Psychology was dominated by a particular form of discourse for most of the twentieth century furnishes the main criterion for the selection of psychological categories discussed in this book. The history of these categories is a vast domain, so it is necessary to be selective. I have selected categories whose history is intimately tied up with that of 'behavioural' discourse in general.[17] Most obviously, this is the case in Chapter 6, which is mainly concerned with the emergence and establishment of the modern category of 'behaviour' and, secondarily, with that of 'learning'. Whereas the latter involved the creation of a new domain of psychological inquiry by an act of abstraction that was essentially a shot in the dark, the story of 'behaviour' is more complex. It had its roots in earlier conceptions of mind as something to be inferred from, not read in, something else that was not mind. But when 'behaviour' became the central component in a new form of social scientific discourse it acquired a diffuse set of meanings and functions that took it far beyond these roots. This process is analysed in Chapter 6.

In Chapter 7 the focus is on two categories whose establishment within the discipline was very strongly influenced by practical imperatives. 'Motivation' was a new concept, formed, like 'learning', by abstracting from profoundly diverse phenomena and reifying the result. It had its origins in the world of management and had manipulative connotations from the beginning. 'Personality' changed its reference in the early twentieth century and came to mean virtually the opposite of what it used to mean. It too entered Psychology via practical fields, especially personnel selection and education, in which members of the discipline were becoming involved. Concepts like 'drive' and 'need' were constructed to provide a theoretical focus for research in the new domains.

Chapter 8 is devoted to a central category in social psychology: 'attitude'. Introspective research on attitudes was quickly abandoned in favour of the concept of 'social attitudes' which was a direct importation from sociology. Using techniques adapted from market research, psychologists successfully annexed this category by giving it a strictly intra-individual interpretation and by developing methods for measuring attitudes. These depended on assimilating the category of 'social stimuli' to older conceptions of stimuli as physical and biological events. The chapter closes with a consideration of differences between the category of 'social attitude' and the concept of ideology which made a brief appearance in social psychology in the wake of World War II.

In Chapter 9 the discussion shifts to the most general categories of psychological discourse: stimulus and response in the first instance and 'variable' somewhat later. These categories have functioned as a kind of metalanguage into which diverse schools of psychological thought could be translated for purposes of empirical comparison. They were derived from specific forms of experimental and statistical investigative practice, and their effect is to impose the form of that practice on all representations of psychological reality. More particularly, the chapter traces the history of the category of 'the variable', from its statistical beginnings, through its psychological reification as an 'intervening variable', to its function as the key term in a language of psychological engineering. This represents the final development of a theme which runs through all the chapters from 5 onwards: the tendency to ground the meaning of psychological categories in the investigative practices of psychologists.

The last chapter (10) draws together such themes from previous chapters and returns to some of the issues raised in this introductory chapter. The discussion centres on the question of whether psychological categories can be said to constitute 'natural kinds', whether they mirror the structure of a psychological reality that exists independently of them. After considering the social contextualization of these categories and their referential role, that question is ultimately answered in the negative.

This book has a specific temporal focus determined by its concentration on categories that have been important in the 'behavioural' discourse of American Psychology. Those categories all took on their modern shape approximately during the second to fourth decades of the twentieth century. Hence, it is that period which is given the closest attention here. Most of the material in Chapters 6 to 9 pertains to those years because this was the time during which American Psychology actually found its language. If one compares texts published before this period with texts published near its end the change is quite striking. There is much discontinuity in the categories that define the subject matter of the discipline. Most of the categories deployed by the later texts – the categories discussed in this book and some others – do not occur in the earlier texts. During these years the discipline redefined its subject matter. But this was not just a matter of shifting from 'consciousness' to 'behaviour'; it involved the upsurge of entirely new domains, like 'personality' and 'social attitudes', and the demise of others, e.g. the will. By contrast, if we compare texts over the next thirty-year, or even fifty-year, period there is much less change in the category language of the discipline. There are changes in the theories *about* the phenomena of interest, but the distinctions between the different kinds of phenomena are still based on essentially the same set of fundamental categories, 'cognition' being the notable exception.

The thirty-year period, approximately defined by the dates 1910 and 1940, was a time of revolutionary change. It was revolutionary, not because the theories that explained phenomena were changed, but because the phenomena themselves changed. They changed because the categories that defined them changed. This process of the historical *emergence* of new categories is examined in Chapters 6 to 9. 'Intelligence', which emerged slightly earlier with a different geographical locus, is considered in Chapter 5. Of course, the new categories did not come out of nowhere, and some of that 'pre-history' forms the subject matter of Chapter 4. So the historical perspective of the present study is provided by a period of special significance. It was during this time that the conceptual divisions which later came to be taken for granted were still being negotiated. That process was largely complete by the 1950s, which is where our study ends. A time of relative stability and 'normalization' had begun. There were many developments after that, but they either did not affect the nature of the categories that dominated psychological discourse, or they signalled the arrival of a new period in the history of the discipline. Whether they really did so, or merely served up old wine in new bottles, is not something that can be decided without a thorough examination of what came before.

Notes

1. Curiously, Richards saw some hope of escaping this dilemma in the new psychological language of stimulus and response that was then coming into vogue. Alas, this hope was misplaced, as we will see in Chapter 9.

2. 'Our' here refers to the vocabulary of the discipline of Psychology, not to some Western folk psychological domains that may well be less extreme in this respect (see White, 1992).

3. The sense–reference distinction has its origins in the work of the logician Frege (1848–1925). This work stimulated much further discussion and several variants of the distinction (see Baker and Hacker, 1984). My use of the distinction is only loosely related to these.

4. On the fallacy of human categories as reflections of nature, see Lakoff (1987).

5. The enormous weight of pre-understanding carried by psychological concepts has been extensively demonstrated in the work of Smedslund (1984, 1991). Unfortunately, his attempt to seek a way out via a universal 'psychologic' displays a certain blindness to culture and history.

6. A more subtle reason may lie in the way that psychology became the social science that catered to a broader ahistoricism characterizing societies and periods that were strongly anti-traditional. Perhaps this is one of the reasons why, from its earliest years, psychological science flourished in the US as nowhere else.

7. For further discussion of this issue, see Danziger (1990b), as well as Smith (1988) and Young (1966).

8. There is further discussion of the reflex in Chapter 4.

9. I prefer the term 'categories', because its use in the English-language literature is closer to my intended meaning than 'concept', which suffers from a multitude of undesirable connotations and ambiguities. However, in what follows I sometimes use the latter term as a synonym for the former.

10. One finds the same approach in histories of so-called 'persistent problems' of psychology (MacLeod, 1975).

11. Much of the extensive literature exploring the historicity of human psychology has revolved around the topics of 'emotion' (Stearns and Stearns, 1988) and 'self' (Danziger, 1997).

12. We will return to this question in Chapter 10. See Hallam (1994) for a useful discussion.

13. I am indebted to the formulation of Roger Smith (1992: 224) here. His study of the history of the category of 'inhibition' exemplifies the advantages of the discursive approach.

14. See Chapter 8. The genre of biography is not affected by this, because its perfectly legitimate concern is with the intelligibility of individual lives, not the explanation of historical trends.

15. A quick check on whether a particular category belongs in this group is to look it up in the comprehensive *Dictionary of Philosophy and Psychology* published in 1901 (Baldwin, 1901). If there is no entry for it, it is almost certainly a twentieth-century psychological category.

16. Where the reference is to both I use the lower case.

17. There are many psychological categories, like perception, memory, cognition, that fall outside the restricted scope of the present study. Of these, perception has been relatively well served by existing historical accounts. But it would hardly be possible to do justice to the others with anything less than a substantial monograph for each.

2

THE ANCIENTS

A few years ago *Isis*, the journal of the History of Science Society, devoted a special section to 'The Cultures of Ancient Science'. Most of the articles in that section focused on the problem of 'Greek Science' and its relationship to modern science (Lloyd, 1992; Pingree, 1992; von Staden, 1992). There was a clear consensus that more recent historical scholarship was quite incompatible with nineteenth- and earlier twentieth-century views that credited the Greeks with the invention of science. Not only had the meaning of 'science' and all its categories changed fundamentally, but there was little or no historical continuity to be discovered between then and now. Nowadays, we have become much more ready to accept the Ancients on their own terms, rather than turning to them for a spurious origin of our own notions. Ancient science is fascinating in its own right. We demean it in the service of dangerous myths of Western origins if we simply mine it for fanciful 'anticipations' of our own ideas.

As already indicated in Chapter 1, we face a similar issue in the historiography of psychology. Because Aristotle was responsible for a book about 'the soul', he was long credited with being the first to write systematically about psychology. Textbooks on the history of psychology commonly begin with the Greeks, ignoring the fact that the very notion of 'psychology' in the modern sense, forming a distinct field of study, can hardly be said to have existed before the eighteenth century (see Chapter 3).

Such cavalier treatments of the highly problematic question of historical continuity usually rely on an uncritical equation of ancient and modern categories. But when they were translated from Greek into Latin and from Latin into various modern languages the categories employed by Aristotle and his compatriots profoundly changed their meaning, not to speak of the changes that occurred within one language over the centuries. Thus, Aristotle's *psyche* is not the *anima* of his Latin translators, and even less is it the *soul* of the Middle Ages, let alone the *mind* of the moderns. Less inclusive categories underwent similar profound changes, if only because the entire conceptual network of which they formed a part had changed (Danziger, 1990b).

There are therefore strong grounds for not including the ancient period in any history of psychological language. However, there are also reasons for devoting at least some attention to this topic. First, there is the existence of an unfortunate tradition in the historiography of psychology, already referred to. Because that tradition has been biased so heavily in favour of historical continuity, some of the more glaring discontinuities should at least be mentioned in order to restore some balance. I do not wish to deny the existence of all historical continuity in principle. My position is that continuity must be rigorously demonstrated rather than assumed, and that it has certainly not been demonstrated in the examples discussed in this chapter.

A second reason for spending a little time with the Ancients is more important. It is a reason that will still be valid when the last traces of the old distortions have disappeared. Nowadays, we accept that knowledge of other cultures, in other parts of the world, can tell us quite a lot about ourselves. By studying the differences between them and us we gain insights, not only into their world, but also our own. Aspects of our own culture, that we had taken completely for granted and hardly been aware of, now move into prominence and change our view of ourselves. We look to social anthropology to provide such insights. But there are cultures, capable of presenting us with a valuable sense of 'otherness', which are conventionally studied by historians rather than by anthropologists. These cultures are separated from us by time rather than by space, and so the methods for studying them are somewhat different. But although we cannot interview or observe their members, the texts and artefacts they left behind often allow us to enter into a fascinatingly different conceptual and material world. That can be a valuable antidote to one great danger attending the reign of 'behavioural science', namely, that its historically contingent and culturally parochial categories will be mistaken for universal principles having eternal validity.

About three centuries ago, there occurred the beginnings of the conceptual changes necessary for the emergence of psychology in the modern sense. In terms of the history of psychology this was a revolutionary development. Before this point, nothing like modern psychology had even been thinkable; afterwards it was. Before this time, there was no network of categories within which a space for the possibility of psychology in our sense could open up. In the next chapter I will describe the new categorical framework from which there is a continuous line of development up to the twentieth century. But because this framework is so deeply embedded in modern culture, it tends to have an obviousness, a taken for granted quality, that makes it difficult to step outside it. To appreciate the fact that it replaced a very different framework, it is necessary to step back in time, even if only briefly, in order to get some sense of a few of the alternative conceptualizations that once existed.

In pursuit of this limited goal I will concentrate on three interconnected topics. First, there is the question of human persons becoming objects to themselves. That question lies behind much of the confusion about the supposedly ancient roots of psychology. Psychological discourse presupposes that individuals have learned to relate to themselves in some sense as objects, that they have learned to introspect their own mental states, or self-consciously monitor their own actions, or describe their own character traits in a common language. These are all examples of *psychological* self-objectification. For us, they are the most familiar examples. For that reason we should guard against the temptation to interpret *all* cases of self-objectification psychologically, assuming that all self-objectifying discourse is necessarily psychological discourse. This is the error we are invited to make by many historical treatments of the ancient roots of psychology. The Ancients certainly developed ways of thinking and acting reflexively, but only by looking at these practices will we be able to decide how close they came to modern psychological reflexivity.

The second topic singled out for attention is that of reason. That is because some of the most fundamental differences between ancient and modern conceptions about people revolve around this category. These differences are discussed in the next chapter. For the present, it will suffice to prepare the ground by means of illustrative examples from the ancient vocabulary pertaining to human reasoning. These will all be taken from one source of unique historical importance, the Aristotelian texts. The content of those texts was very much alive in the period immediately preceding the conceptual transformation to be discussed in the next chapter.

If reason constituted one pole around which ancient self-objectifying discourse revolved, the affections or passions constituted the other. Although these were perhaps the most obvious 'psychological' categories in the classical texts, they faded away and died precisely at the time that the modern psychological categories began to achieve prominence. The reasons for this discontinuity will be explored in the next chapter. Here it will simply be a question of selecting enough background information to provide a point of departure for a consideration of modern developments.[1]

Persons as objects to themselves

One way of dividing up the use of psychological categories is by personal pronoun (Shotter, 1990). We can give accounts in the first person, explaining our actions by reference, for example, to an individual intention. We can also address another person, and perhaps attribute to them a particular belief or fear. Or we can talk in the third person, describing an individual, or something about an individual, just as we might describe any other kind of object. As already indicated, our interest is in the genesis of categories used in the objective mode.

We are accustomed to a plentiful supply of such categories, and we readily transfer them to the first or second person mode. Anyone may refer to themselves or their partner as being an extrovert, or having dependency needs, for example. That involves a kind of self-objectification which we have come to take for granted. But we should not assume that it could be taken for granted at all times. If we read Homeric and other ancient texts attentively we will be struck by the absence of references to the internal mental states of characters (Jaynes, 1976; Snell, 1953) and by what has been called their 'unreflective awareness of "self"' (Sullivan, 1988). At this point, self-objectification seems either to be rudimentary or to assume forms that are quite alien to us. A considerable distance separates the impetuous Homeric heroes from the intellectually sophisticated pupils of Aristotle. Was anything of psychological relevance involved in this change?

The Ancients may well have taken important steps towards self-objectification, but this does not mean that the specific categories they used for constructing self-objects were anything like the psychological categories we know. The mistake commonly made in histories of psychology is the assumption that all self-objectification must necessarily be psychological in character. That assumption is distinctly implausible in the case of the Ancient Greeks, because their language lacked not just some but virtually all the key substantives that define modern discourse on this topic. There were no words for 'the self', for 'mind', for 'consciousness'; and other key words had meanings very different from the meanings they acquired closer to our own time (Wilkes, 1988). 'Psyche', or soul, for example, was something that a tree or even a magnetic substance could have. This means that we run the risk of seriously misinterpreting classical Greek texts if we simply assume without more ado that they constitute a discourse about 'the self', as that term is understood today.

In the course of exploring the historical constitution of the ethical subject Michel Foucault (1986) directed attention to a considerable classical literature on the topic of self-care. This literature is part of, and emerges out of, a more extensive body of writing on the good life, on how to conduct oneself in order to live a life worth living. Such a project entails a reflexive examination of one's own conduct. But making one's conduct an object of scrutiny is not the same thing as separating a substantial self from its actions. For that there would have to be a clear distinction between an individual's actions and some entity assumed to exist apart from and behind those actions. What we get in the classical literature is the reflexive form 'caring for oneself' (*epimeleia sautou*). Although the subtitle of Foucault's volume, 'The care of the self', seems to imply a substantive self concept, that is not what is intended: 'The care of the self is the care of the activity and not the care of the soul-as-substance' (Foucault, 1988: 25). Foucault's primary interest lies in the historical constitution of the self in the sense of an ethical subject. But his main access to this topic is through an analysis of the literature of self-care. He therefore uses the term 'the self' in two senses: in reference to a postulated subject of moral action, and in reference to something that is addressed in the relevant classical literature. The latter is not to be equated with the modern, psychological, self concept, as we will see.

Foucault identifies some features of a process by which persons gradually became objects for themselves. The classical ideal of knowing oneself developed in the context of specific practices of acting on oneself, referred to by him as 'technologies of the self' (Foucault, 1988). Such 'technologies' included, for example, the keeping of a diary and the writing of letters to friends in which a degree of self-disclosure was systematically aimed at. However, we must be careful not to exaggerate the degree of self-disclosure involved here: this type of writing 'stresses what you did, not what you thought' (Foucault, 1988: 30). It takes the writer's past and future actions as its object, not the writer as an entity beyond those actions.

It should also be noted that in taking one's own actions as an object one was engaging in a *social* practice. This is quite obvious in the case of letter writing, but keeping a diary meant following known rules regarding its form and content and often engaging in a kind of imaginary or postponed communication with some other. Quite generally, self-reflection relied on the guidance of another person recognized as being specially equipped for this role. An early prototype for such a relationship is presented in the Platonic dialogues, most explicitly in Alcibiades I, in which Socrates offers to guide the self-improvement of a younger man. The context for self-examination is pedagogical. But there is also an old tradition which places self-care within medical thought and practice (Foucault, 1986: 54ff.). So there were two powerful metaphorical frameworks within which the self concept could develop: in the pedagogical metaphor the self appeared as a locus of ignorance and confusion, as the object of training and instruction; in the medical metaphor the self appeared as a locus of illness, feebleness and vulnerability which became the object of treatment.

What these social contexts provided were points of view from which one's own actions could be examined. The injunction to reflect on one's actions would imply nothing more than the reinforcement of traditional mores if it were not joined to a broader framework within which the examination was to take place. Metaphors derived from pedagogical and medical practice provided a cognitive framework within which individuals, and not just their actions, could become objects to themselves.

Once this happens, there is often a tendency to separate out and to reify a part of the person that is thought of as the special repository of goodness and wisdom. One can see this quite clearly in the interaction of Socrates and Alcibiades already referred to. 'I wish that you would explain to me in what way I am to take care of myself,' asks Alcibiades (Jowett, 1892: 503), and Socrates replies by invoking a metaphor that is to recur again and again in subsequent discourse about the self, right up to the present day. It is the metaphor of the mirror. Socrates likens a person getting to know himself to an eye seeing itself, and this can only be accomplished with a mirror. But only a very special mirror will do, namely, the eye of another person. 'Then if the eye is to see itself, it must look at the eye, and at that part of the eye where sight which is the virtue of the eye resides' (Jowett, 1892: 505). What Socrates suggests is that just as the virtue of sight resides in a special organ, the eye, so moral virtue resides in a special part of the person. If one wishes to improve the moral quality of one's life one must examine this special part and not simply the sum total of one's worldly deeds. In other words, a part of the person has now been categorized as an abiding object of observation and intervention for both self and others.

In this discourse persons have certainly become objects for themselves. But we must be careful not to confuse this state of affairs with the modern concept of the self. First of all, we miss any concern with what would become an obsession in the modern period: the question of individuality, of the unique qualities that establish personal identity and distinguish individuals from each other. The virtue which resides in the Ancients' soul is not its capacity for fully realizing its unique self, its individualized potential, but rather its possibility of discovering and tuning in to the order inherent in the world.

Secondly, we find that the classical writers look for the expression of the personal core, not in the private or the inner life of the individual, as we moderns are inclined to do, but in his public life. In the late classical period there are exceptions to this, especially among the Stoics, who advocated periodic retreats from the world as a way of getting in touch with oneself. But overall, the classical era does not draw the division between a public and a private sphere with anything like the sharpness that we are used to. For these reasons there are definite limits to the development of 'technologies of the self' during this period. Auto-biographies, for example, are virtually unknown, and the few existing examples of the genre do not take as their object a unique private self that persists over the life span (Weintraub, 1978).

The social contexts to which we have traced an emerging self-objectification do not contain prominent religious elements. This does not mean that such elements were absent, only that they did not define the meaning of these situations in the way they defined the meaning of explicitly religious practices, rituals, etc. Nor does it mean that a kind of self-objectification did not develop in a religious context. But the differences between the latter and modern naturalistic concepts of the person have long been recognized. It is when they are at their most naturalistic that the Ancients become attractive as progenitors of our own naturalism. Unfortunately, this affinity can all too easily lead us to mistake their naturalism for ours. Our naturalism has become intimately tied up with physicalism of a kind that originates in a rigorous separation of the physical and the mental, of body and consciousness. That separation was utterly foreign to the classical literature. Accordingly, there was no distinction between 'primary', physical, attributes of things and 'secondary', mental attributes. Aesthetic and moral qualities could be as much part of the objective world order as physical qualities. There was no lining up of the objective and physical on one side of a great divide against the subjective and mental on the other. This is reflected in the Aristotelian category of reason to which we must now turn.

Reason

Aristotle made a fundamental division between those characteristics of the human *psyche* which it shared with the *psyche* of other living things and those which were peculiar to humanity. His Latin translators and commentators generally rendered the latter by the term *intellectus*. This usage survived into the early modern period via Aristotelian scholasticism. 'Intellect' was a specifically human attribute, fundamentally different from anything to be found at the non-human level. It was not unusual for this attribute to be identified with the human capacities for logical inference, conceptual thinking and abstraction.

However, the crucial point is that this category could refer both to a rational order of things and to the human capacity for understanding that order. The Greek term *nous*, which had been translated by the Latin *intellectus*, had defined something in the human soul that participated in objective reason (*logos*), the rational order of the world. We still get a faint echo of this notion in early modern references to the creator of the universe as the 'divine intelligence'. Such theological interpretations were based on a more general figure of thought that united in one category a human capacity and the features of the world upon which it was exercised. Aristotle considered that although

> being an act of thinking and being an object of thought are not the same . . . in some cases the knowledge is the object. In the productive sciences . . . the substance in the sense of essence, and in the theoretical sciences the formula or the act of thinking, *is* the object. As then thought and the object of thought are not different in the case of things that have not matter, they will be the same, i.e. the thinking will be one with the object of its thought. (Aristotle, 1984, II: 1698–1699)

The objects of *nous* were the fundamental principles according to which the world was constructed. To the individual intelligence there corresponded the 'intelligible objects' of the world, and with the exercise of that intelligence these objects lived in the individual. There could be no understanding of *nous* without an understanding of the objects that gave it content. The classical, Aristotelian, notion of intellect depended on a belief in a 'right' and necessary order of the world. The principles of that order were to be distinguished from matters of empirical contingency, things that might also have turned out differently. Only insofar as these principles were glimpsed by an individual could individual intelligence be said to be operating.

As we will see in the next chapter, a very different conception of reason replaces the Aristotelian conception in the modern period. A purely instrumental understanding of intellectual activity supervenes. What reason can do is to find the best means for achieving an individual's ends, not to discover the best ends. In this scheme there is no counterpart to the classical conception of *nous*. Rationality is not something that can be attributed to the world, only to individuals. Things just are the way they are, though people are equipped to make the best of them. In due course this equipment would be attributed to individuals' biological constitution, but for this attribution to be made it was first necessary for people to get used to thinking of the intellect as a piece of equipment, an instrument like an arm or a leg, to be employed in the service of individual ends. Such a notion would have seemed strange indeed to someone accustomed to the classical perspective.

From that perspective the modern conception of intelligence, based as it is on the prior notion of the instrumentality of reason, would seem to involve a loss of the crucial distinction between intelligence and mere cleverness. If we allow the translation of *nous* as intelligence, some such distinction is already to be found in Aristotle, who also recognizes another human quality, *deinotes*, which is generally translated as cleverness. Now, *deinotes*, defined as 'the power to perform those steps which are conducive to a goal we have set for ourselves and to attain that goal' (Aristotle, 1962: 1144a25) sounds suspiciously like the modern conception of instrumental reason. The merely clever person may know how to choose the most effective means to achieve a given end but is a fool when it comes to the rational evaluation of the ends themselves. Of course this is not how we would expect the Aristotelian *nous* to manifest itself. But even *nous* has its limitations. It is defined by the understanding of abstractions, of 'first principles', and fine though this was, Aristotle knew that there was a lot more to living intelligently than that. So other distinctions have to be introduced. One of these leads to a category that is clearly related to some of the everyday rather than the scientific uses of 'intelligence'. This is the category of *phronesis*, which has no equivalent in modern English usage.

Unlike the inhabitants of Greek city states, the monks who interpreted the categories of Greek philosophy in the Middle Ages tended to be preoccupied with theoretical rather than practical or political intelligence. Later scholars often had similar inclinations, and so there developed a curious division between academic writings on the topic of the 'intellectual' faculties and everyday usage to which the term 'intelligence' was consigned – 'abandoned to the psychology of the streets,' as Charles Spearman (1923: 19) put it rather suggestively.[2] (He saw himself as the noble rescuer who would bestow academic respectability upon this poor waif.) However, if we go back to the classical sources we find quite another evaluation of the practical intellect. Human excellence could be displayed in action as much as in abstraction, and in either case its achievement required the operation of rationality. But not in the same way. Theorizing in science and philosophy proceeds from particulars to abstractions, but human action always occurs in particular situations, so that even the most marvellous abstractions do not necessarily help us to act well. For that we have to have a capacity for responding appropriately to particular cases, we have to have 'good sense', the term which some of Aristotle's translators think comes closest to *phronesis*. Whereas *nous*, the prototype for the later category of intellect, involved insight into matters that often had no obvious social character, e.g. mathematical abstractions, *phronesis* was inherently social. The paradigmatic example for the exercise of *phronesis* was political action. Perhaps that is why the term had no appeal to later generations whose experience of politics left a lot less room for good sense than had Athenian democracy.

In everyday usage, however, the attribute 'intelligent' has come to be applied in ways that recall the concept of *phronesis*. It is quite appropriate to speak of an intelligent policy, of someone making an intelligent decision, of handling a situation intelligently. One of the reasons for the scepticism that the twentieth-century psychological concept of intelligence often encountered among the lay public was its apparent failure to cover such cases.

The distinction between theoretical intellect and practical good sense is only a small part of a complex network of concepts within which Aristotelian theorizing attempted to capture the essential meaning of the kind of talk about human excellence that was familiar to its audience (see Reeve, 1992: ch. 2; Sparshott, 1994: 196–237). Among the most fertile of these concepts were *sophia* (wisdom) and *techne*, involved in the making or production of things. Another interesting distinction was that between the part of the rational soul that reasons for itself and the part that merely listens to reason. Natural slaves have the latter but not the former.

The Aristotelian conception of reason opens up a vast domain of which I have merely presented glimpses.[3] These should suffice to convey an impression of a rich conceptual landscape whose features and contours are quite different from what we find in modern psychology. As late as the seventeenth century, an essentially Aristotelian conceptual network still defined intellectual orthodoxy when it came to reflection on human reason. It provides the background against which the significant features of modern developments should be highlighted.

Aristotelian affections

Earlier on, we followed Foucault in noting that in the self-care practices of antiquity individuals became objects of their own regard. Within such a context, concepts of the human person had necessarily to be dual in character. On the one hand, there had to be concepts that would make intelligible the individual's desire for improvement, for better under-standing, for taking care. Such concepts generally referred to the individual's rationality. But on the other hand, it was also necessary to conceive of aspects of the individual which were the object of improvement, the targets of control. These aspects came to be known as the affections, or passions. They were experienced as things that happened to people, things that could grip them, in spite of their better rational judgement.

In the Aristotelian texts, such aspects of the person are discussed in three different places, supplying three different contexts: the *Rhetoric*, the (Nicomachean) *Ethics*, and the book *On the Soul*.[4] When we compare these texts, we find that each of them treats the topic in a different way. In each case the discursive context determines the content.

The *Rhetoric* is devoted to the principles of persuasion, either in a court of law or in a political forum. For this purpose it discusses 'the emotions [which] are all those feelings that so change men as to affect their judgements, and that are also attended by pain or pleasure' (Aristotle, 1984: II, 2195). So here the criterion for grouping certain things together is that they all affect people's judgement. There is an implicit distinction between judgements and certain feelings which affect them. The Aristotelian text enumerates these feelings, mostly giving them a bipolar character. Thus we get anger–calmness, friendship–enmity, fear–confidence, shame–shamelessness, kindness–unkindness, pity–indignation, as well as envy and emulation. The choice of 'emo-tions' is governed by what is considered useful to the public orator, but so is the distinction between judgements and what affects them. Institu-tionalized forms have defined the space within which the orator has to operate. Certain acts of decision making have been institutionally separated from the process of deliberation preceding them. The public orator is permitted to intervene only during the earlier phase but tries to influence what happens in the second phase. A text on the art of rhetoric should provide him (no women allowed) with a conceptual scheme for organizing his actions within this institutional space, and this is what Aristotle's *Rhetoric* is designed to do.

In the *Nicomachean Ethics* the discursive context is quite different. A very specific practical interest has now been replaced by a more general one. The parts of this text that would strike the modern reader as 'psychological' are addressed to 'the student of politics'. Such a person, we are told, should know something about the soul, just as one 'who is to heal the eyes must know about the whole body also' (Aristotle, 1984:

II, 1741). The reference to healing makes it clear that practical concerns have not disappeared, but they are now considerably broader than the narrow goals of the orator. A more general question – how to achieve 'excellence' (or 'virtue', as the older translations would have it) – now determines the agenda.

As a consequence, it is noticed that there are certain things which sometimes prevent us from achieving excellence or virtue in spite of ourselves. The analogy of a 'paralysed' limb is invoked – its owner wants to move it to the right, yet it moves to the left. So there are elements of the soul which go their own uncontrolled way. Some of these elements have to do with processes of nurture and growth which we are powerless to influence at all. Then there are elements which we are able to control to some extent, like passions and desires. The distinction is therefore between human 'reason', which aspires to the good life, and other elements in the soul which must be regulated if the good life is to be achieved. According to Aristotle, the ideal is not the suppression of the passions but their expression in moderation. In modern terms, we would have to say that 'reason', no less than the passions, is endowed with 'motivational' attributes. There is a natural striving for excellence or virtue, for the good life, for happiness, just as there are particular desires which at times interfere with this striving. The distinction is one between different kinds of striving (orexis), not between striving and something else.

A major difference between the rhetorical and the ethical context is worth noting. Both are essentially practical in nature, but whereas in the Rhetoric Aristotle was concerned with ways of influencing others, in the Ethics he is much more interested in improving the self. That clearly determines the way in which individual striving is conceptualized. The public persuader gets what he needs – a finite list of specific human qualities that he can work on. For the person seeking moral enlightenment, however, such a list is of little help because, as Aristotle points out, moral judgements are not made on the basis of natural qualities but on the basis of excellence or virtue. So the ethically interested person is taught to think of almost any quality in terms of the opposition between reasonable moderation and unreasonable excess (or sometimes deficiency). Later on, that ethical opposition would become reified in terms of a conflict between the rational and the irrational part of the human person.

In another discursive context Aristotle himself introduces some such distinction, but the scheme he presents is different from the ethical one. In the work On the Soul there are no practical considerations. This time the only professed interest is in the truth about the soul as such, so we are presented with yet another scheme of classification, a scheme that derives from Aristotle's beliefs about what the Greeks called psyche. This entity has no modern equivalent and is certainly not to be confused with the Christian soul or the post-Christian mind (Sorabji, 1979). For

Aristotle, the possession of *psyche* distinguished the living from the non-living, so that it was to be found in plants and animals as well as in humans. However, in his book on *psyche* (traditionally rendered by the Latin *anima* or the later 'soul') Aristotle is concerned with the differences between the 'souls' of plants, animals, and humans. The underlying question that gives direction to this inquiry is one about the place of humans in the world of nature.

Aristotle lays the ground for answering this question by distinguishing between five 'powers' of *psyche*. These are: the power of absorbing nourishment for growth, the power of sensing, the power of movement, the power of appetition (desiring), and the power of thinking. The 'souls' of plants have only the first of these powers, most animals have the next three, and only the human soul has all five (Aristotle, 1984: I, 658ff.). Thus the distinction between cognition and desire serves to establish the superior status of humans in the order of nature.

What makes this scheme quite different from modern arguments with a similar practical outcome – Descartes' for example – is its meta-physical basis. The natural 'powers' that Aristotle worked with are not at all like the physical machinery of the moderns. Every such power has an inbuilt tendency towards a certain state or end, a certain 'appetite' or directed striving. The power of vision, for example, strives for exposure to visible things, the power of locomotion includes a spontaneous tendency to move, and the power of thought implies actually engaging in thinking whenever possible. *There is no separate category of 'motivation' in this scheme*. That category only became necessary when all psycho-logical activity came to be classified as a kind of mechanism, analogous to inert physical machinery. Such a mechanism *always* needs a push or 'motive' to get it going. That was introduced in the eighteenth century, as we will see in the next chapter. In analysing activity, the Aristotelian scheme did not separate out a mechanical action component and an energizing component. What lay behind activity were certain 'powers' that were as much energizing as they were enabling. The power of thinking was no different. It implied a tendency to reason that did not require a separate motive to get it going. The power of appetition did not act like a source of mechanical pushes for all the other powers. It involved a tendency to seek whatever constituted 'the good' for the creature. In the case of humans, that included moral goods which were objective, as much part of the order of the world as the objects required by animals for their survival. In Christian versions of this scheme the category of 'the will' was often invoked here.

Some post-Aristotelian themes

In the post-Aristotelian literature of antiquity 'affections', or 'passions', were assigned a different place in the make-up of the individual. The moral teaching of Stoicism, in particular, emphasized rigorous self-control, rather than Aristotelian moderation. The things to be controlled were now systematically conceptualized as a separate class of undesirable 'movements of the soul'.[5] Four basic passions were recognized: pleasure, pain, fear, and desire. The Greek concept of *pathos*, applied to things that one underwent or suffered, had been given a philosophical interpretation by Aristotle as one of the ten basic categories of existence. It also had a more specific meaning. The passions could distort the normal functioning of the person. They were even thought of as a kind of disease of the soul. For the Stoics, the unity and rationality of the soul remained paramount. Passions were still beliefs or judgements, so that the opposition was not between cognition and passion, but between natural and unnatural expressions of the soul. In the Stoic view: 'we are responsible for our emotions, just as we are for our more considered actions' (Annas, 1992: 116).

Mediaeval Christian theology elaborated its own doctrine of the powers of the soul, reinterpreting the classical authors to suit a different agenda. In particular, the opposition between sensuous and intellectual striving and between endured passion and active will became entangled with the opposition between flesh and spirit. St Thomas Aquinas held that the sensuous appetites, or passions, were not attributes of the (immortal) soul as such, but only affected the soul insofar as it was tied to the body. That idea incorporated a long tradition of blaming the body for feelings that were unwelcome yet hard to control, a tradition that was to survive in secular form right up to the twentieth century.

Scholastic doctrine is also notable for its systematizing efforts. In the writings of St Thomas Aquinas (1947) these led to an elaborate classificatory network which assigned a proper place to such diverse experiences as hope, despair, fear, courage, desire, pain, love, aversion, and several others. All these were 'passions'. The practical interest in controlling human experience and conduct is still prominent – Thomas rates them all as either good or evil. But there is also a pronounced effort at conceptual control. The labels for the passions are lifted from their place in ordinary usage and caught in the scholar's finite nomological net where they are assigned their systematic place. Backed by the institutional power of the Church, there now existed an authoritative doctrine which could be used to instruct people about how they were to regard their affective life.

As late as the seventeenth century, there are few basic changes in this doctrine. Descartes' *The Passions of the Soul*, published in 1649, is notable for its total separation of soul and body and its mechanistic view of the latter (Descartes, 1931). That radicalizes the existing tendency to make the body responsible for the passions. The latter are now simply experiences of the soul caused by the body. A new opposition comes to define the passions. The 'passions of the soul', originating in the body, are now distinguished from the 'actions of the soul', which depend solely on the soul itself and owe nothing to the body. These 'actions' are described as 'all our desires', and they include acts of will resulting in overt behaviour as well as pure thoughts. The passions include 'perceptions' of bodily appetites, like hunger and thirst, as well as 'feelings or emotions' caused by the body. For Descartes, there could also be perceptions, feelings and emotions that do not originate in the body but in the soul. He therefore employs two principles of classification, one experiential, the other metaphysical. Experientially, we know the difference between perceptions and feelings, and we also refer them either to the outside world or to ourselves. But, metaphysically, there is a fundamental distinction between experiences originating in the body and experiences originating in the soul. Descartes' metaphysical criterion enjoyed a strong revival two centuries after it was first proposed. The effects of that revival were still prominent in twentieth-century conceptions of the emotions.

In many respects, Descartes' treatment of the 'passions' followed tradition. He disagreed with St Thomas' classification and offered his own, deriving all the passions from six primitive ones: wonder, love, hatred, desire, joy and sadness. However, he clearly shared the conviction that passions were distinct entities to be caught in a classificatory net like animal specimens. His book on the passions was based on his earlier correspondence with Princess Elizabeth of the Palatinate, a political refugee who looked to him for advice on how to cope with the difficulties of her personal situation. He also sent the book to Queen Christina of Sweden, another troubled soul whom he was counselling at the time. As in the past, Descartes' conceptualization of the passions is embedded in a context of moral concern. The passions are that which must be controlled if the good life is to be achieved. They are assigned their place by the fundamental opposition between a superior part of the individual which does the controlling and an unruly inferior part which ought to be controlled. Descartes, however, refuses to identify these parts as higher and lower layers of the soul. Only the superior part is soul; the inferior part is body.[6] The passions had always been undesirables within the soul, but now their causes are banished to a nether region outside the soul.

Note that passions now have *causes*. There is a hypothetical chain of physical causes and effects within the body involved in their generation. And if the rational will does not intervene, this chain of efficient causes extends to the skeletal musculature and results in motor activity which Descartes does not distinguish from action. If one acted purely under the influence of a passion one's behaviour would be quite mechanical. Descartes' rigid mind–body dualism introduced a fundamental division between *voluntary* and *involuntary* action that was not like anything recognized in the classical literature. In this respect, his work on the passions certainly marked the beginning of a new period.

Let us briefly note the main points that have emerged so far. First of all, it is clear that there was a strong element of continuity in European discourse regarding such phenomena as desire, joy and aversion. For many centuries, such topics tended to be discussed in a context of moral concern dominated by a fundamental opposition between one part of the individual that was higher, better and in charge, and another part that was a source of unhappiness and evil, and that must be kept in control. This was a discourse that aimed to inform people about their own nature in such a way as to facilitate their self-management within given social circumstances. One of the ways in which this worked was through the provision of schemes of classification that would enable people to label and identify their experiences in a manner appropriate to the goal of moral control. Because they were arbitrary, there was never any agreement on the labels covered by these schemes, and there certainly was nothing remotely resembling the twentieth-century distinction between emotion and motivation. What was much more important than the specific content was the mere existence of such schemes and the fundamental polarity between the ruling and the ruled over parts of the individual. Those were the features which ensured the serviceability and survival of conceptions that converged on aspects of humanity characterized as non-rational.

Notes

1. For pursuing many of the issues briefly touched on in the present chapter, as well as related topics, the extensive bibliography in Everson (1991) will be found very useful.

2. Possibly this was encouraged by the devaluation of 'intelligence' implied in St Thomas Aquinas' (1947, I: 405) observation that this form is found in translations from the Arabic, whereas 'intellect' is found in translations from the Greek.

3. For a topical discussion of some of the complexities of ancient conceptions of human and animal reason, as well as references to relevant secondary sources, see Sorabji (1993).

4. There are also brief allusions in the *Topics* which need not be considered here.

5. See Gardiner et al. (1970) for details. On general issues regarding 'the passions', see Solomon (1976).

6. 'For there is within us but one soul, and this soul has not in itself any diversity of parts; the same part that is subject to sense impressions is rational; and all the soul's appetites are acts of will. The error which has been committed in making it play the part of various personages, usually in opposition one to another, only proceeds from the fact that we have not properly distinguished its functions from those of the body, to which alone we must attribute every thing which can be observed in us that is opposed to our reason' (Descartes, 1931: 353).

3

THE GREAT TRANSFORMATION

Many of the fundamental categories of twentieth-century psychology are, to all intents and purposes, twentieth-century inventions. Such concepts as 'intelligence', 'personality', 'behaviour' and 'learning' were given such radically changed meanings by modern psychology that there simply are no earlier equivalents. In other cases, for example 'motivation' or 'social attitudes', the use of the terms themselves was new, describing previously unsuspected phenomenal domains. The coming of modern psychology was associated with a revolutionary restructuring of the network of categories employed in the conceptualization of human experience and conduct.

But not everything was changed. Certain, unquestionably psychological, categories were retained with little or no change in meaning from an earlier period. Concepts like 'emotion', 'motive' (which is not 'motivation'), 'consciousness' or 'self-esteem' made the transition to the modern period without any radical change in meaning. The existence of this more venerable group points to an older layer of psychological concepts that antedated the emergence of Psychology as a discipline. Of course, this older layer also contained such prominent categories as 'will' and 'character' which did not survive the transition to a scientific psychology. Why then did one group survive and another not?

The answer proposed here is that the survivors were part of a categorical network whose basic features were bequeathed to modern psychology by an earlier period. To use an archaeological analogy: in constructing its domain, modern Psychology used building blocks from older settlements insofar as these were still serviceable under the new conditions. However, the image of building blocks is perhaps misleading. It would be more appropriate to speak of foundations. For it was not a pile of disconnected conceptual units that was taken over but a lattice of interconnected parts. In the present chapter we will describe some of the historical roots of these foundations.

Eighteenth-century novelties

If we try to trace back the meaning of the older psychological categories that are still in systematic use today we quickly lose the trail once we go back further than the eighteenth century. Unless we are determined to see modern meanings where none exist, and to close our eyes to crucial distinctions, we will find ourselves in quite unfamiliar conceptual territory, even in the seventeenth century. True, there will be occasional flashes of recognition evoked by this or that element, but these elements will usually be embedded in an alien framework and will not be historically continuous with their later incarnations.[1] For example, in the previous chapter we noted the essentially traditional nature of Descartes' ideas about the 'passions'. Between these ideas and later concepts of 'emotion' or 'motivation' there is a vast conceptual gulf. We cannot travel from one to the other without entering an entirely different landscape.

The very notion of 'Psychology' does not exist before the eighteenth century. Of course, there was no lack of reflection about human experience and conduct, but to imagine that all such reflection was 'psychological' in our sense is to project the present on to the past. Before the eighteenth century there was no sense of a distinct and identifiable domain of natural phenomena that could be systematically known and characterized as 'psychological'. There were theological, philosophical, moral, rhetorical, medical, aesthetic, political categories, but no psychological categories.

When these made their appearance in the eighteenth century the need for a specific label gradually made itself felt. That label was invented in Germany towards the middle of the century and later travelled to France (Dessoir, 1902; Pongratz, 1967; Scheerer, 1989). Before this time, 'Psychology' crops up occasionally in reference to knowledge about spiritual creatures (Lapointe, 1972). It is only from the second half of the eighteenth century that there exists a continuous discursive domain under that label. In Britain, such a domain had emerged at about the same time, but it had come to be known as mental philosophy. Only towards the middle of the nineteenth century did the lexically more convenient 'Psychology' begin to be adopted (Hamilton, 1863).

It was in its British form that eighteenth century psychology survived in the twentieth century. There are two major reasons for this. One has to do with the historical accident that twentieth-century psychology came to be dominated by one national psychological tradition, the American, that was in direct line of descent from British mental and moral philosophy. Early modern American Psychology took many of its categories from nineteenth-century British textbooks, which had inherited those categories, with little fundamental change, from an earlier generation of British texts.[2] In many cases those categories were part of everyday English usage.

A second, and more fundamental, reason for the long term survival of certain psychological categories from eighteenth-century British philosophy lies in their appropriateness to conditions of life that have undergone little essential change during the intervening period. In certain fundamental respects eighteenth-century Britain was the first major example of a modern society. It was characterized by a new social order, based on free wage labour and capital, the ubiquity of commercial and contractual relationships, the principle of representative government, individual enterprise, and scientific rationality. Under these conditions the old moral discourse began to lose its force and relevance. A new moral discourse, more in tune with the times, derived its principles from knowledge about what was now called *human nature*, not from revealed truth or rational deduction from metaphysical certainties. A new set of categories was developed for the description of this human nature, which, one is not surprised to discover, would have been rather well adapted to life as a man of property in eighteenth-century Britain. These new categories involved a fundamental reconstruction of ancient conceptions about both reason and the passions, and some of the products of that reconstruction were to prove remarkably durable.

The construction of a new moral discourse involves a complex historical process. Over a relatively long period, countless individuals increasingly encounter situations in which old ways of making sense no longer work. Quite unintentionally, and usually without awareness, subtle changes creep into the way words are used, new terms appear and novel perspectives emerge. Sooner or later, these changes are reflected in written texts which later provide historians with their raw material. Such texts will belong to a variety of genres – literary, medical and scientific, educational, philosophical, and so on. In principle, material from any and all of these genres is relevant for the reconstruction of the historical process.

Nevertheless, the present chapter is limited to a consideration of texts that can be described as 'philosophical' in character. There are several reasons for this restriction, the first being economical. To trace all facets of the kind of transformation that is of interest here would require a lifetime of work from many scholars. In this chapter, however, the aim is only to pick out certain themes that are directly linked to later developments in psychology. No doubt one could point to innumerable indirect links, if one looked for them. But, because of the way in which the discipline of Psychology arose, the direct links mostly involve philosophical texts and writings in the medical-biological domain. The latter will be explored in the next chapter. For the present, we will concentrate on the philosophical genre. This genre is also particularly useful in pursuing our general goal of tracing the historical construction of psychological categories. Philosophical texts strive for conceptual clarification, and in doing so they often systematize and make explicit what is left indistinct by other writers. Such texts also tend to address matters that are taken for granted elsewhere and therefore provide valuable insights into the process of category construction. Relying on these useful features of the philosophical genre does not, however, mean that philosophers are assumed to be the individual creators of the changes that their publications allow one to document.

From passion to emotion

In the first place, the fundamentally changed social circumstances had made it imperative to re-evaluate the passions. So far from being undesirable, a certain kind of passion seemed in fact to be necessary for the success of the kind of society that had now emerged. This insight was provocatively presented in the form of a fable for the times that caused an enormous commotion. It was called *The Fable of the Bees*, and it bore the telling subtitle: *Private Vices, Publick Benefits* (Kaye, 1924). Its author, Bernard de Mandeville, a Dutch physician who had settled in London, had summed up a current dilemma by telling of a great and prosperous hive of bees who were upset by the fact that vices like pride, envy and vanity were so widespread among them. But when a higher power turned them all into virtuous and honest individuals, the hive quickly lost both its greatness and its prosperity. Two essays appended to the fable's second edition in 1723 drove home the moral: public benefits result from private vices.

The fable released a veritable flood of responses. By 1759, no fewer than 145 of these had appeared (Kaye, 1924), an extraordinary result for the time and a clear indication that its author had struck an exposed nerve. Among the critics were several of Britain's foremost philosophers, and the influence of the fable was still important half a century later.[3] One of the philosophers who responded to the challenge of the fable in terms that are especially relevant to the reconceptualization of the passions was Francis Hutcheson, Adam Smith's teacher. He made a distinction between 'calm' desires that led to the pursuit of very general goals, like wealth and power, and more specific affections of the mind which were often linked to 'confused sensations' and 'violent bodily motions' (Hutcheson, 1969). Only the latter were true passions, while it was the former which constituted the private origin of 'public benefits'.

A similar move had been made just two years earlier by Bishop Butler, who was then a much respected authority on questions of moral philosophy. Butler thought there was a big difference between 'cool or settled selfishness' and 'passionate or sensual selfishness' (Butler, 1950: 13). It was only the latter which was to be condemned, while the former was quite beneficial, both to the individual and to society. There were really two kinds of motivated action. The first kind involved specific impulses directed at particular objects, without regard to the ultimate consequences for the individual. The second kind constituted what Butler called 'an interested action'.[4] Such actions were governed by 'the cool principle of self-love or general desire of our happiness and private good' (1950: 52). This distinction was not merely a convenient device for purposes of classification; it was thought to correspond to fundamental elements of human nature. Therefore, much of the conflict previously seen in terms of the war between reason and the passions was now accounted for in terms of the clash between sensuality and 'self-love' or 'interest'.

The distinction between two classes of non-rational affections of the soul followed the general scheme of the empiricist philosophy as laid down by John Locke. According to this scheme, mental contents were to be divided into one category that was the product of direct sensory experience and another category that constituted the results of mental reflection on this sensory basis. Locke had been primarily concerned with epistemological questions. The eighteenth-century moral philosophers devoted more attention to the operation of Locke's distinction in the field of conduct and its regulation. Here a parallel distinction had to be made between those impulses to action that affected the mind directly through the senses (internal as well as external) and those that were the result of reflection. The former constituted the 'violent' passions, while the latter took the form of 'calm', 'cool' or 'gentle' passions or interests. These were thought of as being gradually formed in the course of individual development, as the result of reflection on past actions and their outcomes. It was by learning from their personal experience that individuals developed an active concern for their general self-interest.

Not many years after Butler and Hutcheson had driven a deep wedge between two kinds of passion, David Hume, a more profound and ultimately more influential philosopher, adopted a similar distinction between what he referred to as *calm* and *violent* passions. However, he adds a clarification which shifts the basis for the distinction. He will not be concerned, he says, with the immediate effects of pure sensory impressions, only with 'reflective impressions', that is, those which are already affected by past experience (Hume, 1978: 276). That means the distinction between 'calm' and 'gentle' passions cannot be traced to the Lockean distinction between sensation and reflection (Ardal, 1966). What then is to be the new basis for distinguishing among the passions?

A clue to the answer is provided by Hume's frequent use of a word which hardly figured at all in previous discussions of the topic. That word is *emotion*. It was a fairly recent derivative of *motion* that had been used to describe either a physical or a social agitation. By analogy, it was also applied to mental agitation or excitement. But at this point it lacked any kind of systematic status, being no more than a slightly picturesque descriptive term. That is still how Hume uses it, but the context in which he employs it gives it a fresh prominence. On the surface, the context is provided by a further development of the distinction between calm and violent passion. Hume argues that this distinction conflates two characteristics which should be kept distinct: the present violence with which a passion manifests itself, and the strength of the passion as a motive for action:

> Men often counter-act a violent passion in prosecution of their interests and designs: 'Tis not therefore the present uneasiness alone, which determines them. In general we may observe, that both these principles operate on the

will; and where they are contrary, that either of them prevails, according to the *general* character or present *disposition* of the person. . . . 'Tis evident passions influence not the will in proportion to their violence, or the disorder they occasion in the temper; but on the contrary, that when a passion has once become a settled principle of action, and is the predominant inclination of the soul, it commonly produces no longer any sensible agitation . . . it directs the actions and conduct without that opposition and emotion, which so naturally attended every momentary gust of passion. We must, therefore, distinguish betwixt a calm and a weak passion; betwixt a violent and a strong one. (Hume, 1978: 418–419)

Here there emerges in outline a distinction that has become quite familiar to us, but that had remained nebulous in the writings of Hume's predecessors – the distinction between a motive and an emotion. Hume still talks of passions, but that category is now seen as mixing up several different things: it mixes up temporary states and settled dispositions, and it mixes up motive causes (which vary in strength) and mental agitations (which vary in intensity). As Hume's point of view came to be shared by more and more people, these distinctions were seen as much more significant than the old distinction between reason and the passions. Eventually, that resulted in the demise of 'the passions' as a category of scientific discourse and its replacement by *emotion*. But because the passions had such a weighty historical tradition behind them and were deeply embedded in ordinary usage, that took some time. The process was not complete until the second half of the nineteenth century.

In the meantime, people wrestled with the co-existence of the old and the new terminology. Initially, the distinction between motive cause and mental agitation was suggested as a basis for discriminating among passions and emotions. In 1762, Henry Home (better known as Lord Kames) addressed this question:

Are passion and emotion synonymous terms? This cannot be averred. No feeling nor agitation of the mind devoid of desire, is termed a passion; and we have discovered that there are many emotions which pass away without raising desire of any kind. . . . An internal motion or agitation of the mind, when it passeth away without raising desire, is denominated an emotion: when desire is raised, the motion or agitation is denominated a passion. (Kames, 1970: 53–54)

Note how passion is no longer a fundamental category. The basic categories are emotion and desire, and passion is now merely the name for their combination.

By the early nineteenth century, there was at least one influential system of mental philosophy in which the term 'emotion' had advanced to being the name for all non-intellectual states of mind. In Thomas Brown's system the passions no longer have a place. Instead, he is able to rely on the secure position which 'emotion' had by then achieved in everyday understanding: 'Every person understands what is meant by an *emotion*,' he tells his audience, when he introduces his basic distinction between intellectual and non-intellectual states of mind, the latter being referred to as emotions (Brown, 1831, I: 165).[5] In this scheme there are three categories of emotion, the immediate (example: admiration), the prospective (example: hope), and the retrospective (example: remorse). By and large, desires are classified as prospective emotions. Although Brown's promiscuous use of the term 'emotion' was unusual, the category was now well established. It continued to be evoked throughout the nineteenth century in reference to a major class of psychological objects.

There is a context for the rise of 'emotion' that should not be overlooked. If Hume made the distinctions he did, it was not just because he was a very bright fellow, which he undoubtedly was. There was a change of perspective, a change of world view, that formed the background for his originality. And if the opposition between reason and the passions seemed in the end to lose its hold, this was not just because of the fractionation of the passions; the other side of the polarity, reason, was presumably also implicated. The conceptual change that created the modern concepts of motivation and emotion involved much more than one or two specific distinctions. Important though these were, they were made possible by a rearrangement of a whole network of concepts covering the explanation of human action.

Instrumental reason

So far, we have concentrated on the passions, but it is obvious that no one could have believed in any effective opposition between reason and passion unless they assumed reason to have some kind of causal power. Individuals sometimes acted under the influence of passion, but that influence could be counteracted by the force of reason. Virtually everyone took this for granted right up to the end of the seventeenth century.

But then the fortress of reason began to crumble. An early breach was made by Francis Hutcheson. It seemed to him that when we ask for the reasons of an action the answer may be either in terms of the real causes of the action or in terms of what makes the action 'reasonable' or worthy of approval or disapproval. The two are not the same. If someone is asked why he joined the army he may offer good patriotic reasons, but the actual causes of his action may be far less exalted: being broke or running away from home, perhaps. Thus, Hutcheson (1969: 217ff.) distinguishes between 'exciting' and 'justifying' reasons. The latter are rational propositions, which, according to Hutcheson, never moved anyone to action. That power belongs to the affections or passions, for only they can function as *motives*. He uses a telling analogy: 'Rhubarb strengthens the stomach,' we say. That proposition may justify our fondness for rhubarb, but it cannot strengthen the stomach – only the natural action of the rhubarb can do that.

The dethronement of reason is completed by Hume. What had been a useful distinction for Hutcheson now becomes an absolute principle governing the explanation of human conduct: 'reason alone can never be a motive to any action of the will . . . it can never oppose passion in the direction of the will' (Hume, 1978: 413). Behind such confident pronouncements lies a revolutionary recasting of the entire network of basic categories used to make human action intelligible. Hume still uses traditional terms, like 'passion', 'will' and 'reason', but they no longer mean what they used to mean. We have already seen how 'passion' had become morally neutered to include any 'calm' and 'settled' disposition capable of acting as a motive. Concomitant changes in 'will' and 'reason' were even more profound.

What had held the concept of the passions in place over the centuries was the polarity between them and reason. The passions were what they were by virtue of their opposition to reason. But reason, it must be remembered, was not simply an individual attribute (see Chapter 2). Rather, it was the individual's link with the universal. From the necessity of the laws of reason flowed the order of values that governed the human world. This order was fixed and objective, though individuals could be deficient in their understanding of it. By the High Middle Ages individuals were thought to be endowed with a rational will that enabled them to participate voluntarily in the higher order of the cosmos by controlling their passions. Will and reason were conjoined. While the passions were the home of individual, increasingly material, particularity, the rational will opened the door to the eternal moral order of the universe.

All that was now gone. The eighteenth-century moral philosophers all worked in the shadow of Newton, none more so than David Hume. It was established that the order of the universe was mathematical and mechanical. Many still attached deep moral significance to this order, including Newton himself and Bishop Butler, but the conclusions they drew from this were not the traditional ones. Butler (1950), for example, considered the private experience of pleasure and pain to be a reliable moral guide, for God had affixed pleasures and pains to various courses of action in such a way as to make good actions more likely and bad actions less likely, on the whole. It is not through their reason that individuals share in the divine order of the universe, but through their private and sensuous experience of pleasure and pain.

This process of privatization soon affects reason itself. Hutcheson discovers that when persons act under the influence of what have now been identified as 'calm' desires they follow certain 'maxims' or 'natural Laws'. The good or evil to be expected from the objects of such desire is found to be quantifiable, because it is proportional to the duration and intensity of the pleasures and pains afforded by the objects. Hutcheson (1969: 41) also observes that 'men content themselves in all Affairs with smaller, but more probably successful Pursuits, quitting those of greater

Moment but less probability.' If they now multiply this probability by the net quantity of expected pleasure they will arrive at an estimate of the relative desirability of the object. Where there are both positive and negative aspects associated with the attainment of an object, the estimated value of the one is subtracted from the other in order to arrive at the final outcome measure. This is reasoning all right, but what a difference to the reason that was involved in the exercise of the rational will! When operating in the service of the new category of 'calm' desires reason becomes an exercise in calculation (see Brooks and Aalto, 1981). No longer does it lead to the discovery of an objective order of universally binding truths. It has now become *instrumental*, employed in the service of calm desire. From being the master it has become the servant.

This reversal is celebrated in Hume's famous dictum that reason is and ought only to be the slave of the passions. Reason can no longer act with the force of will, because the determinants of human conduct are now seen in terms fashioned after Newtonian natural philosophy. Hume was a convinced determinist. Human action, he claimed, resulted from the workings of a mental machinery that followed regular and predictable patterns. There was no difference in principle between causality in the physical sphere and causality in the mental sphere. In both cases causal determination involved merely the regular succession of perceived events. No 'hidden powers' could be made responsible for the regularities presented in experience. On the psychological level this meant the elimination of any concept of human agency. Individuals acted under the influence of their passions, and reason merely calculated the optimum path for this action. By now, Hume had moved too far out for his contemporaries. But two centuries later, such ideas were no longer shocking.

Motives and the contingency of action

The will was now reduced to a vehicle for the transmission of mental impulses to the motor apparatus. Very little could or need be said about it. In fact, if one was to be completely consistent in applying the new scheme, the will was a redundant concept. On the other hand, the category of *motive* acquired a new importance. Because the will could do nothing on its own, it always required a motive to push it into activity. But motives were not reasons. They could no longer be defined in terms of goals chosen by an agent. Instead, they were now conceptualized as elements in a linear chain of cause and effect that linked human experience and human action. Now that the rational will had disappeared, its place was taken by specific elements that all shared the property of causing action. The class of such elements was identified by the label *motives*. The word 'motive' had existed before, but it now acquired a new, systematic, status in a coherent scheme for the explanation of human conduct. The hallmark of this scheme was its thoroughgoing determinism.[6] It was Hume's ambition to lay the foundations for a science of human thought and action along the lines of the Newtonian science of nature. In that sense, it is not altogether far-fetched to refer to his 'contribution to behavioral science' (Miller, 1971).

By the middle of the eighteenth century, a new conception of the relationship between human persons and their actions was in the public domain. But the change had been in the making for some time. We have been focusing on the last stages of the change, because it is in these that the nature of the change appears most clearly. However, in the later stages, certain understandings that had been necessary for the occurrence of the change were already taken for granted. To explore these background assumptions we have to step back a bit in time to a period when they were still controversial and therefore under active discussion.

Philosophically, the basis for the changes I have been discussing had been laid by John Locke at the end of the seventeenth century. In 1690 he had announced that 'the will or preference is determined by something without itself' (Locke, 1959: 375), but had still identified this determinant as 'the good'. One might say that he had half broken with the traditional conception. A few years later, his revised text uses a different language: 'The motive for continuing in the same state or action, is only the present satisfaction in it; the motive to change is always some uneasiness' (1959: 331). The determinants of the will, that is of action, no longer have any intrinsic connection with the supra-individual domain of reason or morality; they have a purely individual and private origin in feelings of satisfaction or unease. These latter, also known as pleasures and pains, provide the common attribute of all motives. Whereas in the classical scheme only some actions – those under the influence of the passions – were undertaken for the sake of private satisfaction, now all actions were assumed to be determined in this way.[7]

This privatization of the causes of action was based on a pervasive sense of separation between human agents and their actions. For male members of the propertied classes the new social order had greatly increased the possibilities of personal choice and acting on one's own account. For such persons, at least, considering alternative courses of action in the light of one's personal preferences had become the norm. In the past, one's course of action had generally been prescribed by tradition, by moral rules experienced as universally valid, or by the commands of authorities to whom one was tied by bonds of unquestioning loyalty and obedience. The question of private preference did not arise. For a large but diminishing part of the population that condition continued well into the modern period. But for the privileged strata that provided the producers and consumers of written texts a different experience of action had become more typical. One now felt oneself to be personally in command of one's own actions, and one could indulge in the luxury of allowing free play to one's private preferences. The link between action and preference was *contingent*: one could choose the action which promised the greatest private benefit in the circumstances.

Locke gave expression to this experience by formulating the relationship between individuals and their actions in terms of *property*. In a very famous passage he states that 'every man has a property in his own person', and in particular in 'the labour of his body and the work of his hands' (Locke, 1980: 19). In other words, my abilities and personal qualities, as well as my actions and their products, are part of me only in the way that my house and my garden are part of me. They may be very dear possessions, but I will deploy them so as to gain the most benefit from them; in other words, I will use them *instrumentally*. Locke's philosophy announces a new way of experiencing the individual's relationship to the world, including his own body and its activity. In this philosophy the property relationship is more fundamental than civil society. In the state of nature, which is imagined as prior to society, individuals already treat parts of the world as their property and devote themselves to accumulating more of it. The actions of an individual constitute his original property and are employed instrumentally to increase his possessions.

Of course, the phenomenon of calculated action had long been known and recognized. But its significance had been minimized in various ways, for example by treating it as a character flaw, or by seeing it as a special skill cultivated by rulers or merchants. The new philosophy, however, asserted that calculated, instrumental action was the 'natural' form of human action in general; it was inherent in 'human nature'. That switch entailed a fundamental reconstruction of the categories used to make human persons and their actions intelligible. Reason became instrumentalized, and the ever more important distinction between 'calm' and 'violent' passion evolved into the difference between motive and emotion.

A new sense of self

The reconstitution of the relationship between individuals and their actions implied changes, not only in the explanation of actions, but also in the conceptualization of the human person. Here too, Locke's work signalled a new era. As late as 1890, William James, in discussing the topic of the 'self', still refers to the 'uproar' caused by Locke's views on this question (James, 1890, I: 349). What exactly was the uproar about? Locke had simply raised the question of personal identity: how do I know that I am now the same person I was yesterday or last year?

Although the question was new, it was obviously both meaningful and unsettling for his audience. It was meaningful because in the increasingly commercialized society of post-Revolutionary England social identities conferred by birth, such as class, kinship and occupation, were no longer immutable. Not only were individuals becoming separated from their social identities, but that separation was accelerating at a time when the hold of theologically based notions of personal identity was also beginning to weaken. Where neither social identity by descent nor the immortality of the soul provided a sufficient guarantee of permanence and stability, personal identity had to become something that was questionable.

Locke's solution to the problem was to base it on a continuity of consciousness of self. This consciousness of self accompanies all our experiences as a kind of shadow, 'it being impossible for anyone to perceive without *perceiving* that he does perceive'. He explains that 'since consciousness always accompanies thinking, and it is that which makes everyone to be what he calls self, and thereby distinguishes himself from all other thinking beings, in this alone consists personal identity' (Locke, 1959: 449).

This argument depended on the use of two crucial terms in what was then quite a novel manner. The terms were 'consciousness' and 'self'. As regards the former, it seems to have been virtually a neologism whose first recorded occurrence in English hardly antedated Locke's *Essay* (*Oxford English Dictionary*, 1989, III: 756). Locke had invented a means of describing what was then a new way of experiencing the world, that is, separating the sense of self from the experience of one's inner and outer actions. In this world one never just lives or acts; one is always 'conscious' of one's self living and acting.[8] The self is now a distinct, this-worldly entity, a view which was at first widely regarded as misguided and rather shocking.[9] Locke's many critics (Fox, 1988) generally reaffirmed the more traditional Christian belief that personal identity depended on an immortal *substance*, the soul. But they were fighting a rearguard action.

Locke had extended into the realm of self-knowledge a radically new way of regarding subject–object relations that had emerged in the seventeenth century. In Chapter 2 we noted how the Aristotelian conception of intellect, or *nous*, depended on an intimate connection between human reason and the rational order of the world. In the modern conception, however, intellect became a purely subjective attribute localized in the minds of individuals and not in the cosmos. In the ancient scheme of things, which persisted with certain modifications through the mediaeval period, it was taken for granted that the same spiritual principles were at work in human individuals and in the world around them. The mediaeval alchemist was convinced that his own inner state was crucial to the outcome of his experiments, an outcome that was not conceived in the crudely material terms that a later age was to impose on them. Pre-modern individuals understood themselves as direct participants in an ambient cosmic order. As this sense of

participation broke down, as individuals became increasingly aware of
the depth of the gap between themselves and the world in which they
lived, a new conception of the self could become established. The self
now became the subjectively localized point of origin from which each
individual experienced and acted on a world that had become no more
than a source of those experiences and of the raw material for the
individual's actions.

The Lockean self has been rather aptly named the *punctual* self
(Taylor, 1989), for it is conceived as a point within experience or a focus
of concern which is 'disengaged' and quite separate from any specific
actions and experiences of the individual. Such a view forms the
psychological counterpart to Locke's political doctrines, which were
based on a model of society as an aggregate of strictly separate
individuals, rather than a collective entity.

In subsequent Anglo-Saxon literature Locke's conception became part
of a taken for granted framework for understanding the nature of the
self. This conception may be characterized as *empiricist* because the self
is regarded as an object that can be empirically known and studied,
much like any other object. According to Locke, all knowledge,
including self-knowledge, has a sensory origin. Having received some
'ideas' (mental contents) through the senses, the mind 'reflects' on them
to form other ideas. In addition, 'it turns its view inward upon itself,
and observes its own actions about those ideas it has, takes from thence
other ideas, which are as capable to be the objects of its contemplation
as any of those it received from foreign things' (Locke, 1959: 159). In
other words, one's observation of the contents and the activity of one's
own mind is analogous to one's observation of the external world. In the
empiricist scheme, the way in which we obtain knowledge about the
external world becomes the model for the way in which we are thought
to obtain knowledge about ourselves (Toulmin, 1977). What this means
is that the cognitive relationship between self-as-subject and self-as-
object can, in principle, be just as distanced, and even manipulative, as
the relationship between the self and objects that are external to it.

The basis of self-knowledge had been revolutionized. The change in
the categories of self-knowledge had affected the representation, not
only of the products of such knowledge, but also of the manner in
which they were obtained. Invariably, the empiricist mental philosophers back up their knowledge claims by an appeal to a kind of
observation that is clearly meant to be as dispassionate as that which the
natural philosophers were directing at the external world. Now, however, this dispassionate observation has to be directed *inward* at a world
of mental objects waiting to be discovered just like the physical objects
of the external world. At its most consistent, this attitude leads to the
employment of exactly the same analytic technique for mental
observation as had been so successfully used in the case of the physical
world. Mental contents were to be dissected into their most elementary

components, and it was these that were regarded as most 'real'. Pursuing this technology to the end, Hume concluded that there was no reality to the self as an entity over and above 'a bundle or collection of different perceptions' (1978: 252).

This was not widely accepted, but in Britain that was not enough to discredit the empiricist approach to the mind. The anti-Humean Scottish School of mental philosophy, founded by Thomas Reid, was just as steeped in Lockean empiricism as their opponents. It was in Germany that disagreement with the excesses of empiricism led to a more fundamental rejection of the entire approach. At first, British mental philosophy was quite popular among German writers, but in the latter part of the eighteenth century that changed (Dessoir, 1902). Two kinds of knowledge came to be more and more sharply distinguished: one based on the distanced, dispassionate, observation of nature encouraged by science, the other typified by the more subjective, involved, way of experiencing the world expressed in the new literary and artistic style of Romanticism. As this distinction crystallized, the terms *Empfindung* (sensation) and *Gefühl* (feeling) took on their modern psychological meaning. In the nineteenth century an analogous process occurred in English. Prior to this, 'feeling' had referred to any mental state (see note 5); now it took on the subjective colouring which placed it in the proximity of 'emotion'.

Romanticism entailed a further reorganization of the categories of mental activity. In the classical, rationalist, scheme the salient distinction was between clear and distinct ideas and unclear, confused, ideas. The latter marked what would later be called 'emotional' experiences, but the distinction was based on their *inferiority*, not on their difference in kind. Empiricism devalued this distinction, but it also emphasized the privacy of experience and encouraged self-observation. The need to combine this emphasis with the modern respect for dispassionate scientific observation eventually led to the distinction between feeling and sensation. The latter provided the supposed basis for 'objective' knowledge, the former for 'subjective' experience.[10] Since the nineteenth century, the psychology of sensation and perception and the psychology of feeling and emotion have therefore been constituted as separate fields.

Notes

1. Graham Richards has presented the only extensive discussion of this issue in the literature. He sums up as follows: 'no single tap-root of Psychology is present in the seventeenth century, but there is a range of one-off, discrete anticipations of specific realms of Psychological enquiry, both within and outside the texts in the orthodox canon. These nearly always failed to initiate continuous traditions of enquiry and contributed little to the development of the modern enquiries they anticipated' (Richards, 1992: 92).

2. The most prominent examples of such textbooks are those by Bain (1977) and by Spencer (1871). What was new in them was the latter's evolutionary perspective and the

former's recourse to physiology. In their purely psychological conceptionalization they continued along the tracks laid down by earlier British empiricists.

3. Bishop Berkeley and Mandeville engaged in a public polemic. The links between Mandeville and Adam Smith have often been noted and are extensively explored in Dumont (1977).

4. Butler did not invent this terminology. There was by this time quite a history of discourse about interests as 'countervailing passions' linked to the beneficial effects of capitalist economic activity (Hirschman, 1977). The British eighteenth-century moralists systematized this discourse and elaborated its quasi-psychological implications more thoroughly than their predecessors.

5. At this stage, the term 'feeling' still functions as a synonym for 'state of mind', so that sensations and perceptions are also categorized as feelings. The liaison between feeling and emotion came later. This is discussed in the section, 'A new sense of self' (pp. 46–9).

6. Hume's determinism was no idiosyncrasy. Quite independently, David Hartley was working on another deterministic account of human conduct at the same time, though he only published the final version ten years after Hume's account had appeared (Hartley, 1749). Unlike Hume, Hartley provided a theological rationale for his determinism. This was however ignored by his rather influential nineteenth-century followers, who included James Mill and W.B. Carpenter. In psychology, the legacy of eighteenth-century determinism and mechanism was first preserved in its specifically Hartleyan rather than its Humean form. But in the long run, the influence of Hume, a major philosopher, was much greater.

7. This is not to be confused with earlier doctrines that had proclaimed the ultimate selfishness of human striving. The point here is not the selfishness of goals but the inevitable privacy of their origins. Those eighteenth-century descendants of Locke who believed in a 'moral sense' could recognize unselfish goals; what had become unthinkable for them were goals that did not have a private origin.

8. Locke was clearly indebted to Descartes' derivation of personal existence from personal thought – 'I think, therefore I am'. From a philosophical perspective, Descartes' point was more fundamental, but in the history of modern psychology it is Locke's formulation of questions and answers about the self that marks the beginning of the empiricist discourse that has dominated this field. By contrast, Descartes' commitment to a metaphysical soul substance and a rational will erected insuperable obstacles to the development of anything like modern Psychology.

9. When the English word 'self' first appeared as a noun, around 1300, it had the negative connotations derived from a long tradition of seeing the individual primarily as a sinner. The *Oxford English Dictionary* (*OED*) (1989, XIV: 906) quotes an early example: 'Oure awn self we sal deny, and folow oure lord god al-myghty.' This opposition between the self as an incarnation of wickedness and divine goodness survives for several centuries. An example from 1680 declares that 'Self is the great Anti-Christ and Anti-God in the world' (*OED*, 1989, XIV: 907). But by then there was also a counter-current that had announced itself in the appearance of numerous new 'self' compounds in the English language. Many of these carried positive rather than negative connotations, as in *self-made* (1615), *self-interest* (1649), and *self-confidence* (1653).

10. Philosophically, the seeds of the distinction can be traced to the differentiation of 'primary and secondary qualities' which Locke had adopted. Historically, many other factors enter into the picture.

4
THE PHYSIOLOGICAL BACKGROUND

Psychology and physiology

If a significant number of the fundamental categories of twentieth-century Psychology had their source in empiricist mental philosophy, could one say that this Psychology was a kind of continuation of empiricist philosophy by other means? That would be going too far. First of all, these 'other means' – experimental and statistical technologies – were never mere passive instruments, but played a crucial role in reshaping the conceptual landscape of the discipline. Secondly, modern Psychology relied on the older sciences for more than its technology. Some of its most basic categories had a biological origin. There was nothing arbitrary about the title of the first major textbook of the new science: *Principles of Physiological Psychology* (Wundt, 1874). The topics, the methodology and the conceptual apparatus were all to be found in the physiology of the time. Strong traces of this legacy were still evident a century later.

The dependence of early experimental psychology on previous work in physiology has always been obvious. What has been much less obvious is the appropriate time frame for assessing the nature of this dependence. It is clear that virtually all of the work in the first psychological laboratories stood in a direct line of descent from similar work in mid-nineteenth-century physiological laboratories. One thinks of work on vision, touch and hearing, on reaction time measurement, on the recording of physiological reactions, and so on. However, that is not all there is to the story. The conceptual link between physiological and psychological topics goes back rather further than this practical link. In fact, the boundary between physiology and psychology was not always drawn as sharply as it was in the latter part of the nineteenth century. By that time, physiology had finally embraced a consistently mechanistic approach. Henceforth it would limit itself to the investigation of somatic functions in a purely physicalistic framework.[1] That project was extremely successful, but it did entail the jettisoning of that part of its older mandate which had extended to psychological issues. In a manner of speaking, the newly autonomous physiological psychology had been spat out by nineteenth-century physiology.

Prior to these developments, physiological texts had dealt with psychological issues as a matter of course. Johannes Müller's great compendium, *Elements of Physiology* (1838–42), had devoted large sections to topics that were later to be considered as falling on the psychological side of the boundary between the disciplines. The same was true of the text of his predecessor, Rudolphi (1821–23). Burdach, another prominent physiologist of the time, explicitly defined the task of physiology as including the study of psychological aspects (1826: 4). In Central Europe this tradition went back at least to the monumental mid-eighteenth-century text *Elementa Physiologiae* (translated as *First Lines of Physiology*, 1966) by Albrecht von Haller. In Britain, there was a late efflorescence of psycho-physiological texts even beyond the middle of the nineteenth century, prominent examples being Thomas Laycock's *Mind and Brain* (1860), Sir Henry Holland's *Chapters on Mental Physiology* (1852), and William Benjamin Carpenter's *Principles of Mental Physiology* (1874). This last work was republished in America as late as 1891 and was cited extensively by William James.

The changing nature of the relationship between psychology and physiology had profound consequences for psychological language. Could the same set of terms be used for describing both bodily and mental phenomena, or would two different languages be needed? At one extreme there was the consistently dualistic position which regarded with horror any mixing of the physicalistic language of physiology and the mentalistic language of psychology. Nineteenth-century physiological mechanists took this position, but so did many of the moral philosophers who were their contemporaries. Both sides feared contamination by the other. However, ordinary language was not so fastidious in its distinctions and contained many terms that carried a mixed somatic and psychological meaning. Common examples were attitude, motive and temperament. Historically, the separation of physical and mentalistic language was a modern development, and in the nineteenth century it was far from complete. The development of Psychology as an autonomous scientific discipline entailed a confrontation of these issues. Two sets of linguistic boundaries would have to be established: the language of scientific Psychology had to be distinguished from everyday usage, and it had to be found a place somewhere between the non-communicating solitudes of physiology and moral philosophy.

There were two areas of investigation in which the boundary between physiology and psychology was particularly unclear. One was the area of sensation. Studies of the sense organs were certainly physiological, but the activity of these organs involved the property of sensibility which was usually considered to be psychological. The second area with blurred boundaries was that of animate motion. The explanation of the movements of living creatures and living organs had become a primary task of physiology. But these movements often exhibited such marvellous co-ordination and apparent wisdom that the question of their direction by some kind of mind or soul kept on coming up. In such discussions no sharp line between the physiological and the psychological could be drawn. It was only the victory of physiological mechanism and physicalism, towards the middle of the nineteenth century, that established rigid borders around the subject matter of physiology. Even then, physiological reductionism applied to psychological topics could still flourish.

At different times, Psychology adopted physiological categories that differed widely in their degree of generality, from highly specific, technical categories to broad categories whose use was pervasive. We will focus on the latter. Among them the interconnected categories of organism, stimulus, reflex and energy require special attention because of their importance for the emerging conceptual structure of modern psychology.

The first of these, *organism*, is fundamental for the transfer of physiological concepts into psychology. It establishes a category of beings that unites animals and humans and thus establishes the plausibility of assuming similar attributes for both. If humans are taken to be organisms in some fundamental sense, then the defining features of what it means to be an organism will apply to them. During the major part of the twentieth century, the most visible of these features have been those related to the theory of evolution by natural selection, i.e. features like adaptability, 'survival of the fittest', and heredity. But the concept of the organism is older than Darwinian theory. Before that theory achieved its pre-eminent position, the nature of organisms was defined by other features. Those features have not disappeared. Some have simply become invisible through being taken for granted; the role of others is now seen as more limited. Response to stimulation is an example of the first case, reflex action and energy are examples of the second. But this does not affect the historical importance of these attributes of organisms, for the traces of their former importance are still present.

For example, *stimulation* is probably the most pervasive category in all of twentieth-century Psychology, precisely because it is so deeply embedded in the conceptual and historical foundations of the discipline that it has acquired a completely taken for granted quality. Whatever the specific content of modern psychological descriptions or theories, a broad range of them presupposes that their domain of application has already been formulated in terms of the category of stimulation. Accounts of perceptual processes deal with the effects of present stimulation, accounts of learning and memory with the effects of past stimulation. Motives and emotions are often conceptualized in terms of 'internal' stimulation, and a still strong tradition conceives of all human behaviour as a 'response' to stimulation. A great deal of psychological description is based on a pre-theoretical analysis of complex and potentially ambiguous situations in terms of stimuli and their effects. A great deal of psychological theorizing is designed to explain how such

effects work. The relevance of such theories depends on the prior
description of phenomena in terms of the category of stimulation. So
pervasive, and so deeply rooted, is the use of this category that its
implications have become invisible. It is assumed to be completely
neutral and to entail no assumptions about the nature of the subject
matter that is to be described or explained.

That, however, is an illusion. Description of phenomena in terms of
stimuli and their effects imposes a certain structure on the phenomena.
In most instances there are other descriptions that could have been
adopted but have been quietly rejected. Moreover, the category of
stimulation is a historical product which emerged in specific contexts
and for specific reasons. To understand its significance we need to
appreciate the circumstances of its historical formation and its subsequent trajectory. Stimulation has not always meant the same thing. In
the course of its history, the connotations of the term have varied
considerably. At each stage, a different aura of meaning was imposed
when phenomena were subsumed under the category of stimulation. At
every stage, however, this term, perhaps more than any other, expressed
fundamental convictions about the status occupied by subjectivity in the
natural order.

The present chapter explores the 'archaeology' of stimulation by
exposing some of the deeper conceptual strata that have provided the
foundations on which modern variants could be erected. Three layers
are considered here: the deepest is vitalistic, the next involves a transition to mechanistic models in the shape of the concept of the reflex,
and the third represents the incursion of metaphorical physicalism
through nineteenth-century concepts of energy.

Vitalistic roots of 'stimulation'

Both the area of sensation and the area of animate motion were deeply
affected by a fundamental reformulation of physiological problems that
took place in the second half of the eighteenth century. The concept of
stimulation played a crucial role in this reformulation. In one sense,
what happened was less a question of the reformulation *of* physiological
problems than a question of reformulating problems *as* physiological. In
the late seventeenth and early eighteenth centuries the important work
on the operations of the living body had been conducted within a
dualistic framework. Descartes had set the tone. Souls and bodies represented entirely different orders of being. Living bodies were pieces of
physical machinery whose reactions did not require any explanation
beyond those supplied by the science of mechanics. The living structures
that conveyed the effects of stimulation were regarded as mechanical
contrivances that behaved like strings, valves, tubes, and fluids under
pressure. The problem of the production of animate motion was not

distinguished in principle from the problem of the production of inanimate motion. Physiological problems were problems in applied mechanics. At this time, the term 'stimulus' is occasionally found in the medical literature (Möller, 1975) with reference to external agents that produce injuries (e.g. burns and stings) or that alleviate pathological conditions (e.g. the reduction of swellings).

The emergence of the category of stimulation as a fundamental element in the construction of uniquely *physiological* questions is intimately tied up with the switch from mechanism to vitalism that became increasingly pronounced in the latter part of the eighteenth century. Vitalism came in many varieties (Benton, 1974), but here we are only concerned with their common denominator, namely, an insistence that the processes of life could not be reduced to physical mechanism but involved the operation of special principles characteristic of living forms. The much respected Haller, for example, considered that *sensibility* was due to a unique property of living nerves, and that animate motion depended on the special *irritability* of muscles (Haller, 1922). With the advance of physical and chemical knowledge such principles seemed, at best, redundant, and at worst, unscientific and mystifying. However, the bad press which vitalism got from the new breed of mechanists in the nineteenth century should not blind us to the fact that some of the conceptual constructions of the vitalists became part of the common language of physiology. Among these constructions the notion of stimulation played a crucial role.

In the old dualistic scheme, only two kinds of instigators of activity were recognized. These were physical forces and acts of will. The activity of animals was entirely due to the former, while human activity was the result of both. Cartesianism held that the passions were produced by physical events in the body, but they could be opposed by the soul's rational will. This scheme created an unbridgeable gulf between the domain of natural science, concerned with animate and inanimate bodies, and the domain of the soul, left to the tender mercies of theologians and philosophers. The vitalistic physiology of the eighteenth century began to bridge this gulf by constructing a third kind of activity which was neither like the mechanical action of inanimate bodies nor the deliberate rationality of human moral action (Danziger, 1983). It was activity in response to a stimulus, and it was characteristic of living beings, now thought of as *organisms*. Whereas inanimate motion depended on a transmission of physical force through passive structures, so that variations in the effect were entirely accounted for by variations in the impinging cause, animate motion depended on the relationship between stimulus and living body. This meant that the effects of stimuli could not be predicted merely from a knowledge of physical principles. Weak stimuli could have powerful effects, and out of several mechanically possible effects only those occurred which preserved the integrity of the living system.

The category of 'motion from a stimulus' first occurs in the work of the prominent Scottish physiologist, Robert Whytt (1768). Such motions were governed neither by the laws of mechanics nor by the laws of logic, but obeyed their own kind of 'necessity' which had to do with the preservation of organismic integrity. Whether an instigator of vital movement was physical or mental had nothing to do with its status as a stimulus:

> The remembrance or idea of substances, formerly applied to different parts of the body, produces almost the same effect as if those substances themselves were really present. Thus the sight, or even the recalled idea of grateful food causes the saliva to flow into the mouth of a hungry person; and the seeing a lemon cut produces the same effect in many people. The sight of an emetic, nay its very name, or seeing others vomit, will in many delicate persons raise a nausea. (Whytt, 1768: 133)

Responses to stimuli were involuntary, but their causal determination was not a mechanical one. There was recognition of a new category of causally determined activity, where the causality was non-mechanical and the mental or physical nature of the cause was irrelevant. That shattered the old dualism of involuntary and voluntary action, the former having physical causes, the latter a mental cause, the will. It also changed the conception of what mind was:

> The mind, therefore, in carrying on the vital and other involuntary motions, does not act as a rational, but as a sentient principle; which, without reasoning, is as certainly determined by an ungrateful sensation or *stimulus* affecting the organs, to exert its power, in bringing about these motions, as is a scale which by mechanical laws turns with the greatest weight. (Whytt, 1768: 152)

Whytt still retained the concept of a rational soul capable of rational consciousness and volition. But he added the construct of a 'sentient soul' which lacked freedom, and whose rationality was not that of self-reflective reasoning but that of the preservation of the biological organism.[2]

One important consequence of this was that voluntary and automatic actions were no longer seen as belonging to irreconcilably separate categories but that voluntariness and automatism were matters of degree. A particular activity might involve varying degrees of automatism at different times and under different conditions. This was a considerable breach in the conceptual fortress that had protected the realm of the will from any kind of naturalistic encroachment. As we saw in the last chapter, the philosophy of Hume had worked in the same direction, and even more radically. However, Hume's solution took the form of a mechanization of the mind, while retaining the separation of mind and body. Compared to this, the new category of stimulated motion was much more productive. It opened up a space for concrete scientific investigation that undermined the traditional position more subtly and more effectively than a purely philosophical critique.

In the work of William Cullen (1710–90), Whytt's successor at Edinburgh, the possibilities of the stimulus concept were developed further. Where Whytt had mainly been concerned with the role of stimuli in the internal functioning of the body, Cullen stressed the crucial role of external stimuli in maintaining normal physiological activity (Thomson, 1832). Other medical authors extended the category of stimulated action in a more psychological direction. At the end of the eighteenth century, Erasmus Darwin (Charles Darwin's grandfather) produced a comprehensive theory of human behaviour and experience in terms of three fundamental categories: stimulation, muscular contraction, and a central 'sensorial power' (1794–96). Unlike his medical predecessors, he did not limit his stimulus–response analysis to actions like sneezing, swallowing and vomiting, but extended it to everyday voluntary activity. He was able to do this by drawing on the principle of association developed within empiricist philosophy. This fusion of the physiological schema of stimulated motion with philosophical empiricism had considerable potential, but Darwin was ahead of his time. It was at least half a century before such ideas resurfaced in Britain, and in the meantime Darwin had been forgotten by his countrymen. However, he fared much better on the continent of Europe, especially in Germany. Ironically, some of his more original notions arrived back in his own country in the form given to them in Johannes Müller's textbook, already referred to. (Young, 1970).

The attention paid to Erasmus Darwin in Germany took place against the background of a fast developing interest in the stimulus concept in that country. In fact, after the original contributions of Scottish medical men, the further elaboration of the category of stimulation was largely a German affair. Cartesian dualism had never become as solidly established in Germany as in France and Britain, so that there was much less resistance to non-dualistic formulations in German medical discourse (Verwey, 1985). Leibnizian philosophy, with its emphasis on the principle of continuity in nature – the idea that natural differences in kind were traceable to many much smaller differences – was also favourable to the extension of the schema of stimulated motion.

When it was extended from the reactions of specific biological organs to the reactions of the organism as a whole, the concept of action from a stimulus became psychologically significant. Eventually, it was applied to purely psychological causes and played an important role in the development of a naturalistic basis for psychology. Thus, J.G. Herder, a prominent figure in the German Enlightenment, advocated a psychology tied to physiology 'at every step' and made copious use of the stimulus concept in a somewhat muddled attempt at showing the way (Herder, 1778).

Soon there was an enormous expansion of the field of meanings covered by 'stimulus' (Reiz) in the German literature. The term 'internal stimulus' was now used to describe the causal effect of mental activity.

In the writings of philosophically inclined biologists like Treviranus
(1822) the will is said to be the stimulus for bodily movements, an action
that is said to be analogous to that of external stimuli and to be subject
to natural laws. Stimuli are also credited with long term effects through
the changes they produce in bodily organs, including the nervous
system.

By the end of the eighteenth century, J.C. Reil, a major contributor to
the systematization of medical knowledge, was able to distinguish
between various senses of the term 'stimulus' (Reil, 1910). In line with
Haller, there was the distinction between sensory and motor stimuli, but
there were also other distinctions. Among these, two are worth mentioning. First, there was a distinction to be made between external,
physical, stimuli, and those stimuli that acted within the organism. The
latter need not be physical and occurred in connection with such
phenomena as the association of ideas. Secondly, there was a distinction
between stimuli in general and those stimuli that corresponded to the
specific sensitivity (*Reizbarkeit*) of a particular organ, light for the eye
and sound for the ear providing obvious examples. The idea of specific
sensitivity was taken up by a later generation of physiologists, like
Johannes Müller (1826), and for a time it provided a theoretical framework for empirical work on sensation and even space perception. In its
later incarnation it came to be known as the 'doctrine of the specific
energy of nerves' (Boring, 1942).

Ramifications of the reflex concept

In its early history, the category of stimulation had acquired a rather
broad meaning derived from a vitalistic understanding of causal processes in living organisms. After about 1830, however, vitalism was in
decline, experimental techniques were becoming more precise, and
scientific explanation became more closely identified with the search for
elements. These changes manifested themselves both in the investigation
of sensory physiology and in the investigation of animal movement and
led to profound changes in the practical deployment of the concept of
stimulation. Here we will focus on developments in the area of animal
movement because, in the long run, these had the most far-ranging
repercussions for the history of psychology.

During the last two-thirds of the nineteenth century, and into the early
twentieth century, the scientific study of animal movement was dominated by the concept of the reflex. Stimulation was of course an integral
component of this concept, but its meaning had undergone a profound
change. Attention had shifted from the broad features of biological
causation to more specific effects. It could now be taken for granted that
the effects of external agents depended on the organization of the living
system, and this recognition was expressed in the retention of the term

'stimulus' in physiology. But questions about the overall integration and functioning of the organismic unit now took second place to questions about the *elements* of the living organization. That implied a change in the way in which this organization was conceived. Increasingly, in the early nineteenth century, the organism was understood in terms of separate functional elements, each with its own spatial localization in the body. Physiological investigation became dedicated to the isolation and identification of such elements.

This emerges very clearly in the work of Marshall Hall on muscular responses that depended on stimulation of the spinal nerves. His experiments on spinal animals were not radically different from earlier work, but his conceptualization certainly was. He attributed the responses of these preparations to the activity of an 'excito-motory', or 'true spinal' system of nerves, which was to be sharply distinguished from the 'sentient and voluntary' part of the nervous system located in the cerebrum. Whereas the reactions mediated by the latter involved conscious sensation and were often 'spontaneous', in the excito-motory system 'there is always the application of an appropriate stimulus, or cause of excitement or irritation; this is followed by the contraction of peculiar sets of muscles' (Hall, 1836: 21). Hall referred to this as 'the reflex function of the spinal marrow', a function composed of many specific reflexes. One could now speak of a reflex in the singular. Reflexes also acquired an anatomical localization in specific nervous pathways. Soon, the concept of the *reflex arc* would become popular. That meant a hard-wired connection from a particular sense organ via sensory nerve, specific spinal segment, and motor nerve to a specific set of muscles.

The decomposition of the reflex function into separate reflex elements led to the replacement of the general function of sensitivity to stimuli (sensibility) by an aggregate of specific stimulus–response elements. It was now assumed that stimulation achieved its effects through potentially identifiable *elementary* units. However complex stimulating situations and their associated actions might be, they were ultimately composed of sensory and motor elements.

These changes were part of a more general transformation in the way of regarding the living organism. Whereas vitalistic physiology had tended to look at specific functions in terms of their contribution to the overall integrity and purpose of the living system, the new physiology was fascinated by the mechanisms at work in the sub-systems. It now seemed more rewarding to trace the material basis of such mechanisms than to speculate about how everything fitted together. The organism was now an assembly of 'parts and pieces in movement' (Figlio, 1977). Such changes went hand in hand with changes in investigative practice. Vitalists like those we discussed in the previous section had certainly conducted experiments, but their experimentation was intended to answer broad questions, often by embedding it in a great deal of purely observational material. In the nineteenth century, physiological experimentation became increasingly dedicated to answering highly specific questions. At the same time, the experiment became, first, the method of choice, and then the only really scientific method for the expansion of knowledge. An attitude of bold interventionism had replaced the older sense of awe before the marvels of life.

In Hall's version, reflex action explicitly runs off without conscious sensation playing any role. The reflex function is now localized in one part of the nervous system and consciousness in another. Stimulation was no longer regarded as achieving its effects through its link to sensibility but through its link to motor response. The connection between external influence and physical motion had become primary, and the role of mind or consciousness in mediating this connection had been downgraded.

This involved a kind of dualism which had been in abeyance during the period of vitalism. But the issue was not settled overnight. Johannes Müller, a vitalist who studied reflex action at the same time as Hall, always maintained that reflexes were mediated by some form of sensation. Two camps quickly formed around this question, both in Britain and in Germany. On the one side were the dualists, like Hall and his chief ally, R.D. Grainger, who advocated a sharp distinction between *stimulation*, conceived purely physically, and *sensation*, involving consciousness. On the other side were those who clung to an older conception of stimulation that necessarily included some form of sensation.[3]

One very important consequence of this controversy was a clarification of the meaning of *sensation*. In the late eighteenth and early nineteenth centuries this term had often referred to any kind of impression on a living organism, so that there was no sharp distinction between sensation and stimulation. In fact, the term 'impression' was often used to cover both. In Germany, the reality of 'unconscious sensations', derived from Leibnizian *petites perceptions*,[4] was widely accepted. Essentially Aristotelian notions had not been completely replaced by Cartesian dualism, so that individual consciousness was *not* regarded as the defining criterion of mind. Mid-nineteenth-century physiological mechanism forced the issue by insisting on a physicalistic language in which 'sensation' had no place.[5] Stimulation and sensation were decisively separated, the former reacquiring a purely physical meaning, and the latter being limited to conscious events. It should be noted, however, that this distinction reflected the interests of idealist philosophy as much as those of mechanistic physiology (see note 3). It was a very Victorian solution which enabled the physiologists to get on with their work on the nervous system without appearing to threaten a moral order based on the presupposition that individuals were free to make conscious choices.

For the relationship of physiology and psychology these changes were a source of both estrangement and opportunity: estrangement because there was no longer any place for psychological concepts in the new physiology, and opportunity because a new psychology might be constructed with the help of an invigorated physiology. In the long run, what proved most useful for the establishment of Psychology as a discipline was not so much the new physiological knowledge as the advances in experimental technology that had produced this knowledge. However, this did not become apparent until the last quarter of the nineteenth century, when the new psychological laboratories were established. Before that, there were several determined attempts at establishing a new kind of psychology by using some of the new physiological *concepts* to reformulate psychological issues. Among these concepts, by far the most important was that of the reflex. For nearly a century, from about 1850, it exerted a powerful influence on the conceptualization of psychological issues.

From the beginning, there was impatience with Hall's dualistic limitations on the scope of the reflex concept. The first to claim vast territories for this concept was Thomas Laycock, a mid-nineteenth-century medical authority based at Edinburgh. Rather unusually, he had acquired a definite interest in German philosophy of nature during his early studies at Göttingen. Applying the Leibnizian principle of continuity, he was convinced that the mode of action of the nervous system could not vary fundamentally at its different levels. If reflexes constituted the principle of nervous functioning at the spinal level, as had recently been established, then the cerebrum too must operate on the basis of reflexes (Laycock, 1845). This meant that Hall's rather limited concept of reflex function had been transformed into a general principle governing the entire behaviour of advanced animal organisms. Laycock's version of this idea was only the first of many.[6]

His student, Hughlings Jackson, became a much more influential neurologist than Laycock himself and established the usefulness of the extended reflex concept for clinical practice. He analysed disorders like aphasia in sensori-motor terms, and proposed that, in general, the mental symptoms of cerebral disease were 'due to lack, or to disorderly development, of sensori-motor processes' (Jackson, 1931). Similar views were held by other major figures in late nineteenth-century neurology (e.g. Ferrier, 1876). The appeal of the generalized reflex scheme was not limited to Britain. In 1863 the Russian physiologist, I.M. Sechenov, published a monograph entitled *Reflexes of the Brain* (1965), in which he attempted to analyse a range of higher order functions in terms of the reflex schema. His ideas remained largely unknown outside Russia, but they had an enormous influence on his student, I.P. Pavlov, who became the central figure in the early twentieth-century popularization of the reflex concept. Among Central European physiologists, the generalized conception of the reflex had also become firmly established in the late nineteenth century. Freud's early teachers, Brücke, Meynert and Exner, were all committed to this conception (see Ammacher, 1965; Ellenberger,

1970), and its effects are easily detectable in Freud's own early foray into speculative psycho-physiology (1954).

For early twentieth-century American psychology, it was Sir Charles Sherrington's work that provided a major source of authority in using the reflex as a general category of behaviour. Sherrington had success-fully combined the elementaristic with the generalized use of the reflex concept in his experimental studies. He had shown how specific reflexes combined to produce 'integrated' responses of the organism as a whole, particularly the maintenance of its posture. Moreover, he had gone so far as to assign a psychological meaning, 'conative feeling', to reflex reactions guided by distance receptors which involved 'the musculature of the animal as a *whole* – as a single machine' (Sherrington, 1961: 326; original italics). The way was now clear for the use of the reflex as a general *psychological* category applicable to the behaviour of all organ-isms, including humans. We will look at this development in Chapters 6 and 7.

The metaphor of mental energy

The generalization of the reflex schema favoured the use of physicalistic metaphors for describing and explaining the workings of the mind. If an essentially physical reflex function was responsible for all the actions of higher organisms, then their mental attributes must also be dependent on this function. That dependence became intuitively understandable when one described mental and physical processes in the same, essentially physical, terms. Concepts of *energy* were particularly well suited for this purpose, because, although they had become thoroughly physicalized, one could still talk of mental energy without raising too many eyebrows. The principle of the conservation of energy, and the associated trans-formation of different forms of physical energy into each other had become established in physics by 1850. After that, talk of mental energy made it possible to invoke the analogy of the transformation of heat into mechanical energy when trying to explain the influence of bodily on mental events, and vice versa. An early suggestion along these lines was made by W.B. Carpenter (1857), a prominent contributor to the discussions that developed around the reflex concept.

Just before mid-century, the Berlin physiologist, Emil Du Bois-Reymond, had provided the definitive empirical demonstration of the electrical nature of the nervous impulse. This had fully legitimized the use of energetic language when speaking of the brain as a physical organ. Reflex processes were now described in terms of nervous 'excitation' and 'inhibition'. Excitation was energy that could be conducted, accumulated and discharged. Late nineteenth-century models of reflex action all made use of this kind of language, and there was a strong temptation to speak of the operations of the mind in the same terms.[7]

One can see this very clearly in Freud's *Project for a Scientific Psychology* (1954). Its central concept was that of a waxing and waning supply of energy or excitation 'occupying' specific neural loci and then being discharged in motor activity. Stimulation, external or internal, is now understood as that which causes the build-up of central excitation. By this time the metaphorical extension of energetic language to mental life had become common, and Freud was no exception. Energetics reappears in psychological form, not only in Freud's 'instinct' theory, but in categories that are used descriptively in psychoanalysis, like 'cathexis'.[8]

The traces of mid-nineteenth-century energeticism within psychological usage were as strong in Britain as in Germany. The language of both major figures of British psychology in that period, Herbert Spencer and Alexander Bain, reflects underlying energetic assumptions. Here we will focus on Bain, whose categorization of psychological phenomena was intimately related to his energeticism. It was through Bain's authoritative texts that this usage became widely accepted in academic psychology.

For Bain, the animal organism is an energy-transforming system which turns the energy derived from food into 'vital energy' that flows into the muscles and is expended in the movements of the organism. The nervous system is no longer a passive conductor of the effects of stimulation but a storehouse of energy that seeks an outlet. Bain accepts 'the physiological fact of a central discharge of nervous energy where no stimulus from without is present as a cause'. Together with other observations, this leads 'irresistibly to the conclusion, that there is in the constitution a store of nervous energy, accumulated during the nutrition and repose of the system, and proceeding into action with, or without, the application of outward stimulants' (Bain, 1977: 328). There is 'a central fire that needs no stirring from without' (1977: 329).

But this is a fire that is not simply physical. A 'coincidence' of states of bodily agitation and states of mental excitement is assumed to exist. Variations in the one produce equivalent variations in the other. More particularly, Bain considers that a rise in vital energy manifests itself as pleasure, while a fall is experienced as pain. These feelings (pleasure, pain, and hedonically neutral excitement), are the basic elements in *emotion*. They define what an emotion is. But because these feelings are manifestations of fluctuations in vital energy, emotion has now become a psycho-physiological category. As we saw in the previous chapter, the category of emotion arose within mental philosophy. For Hume, Kames and Brown 'emotion' described a mental state. Now, however, the mental states so described are defined as dependent on specific physiological events. Emotion is as much physical as it is mental. This has two important consequences for the way this topic is pursued in the late nineteenth and most of the twentieth centuries. On the one hand, talk about emotion is strongly influenced by the energy metaphor, with its images of 'discharge', 'tension', 'diffusion', etc. On the other hand, the problem of emotion within academic Psychology becomes dominated by psycho-physical questions.[9]

At an even more basic level, the energy metaphor was intimately involved in the emergence of a new distinction between psychological attributes. The energy which psychology borrowed from physiology was purely physical and therefore blind. If organisms were to survive, direction must be imposed on their movements. A separate controlling and directing function was therefore needed to assure the proper channelling of energy. Bain draws a fundamental distinction between 'the directing and the moving powers'. The latter were identified with emotional energy, the former with the will. There was also a third basic power, that of the intellect. But Bain was a good British empiricist, so the intellect's powers were entirely instrumental. This tripartite division of the mind replaced a much older dichotomy between its 'active' and its intellectual powers. The tripartite scheme had originated in the late eighteenth century, when Romantic impulses led to the elevation of feeling as a fundamental category on a par with the will and the intellect. But nineteenth-century energeticism reinterpreted this threefold division. It was no longer the experiential quality of feeling which ultimately defined the third mental power, but its capacity to energize, to *move*.

That, however, entailed a change in the older 'active' power, the will. Earlier on, the will had had the function of translating ideas in the mind into actions in the world. That was no longer necessary, because the physical organism was perfectly capable of motor activity. It had its own energy. What was still needed, however, was something that would give appropriate direction to the discharge of energy in movement. This was the new role of the will. If it was to affect the flow of physical energy, however, its action would have to be thought of in quasi-physical terms. That was accomplished by evoking the image of *channelling*. The will directed action by providing the right channels for energy to flow along. To do this, however, it would have to be assigned a place in the energy economy of the organism. It would have to be regarded as one natural force among others. But in that case, should it still be regarded as a fundamentally distinct category of mental life? Towards the end of the nineteenth century it became increasingly difficult to answer that question in the affirmative, once one had accepted the other popular categories of the current psycho-physiology. The will was in decline, and it would not be long before it disappeared from scientific psychology.

Notes

1. The young German physicalists, Brücke, Du Bois-Reymond, Helmholtz and Ludwig, took the lead in developing an explicit programme along these lines which dominated the development of physiology for the rest of the nineteenth century. In France there had been a more continuous tradition of physiological reductionism. Developments in Britain were slower.

2. This was a great advance on the earlier hypothesis of the German medical theorist, G.E. Stahl, that the operations of the rational soul were involved in the functioning of the body. Stahl was still committed to the dualism of reasoning mind and inert matter.

3. In Germany the controversy culminated in a clash between E. Pflüger, editor of a major physiological journal, and the medically trained philosopher, R.H. Lotze. Pflüger (1853), in a position reminiscent of Whytt a century before, maintained that the adaptive nature of the responses of spinal frogs implied the operation of a 'spinal soul'. Lotze (1853) denied this and drew a sharp line between mechanical responses at the level of spinal reflexes and actions controlled by the conscious soul. Like most dualists, he wanted to preserve an autonomous space for conscious moral decisions. In Britain, a late defender of the Pflüger position was the scientific outsider, George Henry Lewes (1877), who tended to swim against the Victorian stream in other respects as well (see Ashton, 1991).

4. Leibniz had applied his continuity principle to consciousness and perception, making consciousness a matter of degree. Complex perceptions, like the sound of a waterfall, are the product of many minute impressions (*petites perceptions*) that individually are not fully conscious, but that together produce an impression at a high level of consciousness.

5. Another term which used to be indifferent to mind–body dualism, and which was thrown out of physiology at the same time as sensation, is 'sympathy'. For an extended discussion of the controversies which sealed the physiological fate of both terms, see Leys (1990a).

6. See Danziger (1982).

7. The ambiguities of this usage in the case of inhibition have been extensively explored by Roger Smith (1992).

8. The inverted commas around instinct and cathexis are intended as reminders of the fact that these terms are the ones chosen by Freud's translators, not by Freud himself. The terms Freud used were *Trieb* and *Besetzung*. The literal translation of the former is 'drive', of the latter, 'occupation'. Both original terms are more expressive of the underlying energeticism than the English versions. Freud's use of the energy metaphor may have been derived from Gustav Theodor Fechner who used it to justify his invention of psychophysics: 'Just as it takes a certain quantity of kinetic energy to split a log or lift a given weight to a given height, so does it take a certain quantity to think a thought of a given intensity; and energy for one can be changed into energy for the other' (Fechner, 1966: 36).

9. These questions tended to take one of two forms: (a) questions about the recognition of emotions from their physical 'expressive' aspects; and (b) questions about the direction of causal influence between the physical and mental aspects of emotion (the debate about the James–Lange theory).

5

PUTTING INTELLIGENCE
ON THE MAP

Biological roots

In the words of a well-known historian of science: 'Intelligence as currently and conventionally understood by psychologists is a brashly modern notion' (Daston, 1992: 211). Indeed, Baldwin's comprehensive *Dictionary of Philosophy and Psychology*, first published in 1901, does not have a separate entry for 'intelligence'. The reader is simply referred to the term 'intellect', which is defined as 'the faculty or capacity of knowing'. At this point 'intellect' was clearly part of the technical vocabulary of philosophical psychology and was presumed to refer to a distinct psychological entity, but 'intelligence' was a mere synonym without any specific scientific meaning of its own. Two decades later Charles Spearman, the British pioneer of testing intelligence, was still complaining that: 'Right up to the present day a large number – perhaps the majority – of even the best accredited textbooks on psychology do not so much as mention the word "intelligence" from cover to cover' (Spearman, 1923: 2).

Nevertheless, in the early years of the twentieth century 'intelligence' had suddenly become a scientific buzz word, among a significant number of psychologists. British psychologists in 1910 (Myers et al., 1910), and American psychologists in 1921 (Thorndike et al., 1921), organized extensive discussions about the meaning of 'intelligence', never doubting that the term had a distinct reference and paying little attention to 'intellect'.

What had happened? Was this merely a linguistic change, a turn of verbal fashion without any fundamental significance? Or should we regard the verbal change as a sign that more interesting changes were afoot? One such change is obvious: intelligence tests had been invented in the meantime and by 1921 were certainly very much part of the psychological map. But does this tell us why 'intelligence' suddenly acquired a psychological life of its own? In a sense, yes, the existence of a widely popular technology was certainly crucial in creating a distinct referential domain for the newly fashionable term. But then again, no, because have we not merely pushed the question one step back? Why, after all, were the new tests called 'intelligence' tests? They could have been called 'intellect tests', or simply 'mental tests', as their precursors had been called for some time (Cattell, 1890). Why the specificity? To call their tests 'intelligence tests', rather than something else, the testers must have had some preconception of what it was they were testing, or at least wanted to test. Where did that preconception come from?

Perhaps it came from Francis Galton, the nineteenth-century figure who inspired the first generation of Anglo-American intelligence testers? But insofar as Galton uses the term 'intelligence' at all he employs it as an everyday term that is generally interchangeable with 'intellect' and requires no careful definition. The term that he uses more systematically in his studies of human differences is 'natural ability', and this he does define explicitly, though his definition disqualifies it as a synonym for twentieth-century test intelligence: 'By natural ability, I mean those qualities of intellect and disposition, which urge and qualify a man to perform acts that lead to reputation. I do not mean capacity without zeal, nor zeal without capacity, nor even a combination of both of them, without an adequate power of doing a great deal of very laborious work' (Galton, 1962: 77). Now, this is not how intelligence testers defined the object of their investigations. Batteries of intelligence tests were not designed to test for 'zeal', and performance on them was certainly supposed to depend on capacity rather than mere laborious work.

The first point to note then about the conceptual shift from nineteenth-century 'general ability' to twentieth-century 'intelligence' concerns the much narrower scope of the latter. That narrowing becomes quite intelligible when we consider the social context within which each of these concepts was deployed. Galton was interested in life accomplishments of the most general sort, professional success and intellectual recognition. The intelligence testers had been given their start and retained their basis in the school system; it was accomplishment, or rather the lack of it, within the relatively narrow confines of that system which was their primary concern. They were employed to assess *capacity* for scholastic achievement, not 'zeal' or hard work, which teachers could quite easily assess for themselves.

It was not in psychology but in biology that the term 'intelligence' was first elevated from lay usage to systematic scientific discourse. This occurs in the context of analyses of animal behaviour by evolutionary biologists. In 1882 a book appeared that even had 'Intelligence' in the title: George Romanes' *Animal Intelligence*, a title later to be duplicated by E.L. Thorndike (1911). In his book Romanes was concerned with the evolution of mind, and of course the question of reasoning in animals was a key element in that concern. Now, reflection on the nature of human reason had a venerable tradition behind it, but in the new context of evolutionary discourse none of this was particularly appropriate. What mattered now was the notion that the possession of reason was not an all or none matter but a question of *degree*. Contrary to the Aristotelian and Cartesian tradition, humans were no longer alone in possessing reason, they just had more of it. The reasoning that humans shared to some degree with animals was not the same object as the reasoning which distinguished them from animals. For one thing, the necessary link to language was gone; for another, the concept no longer defined common norms but organized ordered differences. But the term 'reason' is too intimately linked to the old conception, so Romanes must substitute a new term to signal the new discursive context. That term is 'intelligence'. After criticizing the traditional definition of reason, he writes:

> More correctly, the word reason is used to signify the power of perceiving analogies or ratios. . . . This faculty, however, . . . admits of numberless degrees; and as in the designation of its lower manifestations it sounds somewhat unusual to employ the word reason, I shall in these cases frequently substitute the word 'intelligence'. (Romanes, 1882: 14)

In the closing years of the nineteenth century this usage became firmly established in evolutionary discourse concerning the relative problem-solving capabilities of organisms. Lloyd Morgan's writings, for example, are full of it (Morgan, 1886, 1891, 1892, 1898).

A decade before Romanes opted for 'intelligence' as the label for a faculty of reasoning inherently variable in its development the conceptual niche for such a faculty had already been prepared in Darwin's own writing. In *The Descent of Man* Darwin had made it clear that his theory entailed differences of degree in what he called 'mental powers' between the species, including humans. He writes:

> If no organic being excepting man had possessed any mental power, or if his powers had been of a wholly different nature from those of the lower animals, then we should never have been able to convince ourselves that our high faculties had been gradually developed. But it can be clearly shewn that there is no fundamental difference of this kind. We must also admit that there is a much wider interval in mental power between one of the lowest fishes . . . and one of the higher apes, than between an ape and man; yet this immense interval is filled up by numberless gradations. (Darwin, 1981: 35)

In common with so many of his contemporaries Darwin immediately extends the concept of inherently graded mental powers to the differences among human groups. He continues:

> Nor is the difference slight . . . in intellect, between a savage who does not use any abstract terms, and a Newton or Shakespeare. Differences of this kind between the highest men of the highest races and the lowest savages are connected by the finest gradations. (ibid.)

For Darwin, variability was a fundamental attribute of what he referred to as 'the intellectual and moral faculties of man', and, he adds, 'we have every reason to believe that the variations are inherited' (Darwin ibid.: 159). He certainly had the framework that contained a conceptual space soon to be filled by the category of 'intelligence', though as yet the label was missing.

Had Darwin been less conservative in his use of language he might have made use of two developments that appear to have had a significant effect on later usage. One of these occurred in France earlier in the nineteenth century when Lamarckian evolutionism had led to a rather lively debate about the possible evolution of reasoning (*raisonne-ment*) in animals. But people were not comfortable with the idea of reason, traditionally the most human of qualities, being perhaps a matter of degree and being at least partially shared with animals. In 1822 Baron Cuvier put the weight of his considerable authority behind the proposal to use *l'intelligence*, rather than reason, in the context of discussions about the quasi-rational accomplishments of animals (R.J. Richards, 1987: 67). This convention appears to have taken hold, giving the term a recognized place in French scientific discourse at a time when it had not yet acquired this status in English. As the conception of human reason became increasingly naturalized in the course of the nineteenth century (Daston, 1992) the term came to refer to human cognition conceived as a multi-layered structure (e.g. Taine, 1872). By the time that Binet entered the discussion at the end of the century the evolutionary link had done its work. What remained was a concept of cognition as essentially layered or graded.

English usage was slow to adopt these French innovations. But a new period began with the publication in 1855 of Herbert Spencer's *Principles of Psychology* (1871), four years before Darwin's *Origin of Species*. Spencer, a dedicated evolutionist, not only announced the vision of Psychology as a biological science, but presented the category of 'intelligence' as a central concept for such a science. 'Intelligence' was the name Spencer gave to a basic process which, he thought, covered both psychological and biological change. The essential point about minds and organisms, for Spencer, was that they had to adapt to their environment. That adaptation was never perfect but entirely a matter of degree. The better the adaptation, the higher the level of intelligence. So the term now describes, not a quality which an act may or may not possess, but a graded series of more and less satisfactory acts. Spencer's universe is one in which every living being is constantly under test, and the adequacy of its response constitutes the level of its intelligence. The specific content of adaptations is relevant only insofar as it permits the construction of a hierarchy of excellence. 'Intelligence' has come to be defined by an inherently comparative concept that refers to an abstract notion of excellence of performance under test.

It is in Spencer's evolutionist philosophy that 'intelligence' re-emerges as a term with a specific theoretical meaning, rather than being simply one of a myriad psychological terms in everyday usage or a mere synonym for the academically respectable term 'intellect'. Intelligence had had a specific meaning in scholastic and Cartesian philosophy, but

the contrast between Spencerian 'intelligence' and its philosophical predecessors could hardly have been more profound. In the philosophical
tradition the term was intimately linked to the fundamental distinction
between a material and an immaterial realm, being specifically used
with reference to the latter. Hence the once common and now archaic
but still intelligible notion of a divine intelligence. It was as spiritual
beings that humans could be said to possess intelligence. By contrast,
Spencer is at great pains to establish the complete unity of the material
and the mental characteristics of living forms. Humans have intelligence
by virtue of their status as biological beings. This status not only
subjected them to the iron law of adaptation, mental as much as
material, but placed them in an order of continuous natural gradations
from the lowest organism to the man of genius.

The image of the world as an arena in which living beings were
constantly tested was not an idiosyncratic invention of Spencer's but
was based on common Victorian convictions that were certainly shared
by Darwin and Galton. Although the latter produced the paradigmatic
contributions that made these convictions scientifically fruitful, Spencer,
the philosopher, had his day when scientific usage gradually conformed
to his terminology. When the Darwinian students of animal behaviour
adopted 'intelligence' as an object for their science they were essentially
adopting Spencerian usage. This intelligence was an inherently graded
biological characteristic concerned with task performance in the abstract.

From the beginning, the category of biological/evolutionary intelligence was deployed to rationalize the grading of human groups in a
hierarchy of excellence. Among the English-language contributors to the
Victorian discourse on intelligence the placing of humans at the top of a
scale of animal intelligence was always accompanied by a division of
humans into higher and lower orders according to this criterion. Invariably, these orders were distinguished by the criterion of race; almost
invariably, by the criteria of gender and social class. At the same time as
it bridged the ancient chasm between humans and animals the new
category of biological intelligence sanctified chasms between different
types of humans. The latter could now be seen as the product of a
natural order whose authority had assumed the attributes of divinity.

Intelligence became a biological category at a time when biology had
become a field for the application of empirical scientific methods. It was
only a matter of time before such methods would be extended to the
study of biological intelligence. At first, these studies were limited to
'animal intelligence', but the Darwinian perspective in general, and more
specifically the Galtonian programme of eugenics, provided a clear
licence for extending the investigation of 'intelligence' to humans. Two
followers of Galton, his biographer Karl Pearson, and the retired Indian
army engineer, Charles Spearman, acted on this licence at about the
same time. In 1904 Pearson published a study on the inheritance of
human mental characteristics, including 'ability', defined in terms of

degrees of intelligence (Pearson, 1904). In the same year Spearman published his first paper on 'general intelligence' (Spearman, 1904a). Two years later Pearson followed this up with a study 'On the relationship of intelligence to size and shape of head and to other physical and mental characters' (Pearson, 1906), and Spearman went on to devote the rest of his life to the study of 'intelligence'. At this stage neither Pearson nor Spearman had any inkling of what was afoot in Paris. Binet's intelligence tests had nothing to do with the scientific début of the term in the English-language technical literature, although they undoubtedly helped its rapid progress. When, from about 1908 onwards, Anglo-Saxon investigators became aware of Binet's tests, which came with the label 'intelligence' attached, they had no difficulty in assimilating them to an already existing conceptual schema.[1]

What modern intelligence was not

Before we return to the relationship between the twentieth-century concept of intelligence and the social practice of intelligence testing we need to look a little more closely at the conceptual work which the modern term 'intelligence' performed. Like every other abstract category label 'intelligence' took its place in a network of categories among which there were certain affinities and distinctions. For an understanding of the semantic significance of each category both affinities and distinctions are important. Affinities can tell us about what is taken for granted in defining a category in terms of one particular polarity, and distinctions provide clues about what is significant for those who use such polarities as a means of orientation. At different historical times and in different cultural settings a wide and variable range of such distinctions has been considered significant, and the meaning of psychological categories has fluctuated accordingly.

What were the distinctions that played a major role in the appeal of modern 'intelligence'? Given the biological origins of the scientific term it comes as no surprise to find that the contrast between intelligence and instinct was often stressed in the work of the late nineteenth-century animal psychologists. 'Instinct and intelligence' was also the title of the first psychological symposium on the modern concept of intelligence (Myers et al., 1910). The salient distinction here is between behaviour that is the result of *individual* adaptability and learning, and behaviour that is based on stereotyped inherited patterns (Of course, different grades of individual adaptability were considered to be inherited too.) The polarity of instinct and intelligence was not simply a morally neutral cognitive framework but clearly embodied a judgement of relative value. Certainly at the human level there was an unmistakable preference of intelligence over instinct and this expressed the superior valuation of the qualities that intelligence represented.

How did intelligence differ from instinct? First, it depended on individual experience; instinctive action was generally thought to owe nothing to individual learning, though it was often highly adaptive. Secondly, intelligent action was flexible and pliable where instinctive action was inflexible and rigid. The distinction had not always been seen in these terms. Older conceptions of instinct had tended to emphasize its 'wisdom' rather than its stereotypy, and classical notions of intellect had generally credited it with a significant supra-individual aspect (see Chapter 2). The tenacity with which the basis for the modern instinct–intelligence distinction was adhered to in the twentieth century, even in the face of awkward empirical observations, makes one suspect that this basis owes more to the culturally sanctioned value of individual flexibility than it does to the demands of scientific work.

But what about the supposed affinity that linked instinct and intelligence as the contrasting poles of a conceptual pair? What did instinct and intelligence share that made it meaningful to compare them within one and the same discursive framework? The answer to this question has already been given in the previous section of this chapter. Once intelligence became a biological category it automatically took its place in a network of such categories that would now help to define its meaning. 'Instinct' was particularly salient because, like intelligence, it addressed the issue of adaptation or fitness.

'Intelligence' was deeply embedded in biological ways of thought and discourse. That is what distinguished it from the much older category of 'intellect' or reason. If 'intelligence' always had connotations of gradation that 'intellect' lacked, this was but one aspect of its membership in a family of biological concepts. The rise to prominence of a quasi-scientific concept of intelligence occurred in the wake of a powerful late nineteenth-century trend to subsume human life under biological categories. Prior to this there had been no need of a concept like the modern 'intelligence', though there had certainly been notions of 'intellect', 'intellectual faculties', and so on.

In one sense 'intelligence' and 'intellect' were actually contraries, for they were the products of opposite impulses. Where 'intelligence' was introduced as part of a discourse based on the continuity between the human and the sub-human, 'intellect' had traditionally been deployed in the course of attempts at explaining the nature of uniquely human attributes. As was noted in Chapter 2, Aristotle had made a basic division between those characteristics of the human *psyche* which it shared with the *psyche* of other living things and those which were peculiar to humanity. The translation of the latter as *intellectus* survived into the early modern period via Aristotelian scholasticism. 'Intellect' was a specifically human attribute, fundamentally different from anything to be found at the non-human level. It was not unusual for this attribute to be identified with the human capacities for logical inference, conceptual thinking and abstraction. Descartes, to whom the division between human and animal life was of course supremely important, even developed the concept of the 'pure intellect' (also rendered as 'pure understanding') which emphasized the irreducibility of intellect to anything like sensory experience or gradual learning. This notion lived on in the influential Cartesian tradition (see e.g. Malebranche, 1980).

That the new, biological, conception of intelligence was incompatible with ancient usage did not escape the notice of those who had a vested interest in that usage. Erich Wasmann, a German Jesuit, was scathing in his condemnation of the notion of an intelligence common to humans and animals and differentiating between them only in a matter of degree (Wasmann, 1897). Nor was his the voice of a scientific illiterate, for he was a well-known researcher in the field of animal behaviour who had published his empirical observations, notably on the behaviour of ants, in the standard scientific journals of Germany, Austria and the Netherlands. But for a man like Wasmann, steeped as he was in the conceptual distinctions of another age, the very notion of animal intelligence was nonsensical, for it was intelligence which made humans human. Needless to say, his reactionary polemics had no discernible effect on the onward march of the modern concept of intelligence, but they do serve to underline the magnitude of the conceptual change that had occurred in this area.[2]

There had actually been two major changes. One was the transformation of intelligence into a biological category, which we are concerned with in the present chapter. But this transformation would not have been possible without the radical subjectivization of reason that we noted in Chapter 3.[3] The classical construction, going back to Aristotle and beyond, had worked with categories that referred to a rational order of things as well as to the human capacity to understand that order (see Chapter 2). Even at the end of the seventeenth century a faint echo of this idea is still to be found in the writings of John Locke, a philosopher who often points the way to later developments. For when Locke (1959) comes to speak of the freshly minted notion of 'the association of ideas',[4] he contrasts two ways in which ideas are connected: by 'chance or custom', and by 'natural correspondence'. The former type of connection occurs as a result of the association of ideas, but the latter type is due to the 'excellency of our reason'. The association of ideas often leads to 'unreasonableness' and even madness; that is, a loss of that rationality which is inherently in tune with the natural order of events.

Locke's lingering belief in a human capacity for discerning the rational order of the world begins to seem dubious in the eighteenth century. The kind of scepticism represented by David Hume in particular tends to abolish the distinction between the merely customary and the truly rational and to make the operation of human reason subject to the mechanics of the association of ideas. This paves the way for a purely instrumental understanding of intellectual activity (see Chapter 3). What reason can do is to find the best means for achieving an individual's ends, not to discover the best ends. Rationality is not something that can be attributed to the world, only to individuals. Things just are the way they are, though people are equipped to make the best of them. In due course this equipment would be attributed to individuals' biological constitution, but for this attribution to be made it was first necessary for people to get used to thinking of the intellect as a piece of equipment, an instrument like an arm or a leg, to be employed in the service of individual ends. Such a notion would have seemed strange indeed to someone accustomed to the classical perspective.

The universal classroom

The break with tradition entailed by the nineteenth-century concept of biological intelligence did not occur only on the level of ideas. The Spencerian image of life as a universe of graded forms expressed an apparently obvious truth in a world transformed by industrial capitalism and colonialism. It also expressed the pious belief that the gross inequalities of that world simply reflected a natural order of things in which rewards were necessarily distributed according to inherent worth or endowment.

Nineteenth-century industrial capitalism not only provided a hospitable environment for the idea of universally graded worth, it also provided the techniques that were to transform this idea into a socially effective technology. Among these techniques were (1) the standardization of human work; (2) the division of work into specialized performances; (3) the subjection of work activity to quantitative measures of output; and (4) the exercise of a regime of discipline designed to separate the content of work activity from its social purpose (workers had to learn to understand and willingly execute tasks that were not embedded in traditional communal activity).

As countries were swept up by the process of industrialization their educational systems adapted to the new conditions of adult life. Textbooks and syllabuses became standardized. The school day was rigidly subdivided into clock-timed 'lessons', each devoted to a different specialized subject matter. Examinations became much more pervasive and formal, and written examinations (which allowed for verifiable quantification of output) came to replace oral examinations.[5] Not only was schooling organized differently, it also became universal and compulsory. That entailed the extension of the new system of work discipline to parts of the youthful population that had not previously come within its grasp. Problems within the system were now greatly exacerbated.

A major set of problems revolved around the issue of accountability. The rationalization of schooling affected teachers as much as pupils. Their work too became subject to standardized norms. Quantitative measures of output could be used to judge the performance of teachers as readily as to judge the performance of pupils. Indeed, as teachers lost much of their traditional local autonomy to find themselves on the bottom rungs of an ever more intrusive bureaucratic structure they were increasingly held accountable for the results of their pedagogic efforts. At another level, tax payers wanted to be reassured that the large funds now going into public education were being used efficiently in terms of the results achieved.

Unfortunately, the results achieved within the recently rationalized school system often seemed unimpressive when measured against the expectations of ambitious parents, anxious administrators and suspicious tax payers' representatives. One of the results of transforming education into a *system* for the manufacture of pedagogic output was that everyone within the system – pupils, teachers, administrators – was potentially accountable for perceived failures to make the system work efficiently. In that situation one defensive argument was always available to anyone taken to account: responsibility for disappointing results could be displaced from the process of manufacture on to the poor quality of the raw material, the innate endowment of the pupils. Because it was generally recognized that people differed in their suitability for various social tasks, the argument that some were inherently unsuitable for academic work could be deployed as effectively by individual pupils accused of morally reprehensible laziness as by teachers and administrators challenged to account for poor outcomes. A discourse of differential 'brightness', 'cleverness', 'slowness', 'dullness' etc. therefore became an inevitable feature of the new system. As the fashion for giving social problems a biological interpretation reached ever wider sections of the literate population towards the end of the nineteenth century one can detect a mounting tendency to associate the traditional social labels of 'brightness' and so on with notions of biological superiority and inferiority. In the work of Pearson (1904) and Spearman (1904a), referred to above, we find an attempt to give this association a scientific basis.

The recently rationalized educational system of the late nineteenth century not only gave rise to the phenomenon of intellectual defect as a social problem, it also generated the means which made possible the development of a social technology for handling this problem. Without the prior development of a rationalized system of school examinations in the nineteenth century there would have been no technology of intelligence testing in the twentieth. It was the new system of schooling that gave universal validity to the notion that intellectual activity could be treated as a kind of *performance* to be judged against precise standards of achievement. Systematic formal examinations gave practical expression to this notion. But then, as we have seen, the problem of accounting for the results of this new social practice had to be faced. Who was to be blamed for poor examination performance, and what was to be done about it?

At this point a clear alternative existed. One could adopt a critical attitude to the system that had produced the disappointing results and advocate its change. A few educational reformers took this path. Alternatively, one could accept the existing system and seek to improve the way it functioned. This was the path taken by the psychologists, and in taking it they devised a technology that really was to put their infant discipline on the map, the technology of intelligence testing.

To understand the birth of this technology one has to keep in mind that at the end of the nineteenth century there existed another system of examination, apart from the academic variety. This was the medical version. Individuals were commonly examined for their social fitness by medical experts – another nineteenth-century development which we do not need to pursue here. This meant that there existed a boundary beyond which the competence of the academic examiner was no longer recognized and medical competence took over. Intelligence testing initially took root by taking advantage of favourable conditions at this somewhat blurred boundary. Medical examination was generally employed to determine whether an individual was to be committed to a medically administered institution like an insane asylum. Academic examination was employed to determine the relative success of large numbers of individuals in educational institutions. Universal compulsory education had however created a sizeable category of individuals who, while dismal failures in school, did not appear to be candidates for an asylum. In due course, special school classes and special schools were created for such individuals, mainly because they were a disruptive influence on the regular process of instruction. But how were individuals to be selected for these special institutions? The sole use of ordinary school examinations for this purpose was questionable because they might simply reflect poor motivation, an unfortunate home environment, conflicts with the teacher, and so on. On the other hand, there would often be nothing about these children that suggested the kind of abnormality for which medical intervention would be considered appropriate. Besides, medical examinations in this area tended to be time consuming, costly and unreliable.

The early intelligence tests were invented to fill this gap.[6] They were a hybrid form that made it possible to play educational and medical practice off against each other by borrowing elements from both. Psychological examiners within the school system mimicked the role of medical experts who had preceded them. In America they also found it expedient to use a quasi-medical language. But the actual technology that was deployed owed more to nineteenth-century education than to nineteenth-century medicine. The most important components of this technology were, firstly, the comparison of answers to standard examination questions with a norm, and secondly, the use of age-graded cohorts as the foundation for norms of performance. The former practice had been developed in the context of increasingly rigorous school examinations; the latter was familiar from the bureaucratic use of syllabuses that established different expectations of achievement for age-graded school classes. From there it was but a short step to Binet's concept of 'mental level', changed by others to 'mental age', thereby implying that intellectual age differences were essentially quantitative rather than qualitative.

For their content the items of the new test drew partly on existing medical practice, especially at the lower age levels, where a child would be asked to carry out simple requests and give evidence of understanding the meaning of common verbal formulations. Then there were school-like tasks, tests of vocabulary, rote memory and rhyming ability, that were used at somewhat higher age levels. Previous psychological investigation also played some role in the choice of item content. The resulting instrument was a heterogeneous amalgam tailored to a specific practical requirement.

Binet labelled this instrument a scale of 'intelligence' precisely because it was not designed to test a distinct psychological entity. Intelligence, he recognized, was a 'word so vague and so comprehensive' reflecting the fact that 'nearly all the phenomena with which psychology concerns itself are phenomena of intelligence' (Binet and Simon, 1916: 42). The best that Binet can do to characterize the common feature of everything that falls under 'intelligence' is to invoke the category of 'judgement'. But what is judgement? It is 'good sense, practical sense, initiative, the faculty of adapting one's self to circumstances'; it is 'a fundamental faculty, the alteration or the lack of which, is of the utmost importance for practical life' (Binet and Simon, 1916: 42). Hardly the stuff of rigorous scientific definition! But of course that was not what Binet was after. He had been concerned to produce a practical device that reflected at least some of the myriad meanings that might be intended when, in everyday situations, a child was judged to be lacking in intelligence. He insisted that his scale did not really measure an entity called 'intelligence', because its component items were not superimposable like linear surfaces. One might calculate an individual's overall score on the scale, though if one was to avoid 'illusions' one should do so merely as a matter of practical convenience.

But Binet's little device soon took on a life of its own. This did not happen on its home soil in France, where there was no enthusiasm for reducing intelligence to a single number (Schneider, 1992), but in America and Britain where Binet's test was quickly translated, adapted and packaged as the new psychology's great gift to humanity – the IQ test. Its technology was appropriated by a group of professionals – Spearman and Burt in Britain, Goddard, Yerkes and Terman in the US –

whose understanding of 'intelligence' was based on the late nineteenth-century biological model discussed earlier in this chapter. Henceforth an individual's total score on an intelligence test was interpreted as a measurement of a real entity, something singular that a person could have more or less of, like height or weight. Not only was this entity unequally distributed among individuals, it was also unequally distributed among social classes (the special concern of the British psychologists) and races (the special concern of the Americans). Similarly to physical characteristics like height and pigmentation, the entity called intelligence was also assumed to be inherited. Inserted into this conceptual framework intelligence testing became transformed from a purely practical device with limited purposes into a pervasive technology applicable to the entire population.[7]

Although both the French and the Anglo-Saxon investigators collected their empirical data in school settings, their intentions were rather different. Binet and Simon limited themselves to the narrow technical task of assisting the educational authorities in implementing their policy of determining pupils' fitness for different programmes. Those who had been inspired by Galton, however, had only a limited interest in this modest craftsman's task. Enthralled as they were by the grand eugenic vision they also wanted to lay bare the roots of human worthiness in general. The category of intelligence would serve to bridge the gulf between relative academic success among school pupils and relative success in life among social classes, races and individuals.

For the Galtonians academic success and failure were of supreme interest insofar as the classroom could be regarded as a kind of microcosm that reflected a crucial feature of the macrocosm of life. The bridge between the two was established by conceptualizing both of them as essentially arenas for competition. The school became the model of life insofar as it could be seen as an arena in which innate endowment was put to the test. But this became possible only when life itself had come to be seen as an arena in which individuals and groups were constantly being tested for their relative 'fitness'. When Galton proclaimed: 'I look upon social and professional life as a continuous examination' (Galton, 1962: 49), he gave expression to the world view that made the dominant version of the modern intelligence concept intelligible.

Quite early on there were two versions, mundane and grand, of this concept. They had in common the notion of an inherently graded scale of performances, but whereas the mundane version regarded any such scale as specific to time, setting and task, the grand version saw one of these scales (intelligence tests) as an emanation of an absolutely general and immutable quality of the individual (Andersen, 1994). But to entertain the notion of such a quality, and to believe that intelligence test performance might be its quintessential expression, one had to share Galton's perspective on life as a continuous examination.

Psychometric intelligence

In due course IQ testing not only became an industry, it also provided the motor for an entire branch of psychology. That development was greatly fostered by the mass use of intelligence tests in the American Army during the latter stages of World War I.[8] Once more there was a convergence of professional interest and practical requirements, as there had been in the case of Binet and Simon's work for French education. But this time the professional interests were represented by a far larger and relatively well organized group of psychologists while the pressures of wartime forced the pace of change. The American Army had been a tiny professional force that was forced to expand as rapidly as possible into a conscripted mass army able to hold its own in twentieth-century industrial warfare. That created enormous problems of manpower selection. American psychologists offered to help with these by adapting the recently developed technology of intelligence testing to military use. At first they were able to play on existing fears of the mentally defective to gain bureaucratic acceptance of a technology that had not been designed for use with adults. But very soon their plans became more ambitious and eventually resulted in the testing of more than one and a half million recruits.

In order to achieve that result the psychologists had to modify their technology. Binet's procedures had stayed close to the model of the medical examination in opting for an unhurried one on one interaction of professional tester and child testee and in leaving room for the examiner's judgement when the child's responses were converted into scores. In the American military context such an approach was clearly unworkable. So the tests were administered to large groups of men at a time (often under conditions of extreme discomfort), and a simplistically codable multiple choice format was substituted for experienced professional judgement in arriving at test scores. Military conditions left their mark on intelligence testing and fostered its conversion into a technology for quickly grading large populations in terms of their mental worth. This conversion provided the indispensable basis both for the ideologically charged debates about observed racial differences in IQ and for the mass use of intelligence tests in the educational system during the 1920s and 1930s.

But the military influence went further than this. Strict timing was introduced and answers to test items had to be begun and finished promptly on command. Army authorities greatly valued speed and obedience, and if 'intelligence' was to be assessed in this context the conditions of testing would have to reflect these priorities. Most important of all, the intelligence test scores of recruits had to be validated against officers' ratings of their intelligence in order to secure military acceptance of the new technology. Psychologists had of course encountered an analogous situation when they first tried to develop instruments for assessing the intellectual level of schoolchildren. If these instruments did not yield results roughly in accord with teachers' ratings no one, including other psychologists, would be convinced by their claim to measure 'intelligence'. Whatever it was that intelligence tests could be said to 'measure' it had to be broadly similar to the understandings prevalent in the specific institutional settings in which large scale validation of the tests had taken place.

But there was also a reciprocal influence which psychologists and their technology exerted on the institutional environments that gave them a base. Insofar as these institutions made any use of what the psychologists produced, the category of 'intelligence', now equated with the results of IQ tests, came to play a bigger role in the way these institutions rationalized their selection policies and decisions. The use of psychological expertise in institutional settings always involved some kind of trade-off and negotiation in which institutional authorities permitted a certain degree of psychological influence on condition that their own priorities were reflected in the psychologists' work. Never was psychological knowledge simply 'applied' in an otherwise passive setting.

Nor were the psychologists merely the passive recipients of institutional influences. Their sense of identity as scientists and their existence as a specific community of experts depended upon two articles of faith: that they were engaged in the investigation of real natural objects and that they possessed the appropriate technical means for generating knowledge about these objects. For early twentieth-century American army and school psychologists the most important natural object was 'intelligence' and IQ tests formed the appropriate technology. The latter conviction was reflected in the (incorrect) belief that statistical correlations among the items of an intelligence test provided unambiguous evidence of the operation of a unitary intellectual power inhabiting each individual. Faith in the existence of intelligence as a unitary natural object was grounded in a whole network of beliefs constituting an ideology of the Social Darwinist type. For at least the first quarter of the twentieth century eugenics was an almost invariable component of this ideology.

Whatever their basis, these convictions provided many psychologists with an ideological backbone that enabled them to resist day to day pressures to modify their procedures in light of concrete institutional requirements. Some 'applied' psychologists, like Walter Dill Scott (Mayrhauser, 1987), were ostracized as being too accommodating by those who regarded themselves as the guardians of the profession's scientific soul. But though the latter were also collaborators up to a point, their ideologically driven stance paid off after the war when American psychology could claim to have established scientific proprietary rights over an entity of great social importance, the national intelligence. As long as hereditarianism, xenophobia, racism and Social

Darwinism were significant ingredients of public life the psychological category of intelligence and its attendant technology assured the new discipline a respected place in the social fabric. As J.M. Cattell, a veteran of American psychology, put it in 1922: 'The army intelligence tests have put psychology on the map of the United States', though he had the wit to add: 'extending in some cases beyond these limits into fairyland' (quoted in Samelson, 1979: 106).

The massive institutional application of intelligence tests perpetuated the split between ideological and practical interests that had emerged when these instruments were applied in a military context. Ideologically, the results of testing were supposed to provide evidence for the existence of a unitary, inherited intellectual power whose unequal distribution would scientifically legitimize political restrictions on immigration, access to educational resources, etc. Practically, testing was supposed to provide the kind of information about individuals that could be used to bring about a better fit between diverse individual characteristics and specific social tasks and expectations, as in vocational guidance or the detection of learning disabilities. Such practical purposes were better served by a multiple rather than a unitary conception of test intelligence (Mayrhauser, 1992). More than any other branch of twentieth-century psychology the area of test intelligence always remained deeply and directly implicated in extra-scientific issues of a political and administrative kind (Harwood, 1983). As a consequence there was always significant social backing both for ideological conviction and for pragmatic considerations among members of the research community. This was likely to perpetuate divisions of opinion about the unitary or multiple nature of intelligence. Moreover, the results of the mathematical technique of factor analysis, which was supposed to resolve such conflicts, themselves depended on non-mathematical decisions that could be influenced by supposedly banished extra-scientific considerations. Unanimity on the nature of intelligence therefore eluded the field.

Matters were further complicated by the fact that ideological influences were historically diverse. In North America the ideological pendulum began to swing away from Galtonian hereditarianism towards a rather simple-minded environmentalism during the second quarter of the century. Psychological research on intelligence followed suit and many studies demonstrating the impact of environmental influences on IQ were conducted (Cravens, 1985). However, it must be emphasized that this development had no very profound influence on the use of the category of intelligence in psychology. Environmentalists generally accepted the IQ as a genuine measure of some significant and unitary entity whose reality they did not seek to question. By shifting the question from the reality of what was essentially a hereditarian construction to its precise genetic status the environmentalists actually helped to legitimize a fundamental component of their opponents' conceptual framework (Samelson, 1975). This prepared the ground for a sterile debate about the 'heritability' of IQ, a debate that can be kept going for ever if the key conceptual questions about the nature of the IQ and the nature of heritability are never asked (Lewontin 1975, 1985; Schiff and Lewontin, 1986; Wahlsten, 1994).

Historically, the crucial step in the scientific survival of the intelligence concept was the establishment of an indissoluble link between a certain view of intelligence and a specific technology. For the discipline there were undeniable political advantages in espousing the psychometric concept of intelligence. The technology of testing provided psychology with its first significant marketable product and established psychologists as the recognized authorities on the nature of intelligence. This was signified quite early in the famous definition, or rather slogan, that intelligence was whatever intelligence tests measured. One reason why 'the intelligence men' (Fancher, 1985) clung to the IQ as the representation of a real and singular entity must surely have been their considerable professional investment in this notion.

Not that there was any lack of suggestions for ways out of the impasse into which the psychology of intelligence was driven by its tie to the technology of IQ testing. However, the alternative psychologies of intelligence which produced these suggestions all sprang up outside psychology's North American heartland and were easily marginalized. A brief enumeration of these alternative psychologies must begin with Gestalt Psychology, one of whose earliest contributions was Wolfgang Köhler's (1925) study of the intelligence of apes. Among other things, this work emphasized a fundamental distinction between cognitive processes that were essentially 'blind' and mechanical and those that were insightful. A related distinction, between 'reproductive' and 'productive' problem-solving activity, was proposed by another Gestalt psychologist, Max Wertheimer (1945). Psychometric intelligence was not concerned with such subtleties because of its exclusive concern with the final outcome or yield of cognitive processes rather than the manner in which those outcomes had been achieved. Because the data of intelligence tests consisted merely of a collection of 'correct' and 'incorrect' judgements the only kind of theoretical concept that they seemed to require took the form of a hypothetical innate limit on performance, i.e. an ability. Thus there developed a somewhat notorious split between the psychology of cognitive performance and ability on the one hand and the psychology of cognitive process on the other. The two had nothing to say to each other, and until the advent of the computer and 'artificial intelligence' the study of problem solving as a process rather than a performance received relatively little support.

The determination to shake off testing technology's stultifying focus on intellectual yield and to look instead at process was also central to the alternative psychology of intelligence developed by Jean Piaget (1950). As in the case of Gestalt psychology, this led to distinctions among qualitatively distinct manifestations of 'intelligence'. In the long-buried but recently rediscovered work of Vygotsky (van der Veer and Valsiner, 1991; Wertsch, 1985) one also finds suggestive hints at an alternative psychology of intelligence. These emerge out of an interest in assessing intellectual possibilities rather than limitations. There is also a break with the tradition that defines ability only in terms of what individuals can do on their own, a tradition which informs the received psychology of intelligence, in both theory and practice.

Looking back at the historical development of the received view, one notices a curious feature that calls for a concluding comment. On what grounds have certain procedures been accepted as providing a measure of 'intelligence' rather than some other psychological quality or qualities? Because their results correlated with those of other such tests or with tests of academic achievement? Undoubtedly, but then the same question arises with regard to these other tests, leading us into a historical regress which is not endless. Sooner or later we always end up, not with a score, but with a judgement, a judgement that a certain performance or a certain individual merits the attribute 'intelligent' or its opposite in some degree. The very first attempts at assessing intelligence had to be validated in this way, and even the power of professional expertise could not long protect a conception of intelligence that diverged significantly from such culturally embedded judgements (Carugati, 1990).

Perhaps then it would have been better to approach the psychology of intelligence, not with the *a priori* assumption that intelligence is a quality which individuals possess, but with the observation that intelligence is something attributed to individuals in certain judgement situations (Goodnow, 1984). That would have led to questions about the nature of the situations in which such judgements are made, the expectations and implicit criteria on which such judgements are based, the variation of such judgements with the characteristics of the performance or the person judged, etc. This is a strictly counterfactual speculation, because nothing of the sort happened. But a dash of counterfactual history can sometimes serve to put into sharper relief the things that were always taken for granted in the historical developments that did occur.

Notes

1. For a comprehensive account of these developments and their historical background see Carson (1994).

2. Charles Spearman (1937), whose scientific career depended on taking the objectivity of the modern category of intelligence for granted, could see no incompatibility between this category and scholastic conceptions of an intellectual faculty. Twentieth-century psychologists sometimes engaged in a little historical tourism, returning home with the claim that they had spotted an ancient lineage for concepts that were always in danger of being regarded as 'brashly modern'.

3. This is a change that has continued to engage social philosophers in the twentieth century, often evoking diametrically opposed reactions. The representatives of modernism have welcomed the change (e.g. John Dewey, 1930: 203), while critical theorists have deplored it (e.g. Max Horkheimer, 1947: ch. 1). Dewey explicitly recognized that the modern term 'intelligence' was not just a technical term but stood for a whole world view. The psychologists' reification of the term would seem to be based on an implicit acceptance of this world view.

4. This topic did not appear in the original 1690 version of Locke's *Essay* but was added to a later edition as a kind of afterthought. Contrary to a popular legend in the historiography of modern psychology Locke was not the founder of 'associationism'. I have discussed this at greater length elsewhere (Danziger, 1990b).

5. For an overview see Calhoun (1973: part 2), and Hanson (1993: ch. 7).

6. This story has often been told. The most detailed English-language account of the original invention of this instrument in France is to be found in Theta H. Wolf (1973). The essentials are carefully discussed in R.E. Fancher (1985). For a translation of the primary source, see A. Binet and T. Simon (1916). American developments are discussed in JoAnne Brown (1992); and in Leila Zenderland (1987).

7. 'What was originally a device for diagnosing the defective became a device for hierarchising the normal' (Rose, 1985: 128). For an analysis of the conceptual problems entailed by these developments, see also Gould (1981: chs 5 & 6).

8. This episode in the history of modern psychology has come in for a great deal of scholarly scrutiny, starting with Kevles (1968) and continuing with a landmark study by Samelson (1979). Important recent contributions are those of Mayrhauser (1991) and Carson (1993). I have drawn on these sources in the following paragraphs.

6

BEHAVIOUR AND LEARNING

The story of twentieth-century academic Psychology is the story of an ultimately unsuccessful struggle against an ever more obvious fragmentation. Intelligence and its testing provided an early example of the discipline's tendency to annex new areas without being able to assimilate them. Psychologists had gained an academic foothold by doing experiments on such topics as sensation, perception and memory. For some time, that remained the respectable core of the discipline, but how test intelligence related to this core was far from clear. It was much easier to annex such a field institutionally than to assimilate it intellectually.

That situation was to be repeated many times over in the course of the twentieth century. Child study, or paedology, as it was known in some countries, was another early example. Originating in joint efforts by physicians and educationists, it became transformed into child psychology, rapidly in the US, more slowly in Europe. But its links to core areas of the discipline remained tenuous at best. The same could be said of educational psychology, another early branch. In the period between the two world wars the discipline sprouted as many arms as Shiva, the Hindu deity. A psychological social psychology challenged its sociological rival, 'personality' and 'motivation' emerged as semi-autonomous fields of research and teaching, industrial psychology flourished, clinical psychology became a reality.

What link was there between these fields, except that they all claimed to be 'psychological'? But did that mean anything beyond a vague sense of a common focus that was based on popular images rather than on solid scientific grounds? Grouping these diverse areas together as branches of one discipline undoubtedly had certain practical advantages. It advanced the cause of professionalization by implying that the more practically oriented branches had a respectable link to basic science, and it legitimized the otherwise esoteric interests of the academics by implying that their work had significant practical applications. But, for the most part, such implications were nothing more than promissory notes to be cashed in at some time in the future. Why should anyone accept these notes, and, more importantly, how could psychologists justify such promises to themselves?

In the period under consideration here, that justification depended to a very large extent on the notion that, ultimately, Psychology was *one* discipline whose various branches would turn out to be linked by *one* set of principles. The grouping together of diverse fields of research and practice under one umbrella would then be more than a matter of historical accident and administrative convenience, it would be the logical consequence of deep theoretical links; common scientific 'laws' would unify the discipline. As a first step in this direction, the various parts of the discipline would need to be tied together by common categories of discourse. Such common categories would establish the claim that there were indeed phenomena of importance that were common to all fields of Psychology. Then one could study these common phenomena in order to discover the principles that unified the discipline.

This was the role played by the categories of 'behaviour' and 'learning' in the history of twentieth-century American Psychology.[1] Of the two, 'behaviour' was more foundational, for it became the category that the discipline used to define its subject matter. Whether one was trying to explain a child's answers on a problem-solving task, an adult's neurotic symptomatology, or a white rat's reaction to finding itself in a laboratory maze, one was ultimately trying to explain the same thing, namely, the behaviour of an organism. Classifying such diverse phenomena together as instances of 'behaviour' was the first necessary step in establishing the claim that Psychology was one science with one set of explanatory principles. 'Learning' was not quite as basic a category, but, historically, its role was so deeply entwined with that of 'behaviour' that one can hardly do justice to the one without the other. For several crucial decades they formed an almost inseparable pair, for the 'laws of learning' provided the core example of those behavioural principles that were supposed to unify the discipline. In the present chapter we will trace the origins of this complex, focusing first on 'behaviour' and then on 'learning'.

The history of 'behaviour' is not only intertwined with the history of 'learning', it is also deeply entangled with the history of behaviour*ism*. Unlike the other categories considered here, it has the unique distinction of having given its name to a *movement*. That leads to certain difficulties. We have to be careful not to confuse the history of the movement with the history of the category. They are far from being the same. Historically, behaviourists had no monopoly on the category of behaviour. It was there as a scientific category before they picked it up and nailed it to their masthead, but even then they were not the only ones to give it prominence. One did not have to be a card-carrying member of one of the behaviourist schools to agree to the definition of Psychology as the science of behaviour. Our primary focus here is on 'behaviour' as a category of disciplinary discourse, not on behaviourism as a movement.

That focus is at variance with most of the extensive historiography on the topic of behaviourism (see, however, Kitchener, 1977). By and large, this historiography concentrates on particular individuals self-identified as behaviourists and particular doctrines to which these individuals were explicitly committed. Such a procedure yields valuable historical insights. But it is more helpful in understanding a minority than in following the commitments of the majority of psychologists who, though influenced by behaviourism, did not identify themselves as behaviourists and rejected many of the movement's specific doctrines. If we wish to come closer to an understanding of the aspirations and self-understanding of a discipline, rather than of a movement within it, we will have to focus on its common practices (Danziger, 1990a) and on the categories of shared disciplinary discourse. 'Behaviour' and 'learning' are particularly important examples of such categories. Others will be discussed in Chapter 9.

Five layers of 'behaviour'

In following the vicissitudes of 'behaviour' it is possible to distinguish five periods. Chronologically, the distinction between these periods is not sharp. As one would expect, they merge into each other. Moreover, each period left a kind of sediment behind, so that later on, one encounters layers of usage that are reminiscent of an archaeological site. Each layer has distinct characteristics and its origins can be approximately dated.

Leaving aside older lay uses of 'behaviour', one finds a first layer of relevant scientific use[2] in the context of comparative psychology. At the beginning of the twentieth century, one can detect a new tendency among comparative psychologists to use the phrase 'animal behaviour' when referring to their subject matter. In the year 1900, Lloyd Morgan, then the best-known representative of the field in the English-speaking world, entitled his latest text *Animal Behaviour*. This was a departure from the titles of his earlier books, covering similar topic areas, that had made use of such formulations as 'comparative psychology', 'animal life and intelligence', etc. A few years later, H.S. Jennings (1906), a rising star of American Zoology, entitled his magisterial survey of the field *Behavior of the Lower Organisms*. A paper by Jennings published in 1899 still bore the title, 'The psychology of a protozoan', but by 1904 he had switched to 'The behavior of Paramecium'. During the first decade of the century the term 'animal behaviour' became well established among those working in the area of what had come to be known as comparative psychology. In 1911, a new monograph series in the area was called simply, 'Behavior Monographs', and a new journal began publication under the title *Journal of Animal Behavior*. While the field was obviously expanding, it should be noted that for many practitioners the term 'animal behaviour' was at first meant to complement, rather than displace, such terms as 'comparative psychology' and 'animal mind'. As

late as 1930, Lloyd Morgan published a book on *The Animal Mind*, while
Margaret Washburn's *The Animal Mind: A Text-Book of Comparative
Psychology* went into its fourth edition in 1936. But by then such
terminology had become unusual.

A second phase in the use of 'behaviour' begins slightly later but
overlaps with the first. At this stage the term makes its entry into
general psychology but without the behaviouristic colouring it was to
acquire later. The first text to announce in its title that Psychology was
'the study of behaviour' appeared in 1912. Its author was William
McDougall, soon to take on the role of one of behaviourism's bitterest
foes. In the previous year, 1911, at least two books had been published
whose titles referred to 'human behavior' as their subject matter (Meyer,
1911; Parmelee, 1911). While one of their authors could be regarded as a
behaviourist before J.B. Watson had proclaimed the label, the other,
Parmelee, could not. In the same year, a relatively conventional psychological text (Pillsbury, 1911) introduced its subject matter by defining it
as the science of behaviour. By the end of 1912, J.R. Angell, spokesman
for the functionalist school of psychology, had delivered a timely
address to the American Psychological Association on 'Behavior as a
category in psychology' (Angell, 1913).

Just two months later, J.B. Watson, a young comparative psychologist,
presented a paper at Columbia University which ushered in a third
phase in the modern history of 'behaviour' (Samelson, 1981). Watson
(1913) called his paper 'Psychology as the behaviorist views it'. The
change was quite drastic. From being a label for a category used in
defining the subject matter of Psychology, 'behaviour' was now given
the distinction of labelling a certain kind of psychologist. It was elevated
above other psychological categories in that it not only referred to an
object of investigation but also supplied an *identity label* that challenged
psychologists either to accept or reject it. From the point of view of the
discipline's history, the most significant aspect of Watson's challenge
was that American psychologists took it so seriously. They could have
ignored it, or shaken their heads in amused disbelief, as their European
colleagues tended to do. But they didn't. For about fifteen years after the
end of World War I, the question of the behaviourist identity sharply
engaged the attention of the American psychological community. As a
result, the category of behaviour acquired a new set of connotations.
There was now a considerable gap between what the term meant in
psychological and in lay discourse.

It is well known that during the 1930s behaviourism acquired a new
lease of life in the form of what came to be known as neo-behaviourism.
For the category of behaviour, this entailed a partial change of conno-
tation. During the previous three decades 'behaviour' had acquired a
certain substantive content that included a commitment to mechanistic
explanation and epiphenomenalism. In the period of neo-behaviourism
such commitments were still common among the friends of behaviour,

but they had become optional. Instead of being defined by implicit claims about the nature of reality, 'behaviour' is now increasingly defined by the *practice* of psychologists. It refers to whatever objects can be constructed by the standard technology of the discipline. Commitment to the norms governing this technology takes the place of direct and substantive metaphysical commitments. Of course, the latter are still present, but they have become implicit and invisible.

This development prepared the way for the fifth and final stage in the twentieth-century history of 'behaviour'. In the years following World War II the term became associated with the new category of 'behavioural science'. The discipline of psychology had never had a monopoly on 'behaviour' and its investigation, and in the post-war period the use of this category became more widespread than it had ever been before. Although psychological usage remained in some sense exemplary for other disciplines, there was now some reciprocal effect on the discipline of Psychology. In the main, this took the form of reinforcing the direction of change that had been initiated in the previous period. More and more, 'behaviour' became a methodologically grounded category.

This overview of the layers of meaning acquired by 'behaviour' provides a rough framework for a consideration of more specific historical and theoretical issues arising at each stage. Because my main focus here is on the *origin* of categories, I will concentrate on the earlier stages.

Mind as inference

If we trace the roots of the peculiarly twentieth-century use of 'behaviour' we arrive at the animal psychology of the first years of the century. What was involved in this early discourse about 'animal behaviour'? For Jennings, a respected pioneer in this area, 'behaviour' owed its role to its juxtaposition with its antipole, 'consciousness'. He begins his early text *Behavior of the Lower Organisms* by noting that 'assertions regarding consciousness in animals, whether affirmative or negative, are not susceptible of verification' (Jennings, 1906: v). For purposes of scientific study we have to turn to something else, namely, behaviour. This is defined as 'the general bodily movements of organisms', and when we study it, 'we are dealing with actual objective processes' and aspire to 'a knowledge of the laws controlling them' (ibid.). Behaviour, being 'objective' in some essential sense, is different from 'consciousness' which is not.

In drawing a sharp line between consciousness and objectivity Jennings was merely following in the footsteps of a number of European biologists who had turned their attention to studying the reactions of organisms to their environment. In this endeavour they encountered a special problem of language. How was one to describe the reactions of worms or molluscs, for example? Traditional usage offered two alternatives: one could use the language commonly employed in referring to the actions of humans. But that language implied self-conscious agents who pursued moral and rational intentions. As long as the conduct of all living things was seen as reflecting the intentions and wisdom of their divine creator, the use of such language in connection with even the humblest of animals did not seem particularly inappropriate. But once that way of viewing life had been displaced by nineteenth-century natural science, the application of a language of intentionality to the actions of the lower organisms seemed ever more incongruous. The alternative was to employ the physicalistic language commonly used to describe the changes of state and position of inanimate bodies. But to most biologists that did not seem appropriate either. Therefore, by the end of the nineteenth century there was considerable discussion about developing a terminology for studies of animal behaviour that would be 'objective' and yet preserve the special qualities that distinguished animate from inanimate action (Beer et al., 1899; Claparède, 1903; Dzendolet, 1967).

What gave this topic psychological interest and relevance was the fact that most biologists still conceived of the special qualities of animal action in terms of the category of 'mind'. At the end of the nineteenth century that was no mere archaism but a line of thought that was strongly supported by contemporary Darwinism. If the human species had been produced by a process of biological evolution, it could hardly be the sole possessor of the whole range of qualities regarded as 'mental'. Lower forms of mentality must be present in sub-human species. In fact, the flourishing of comparative psychology towards the end of the nineteenth century was directly due to the exciting incentive held out by Darwinism, namely, tracing an evolution of mental life that would parallel the evolution of physical life.[3]

Such a project had been undertaken by G.J. Romanes with Darwin's blessing. In his *Mental Evolution in Animals* he presented a 'comparison of mental structures' across species, an undertaking he considered to be analogous to the 'scientific comparison of the bodily structures of organisms' carried out by comparative anatomy (Romanes, 1884: 5). But there was a problem. Bodily structures could be studied by any competent observer, whereas mental phenomena were observable only by the single individual in whose mind they took place. Romanes, in common with virtually all Anglo-Saxon writers on this subject, took it for granted that knowledge of minds other than one's own was based, not on observation, but on inference: 'Therefore all our knowledge of mental activities other than our own really consists of an inferential interpretation of bodily activities' (Romanes, 1884: 16). The study of mental evolution in animals would thus have to rely on inferences from bodily activities that could be regarded as furnishing a so-called 'criterion of mind'.[4]

For Romanes and the other comparative psychologists of the time it was quite clear that the problem of animal minds was only a special case of the problem of other minds in general, whether human or otherwise. It was not merely knowledge of animal minds that had to be based on inference from bodily activities, but knowledge of all minds other than one's own. There might well be special risks and difficulties in making inferences about animal, rather than other human, minds, but this was a difference of degree, not a matter of principle.

Underlying the notion of a bodily 'criterion of mind' was the widespread belief that knowledge of one's own and of other minds rested on different foundations. Only one's own mind could be directly *observed*; other minds had to be *inferred* from observations of bodily activity. Such notions were part and parcel of the empiricist tradition whose emergence was discussed in Chapter 3. They depend on the equation of mind and consciousness and on the Lockean division between two sources of knowledge: sensations and reflection on sensory content. Once mind is conceived as something that can only be known directly through some kind of 'inner sense', or consciousness, then other minds can only be known indirectly through reflection or inference.

Because of the continuing cultural embeddedness of these beliefs it is appropriate to note in passing that this is not the only way in which knowledge of self and other can be conceived. For example, in Continental Europe there was a strong tradition of 'expression psychology' that was based on the idea of inherent links between the outer and the inner aspects of mental life which made directly *shared* experience possible, at least among members of the same species. Instead of beginning with the assumption that experience is basically a private affair, one can begin with the notion that experience is essentially something shared. Then one would regard the partial privatization of experience as the outcome of a process of development that requires explanation. Conversely, if one begins by assuming that experience is necessarily private, it is shared experience that requires explanation. Undoubtedly, implicit assumptions of this kind depend very much on a social and cultural context that is mediated both by intellectual tradition and by the conventions of everyday relationships. In a highly individualistic culture, or sub-culture, experience is usually defined as a basically private event.

Certainly, this was the definition accepted without question by the British comparative psychologists and their American counterparts. The Darwinian project of tracing the evolution of mind was therefore a peculiarly difficult one. Because mind was equated with private individual consciousness, it was inaccessible to others, except by inference from its 'criterion'. Moreover, this inference would have to operate on the basis of observers' experience of their own minds, because that was the only experience of mind anyone could have. Morgan, who followed Romanes, was perfectly clear about this: 'Introspective study must inevitably be the basis and foundation of all comparative psychology,' he advised (Morgan, 1894: 37). The reason is that 'man is forced to interpret the psychology of animals in terms of human psychology, since with this alone he has first hand acquaintance through the study of the nature and sequence of his own mental processes' (Morgan, 1894: 38–39).

The attempt to make the private Lockean mind fit into an evolutionary framework was doomed to failure. But this failure had far-reaching consequences. Initially, it promoted an emphasis on the distinction between conscious mind, which was private, and a new category comprising what Romanes called its 'criterion' and Morgan at first called its 'objective manifestations'. This latter category was made up of 'bodily activities'; not all bodily activities though, only those from which inferences about mind might be made. The procedure of comparative psychology now involved three steps. First, one observed one's own mind, then one observed the bodily activities of the other, and finally one interpreted the latter in the light of the former. It must be emphasized that Morgan, and apparently most of his audience, believed that this was how all knowledge of other minds was arrived at, not just knowledge of animal minds.[5]

But in the case of animals, especially lower animals, the tenuous nature of the inferences made tended to become rather obvious.[6] The class of bodily activities that had served as the 'criterion' of mind, or as its 'objective manifestations', increasingly attracted attention in its own right. Morgan began referring to this class as the 'behaviour' of the animal. Not all bodily activity was behaviour; the beating of the heart or the processes involved in the regulation of body temperature, for instance, were not. The kinds of activity that qualified tended to be those that had served as the criteria or manifestations of mind: approach and withdrawal, discrimination, learning, and so on. One could study these and leave out the troublesome task of mental inference. Increasingly, comparative psychologists found it convenient to avail themselves of the category of 'behaviour' when dealing with these activities. This term was suitably non-committal about the mental aspect, expressing the ambivalence and confusion of most practitioners in regard to the deeper issues involved. By common consent, the study of behaviour was 'objective', whereas the introspective study of mind was not. However, most comparative psychologists at this time explicitly declared that the category of behaviour did not exclude mind. Even Jennings, more objectivist than most, believed that the 'processes of behavior' included 'thought and reason' (Jennings, 1906: vi).

A different conception of mind was beginning to emerge here. The equation of mind with a private individual consciousness was proving to be ever more problematical in the field of animal psychology.[7] But when one considers most of the examples of 'behaviour' that were studied among the higher animals one realizes that this category did not just refer to physical movements. Terms like 'learning', 'discrimination', 'reward', 'habit', etc. were not terms that anyone used to refer to physical displacements and nothing more. They were terms derived from the language of human action, a language on which the philosophical distinction between private mind and public movement had never made much impression. The category of behaviour allowed the comparative psychologists to use this language while paying their respects to an ideal of scientific objectivity. They could also claim to be studying psychological processes like reasoning, memory, perception, and so on, insofar as these processes manifested themselves in animals' actions. The old polarity between physical movement and mind as consciousness was no longer tenable. Once in possession of the category of behaviour, comparative psychologists need no longer be concerned with *inferred* minds, though not all of them immediately accepted that conclusion. The point was that the classes of animate motion which provided most of the content for the category of behaviour already incorporated qualities such as goal-directedness, organization and adaptability that had been attributed to the influence of a separate private mind under the old scheme. With their adoption of 'behaviour' comparative psychologists were on the way to shedding a conceptual framework that presented them with insoluble problems.

One way of resolving these problems without shedding the traditional framework was to adopt a thoroughgoing materialism and declare mind an 'epiphenomenon', a kind of emanation given off by material processes that lacks all causal influence. This is what had been entailed by T.H. Huxley's notion of the 'conscious automaton'. Similar ideas had been developed by D.A. Spalding who performed experiments on animals and established radical materialism as a possible, though unpopular, position to take in comparative psychology (Gray, 1967, 1968).

Of far greater importance for the subsequent history of 'behaviour' was the version of materialism represented by the biologist Jacques Loeb, who greatly impressed the young J.B. Watson at the University of Chicago. Loeb's materialism was not simply a matter of philosophical preference but was intimately linked to his deep commitment to what has been called 'the engineering ideal in biology' (Pauly, 1987). That ideal had its roots in the agricultural biology taught in nineteenth-century Germany, but Loeb transformed it into a guiding principle for all biological research. The goal of such research should be the control of existing forms of life and the construction of new forms. Applied to the behaviour of organisms, this principle led him to the study of tropistic reactions and a rejection of theorizing about hypothetical internal processes, whether mental or physiological. To control and alter the reactions of organisms it was important to study their dependence on external, not internal, conditions. The most direct kind of control could be exercised through the effects of external physical conditions on the physical reactions of organisms. From the engineering perspective organisms were regarded as infinitely malleable. They lacked any capacity for 'voluntary' action, so any consciousness they had would be no more than an epiphenomenon, devoid of causal significance. In Psychology, this point of view would become crucial for the concept of behaviour popularized by the movement known as behaviourism. But before we take this up, we need to take note of the broad significance of animal behaviour studies on the eve of that development.

A naturalistic social science

The adoption of the category of behaviour by comparative psychologists would have remained a minor topic in the history of science had it not been for the fact that this field occupied such a significant place in a certain conception of social science. Around the turn of the century there was a growing interest in applying a scientific approach to social problems, and for many this meant erecting a social science on a biological basis. From this point of view, comparative psychology occupied a key place among the sciences. It provided the crucial link between biological and social science, and its investigations were expected to yield knowledge of basic principles that also operated in human conduct.

This generalization of knowledge about animals to knowledge about humans in society depended on the use of the same categories to describe and explain the activity of animals and the activity of humans. Among the most important of these categories were those of instinct, habit and behaviour. If one spoke of a rat following a familiar path and the conduct of humans at work as both being instances of 'habit', one had already established a strong presumption that these were essentially the same kind of thing and therefore to be explained in the same kind of way. Similarly, the device of extending the reference of 'behaviour' from animal activity to human conduct was attractive to those who had developed a faith in the promise of a biologically grounded social science. Subsuming animal activity and human conduct under the same category of 'behaviour' helped to establish the plausibility of the claim that both could be explained by the same 'laws' or principles.

This is quite apparent in the early, pre-behaviourist, texts with titles referring to 'the study of behaviour', 'the science of behavior', or 'the laws of behavior'. McDougall's (1912) goal was the explanation of human social conduct by means of a finite list of instincts that humans shared with animals. He drew freely on recent studies of 'animal behaviour' to establish his claim that human psychology, defined as 'the study of behaviour', was subject to the same instinctive determinants that operated in animal behaviour. Parmelee (1911) presents 'the science of behavior' in terms of a conventional positivist hierarchy that goes from biological foundations via psychology to sociology. Describing what happens at all three levels in terms of the category of behaviour helps him to establish the claim that the same 'elements' are involved at all three levels. Moreover, he promises that the use of the category of behaviour will perform the same service for human psychology and sociology that it has already performed for animal psychology – it will make them scientific and objective. This consideration is also important for Max Meyer's treatise, *The Fundamental Laws of Human Behavior* (1911), though he looks to physiology rather than animal behaviour for inspiration. Although they differ in their specific agendas, all three authors employ the category of behaviour to establish the plausibility of one or other variant of biological reductionism and to reinforce their claim to have adopted a truly scientific approach.

The biological connection was also important for many psychologists who were closer to the mainstream of American Psychology than these three authors. Representatives of the functionalist school were particularly committed to building a science of Psychology on a biological basis and were therefore greatly interested in the categories of comparative psychology. In an earlier programmatic statement, their spokesman (Angell, 1907: 69) had already expressed his enthusiasm for 'the rejuvenation of interest in the quasi-biological field which we designate animal psychology', and which he proclaimed to be 'surely among the most pregnant which we meet in our generation'. A few years later he focused more specifically on the implications of a biological orientation for the categories of a functionalist psychology, the category of behaviour now playing the central role (Angell, 1913). Noting with approval the 'intelligent apprehension of animal behavior' by comparative psychologists and 'the revolt against the domineering claims of introspection' within psychology, he considered that for functionalists like himself it was 'easy to welcome a category like behavior'. Speaking for this psychological school, he continued: 'Allowing for some conservative reservations, its general tendency would be in the direction of sympathetic acceptance of the behavior concept as a general term under which to subsume minor distinctions in modes of action whether conscious or unconscious' (Angell, 1913: 258–259). Such was the functionalist position on 'behaviour' on the eve of Watson's behaviourist manifesto.

By 1913 'behaviour' was firmly entrenched in an expanding field of discourse that employed the same set of categories for elucidating biological, psychological and sociological issues. Those who participated in this discourse did not see eye to eye on the specific biological categories that held the key to the explanation of human social action. Some gave that distinction to the category of instinct, others to adaptation, still others to reflex. But it was the category of behaviour that was to provide the most convenient general framework for all such discussion. Its promiscuous use expressed an assumption that common principles, spanning the biological, psychological and social levels, were indeed waiting to be discovered. It only remained to identify the right ones.

Moreover, because of its origins among a group of biologists particularly concerned with problems of objectivity, 'behaviour' had acquired scientistic connotations. In stating that behaviour was the object of one's investigations one was also proclaiming one's allegiance to 'science' in the Anglo-American sense, that is to say, natural science and not humanistic science or *Geisteswissenschaft*. Far from being a neutral category, 'behaviour' had become a preferred vehicle for those who shared the conviction that human problems would be solved only by adopting a natural science approach.

These connotations of 'behaviour' converged rather smoothly with certain tendencies that were characteristic of the social sciences in the US. From its emergence in the nineteenth century American social science had been marked by an estrangement from history (Ross, 1991). There was a strong preference for naturalistic rather than historical explanation and a tendency to analyse the present in terms of timeless natural laws rather than particular historical constellations. Social Darwinism represented an earlier manifestation of this tendency, but the pervasive 'evolutionary naturalism' (Cravens, 1978) which took its place was a more effective variant in the long run. Functionalist psychology, which sought to explain all aspects of mental activity in terms of their adaptive value, was very much part of a trend that consistently looked to nature rather than to history for its explanation of human conduct. The category of behaviour provided the perfect vehicle for this fundamental commitment, for it provided a way of describing human conduct that insinuated an essential similarity of human and animal activity. It provided the means for discussing human conduct in a way that abstracted from its moral, political and historical dimensions. In the writings of the friends of behaviour these dimensions frequently had ceased to exist and at best played a non-essential role as added on elements. What was fundamental and essential for understanding human conduct was its link to nature, exemplified in animal behaviour.

Isms and ambiguities

In 1913 the 'ism' was added on to behaviour. What effects did this have on a category that was by then quite well established in certain parts of social and biological science? Most obviously, it imparted a distinctly *rhetorical* quality to the term. Once 'behaviour' had been inscribed on the flag of a *movement*, it became a quasi-political token, a focus for the internal conflicts of disciplines as well as for popular attention and argument (Birnbaum, 1965). In the social sciences one could use 'behaviour' as a battle cry to proclaim one's own militant allegiance to the cause of science and the value of objectivity while denigrating one's opponents as old fogeys held in thrall by yesterday's superstitions. In the popular media one could package all sorts of nostrums as 'behavioural' in order to help one's sales pitch.

Within Psychology, 'behaviour' now became an *arena* in which theoretical conflicts were fought out. These conflicts often took the form of wrangles about what was and what was not to be included in the category of behaviour, about what exactly constituted a 'behaviourist', and about the nature of the 'laws' that were supposed to 'govern' behaviour. The last of these issues quickly became entangled with the fate of the category of 'learning' which is addressed in a later section of this chapter. The question of what it took to call oneself a behaviourist is relevant in the present context only insofar as it illustrates the way in which 'behaviour' had become an arena in which various theoretical issues were fought out. One of these was the issue of introspection. Years before the advent of behaviourism, American psychologists had shown a clear preference for non-introspective data (Cattell, 1904; O'Donnell, 1985), but many of them resisted the idea that such data was to be ruled out of court as a matter of principle. Perhaps one could allow it back in as 'verbal report' and still define psychology as 'the science of behaviour'. It soon became clear that 'behaviourism does not stand or fall with any special hypothesis which behaviourists happen to like' (Woodworth, 1924: 263). Increasingly, it functioned more like a framework that incorporated many of the unquestioned assumptions and unquestionable values of American psychologists. Within this framework there was room for arguing about details.

From the beginning of behaviour's career as a quasi-scientific category there was disagreement about its meaning. Early on, that meaning was closely tied to its relationship to the category of 'mind', as we have seen. Behaviour was that from which mind could be *inferred*. But when the mind was that of an animal, this became problematical. Yet, most of the pioneers of animal psychology remained convinced that mind was somehow *manifest* in behaviour. The question of how this was possible was one that intrigued several American philosophers. E.A. Singer (1912: 209) proposed that 'our belief in consciousness is an expectation of probable behavior based on an observation of actual behavior, a belief to be confirmed or refuted by more observation'. That amounted to a reinterpretation of the problem from a novel, *pragmatist*, perspective. The issue is no longer one of the real existence of mind as an object, but of the foundations for one's belief in such a thing. From this vantage point two lines of development were possible. One could go on to explore the social basis for the attribution of mental qualities. Alternatively, one could revert to a realist position and redefine mind in terms of particular objective qualities in behaviour. The New Realist philosophers, more influential than Singer, took the second road.

For E.B. Holt, (1915: 166) behaviour was an activity of the whole organism that could be 'shown to be a constant function of some aspect of the objective world'. What distinguishes behaviour from mere physical movement is not its accompaniment or activation by a mental event but its functional relationship to some 'objective reference' outside itself. Behaviour is movement that varies with changes in the objective circumstances. That is the difference between a stone rolling from point *a* to point *b* and an organism moving *towards* the light, for example. Intentionality is not due to a mind *behind* the movement, it is discoverable *in* those movements that are behaviour. That, briefly, was the foundation on which Holt's student, E.C. Tolman (1932), was to construct his notion of 'molar' behaviour, to be contrasted with 'molecular' behaviour that consisted of nothing but a chain of muscle contractions. The latter was said to have been the notion of behaviour with which Watsonian behaviourism operated.

But in fact, both Watsonian and molar behaviourism recognized either conception of behaviour, depending on the rhetorical context. When they wanted to emphasize their credentials as natural scientists the molar behaviourists would insist on the physical basis of molar behaviour, and when Watsonian behaviourists referred to the practical applications of their theories, that were so important to them, they had to speak of actions, like memorizing, drawing, writing, rather than physical movements. As many have observed (see Kitchener, 1977; Lee, 1983), behaviourism's use of the category of behaviour has always been marked by *ambiguity*. The reason for that lies in the basic incompatibility of the twin goals of the movement. Behaviourists desperately wanted to be recognized as natural scientists, and, to the degree that their image of natural science included good old-fashioned mechanistic materialism, they would emphasize that behaviour was ultimately reducible to physical movement. But they also wanted to build a practical science of social control, and that had to operate with purposeful action rather than with physical movement. It was only when the crude physicalism of an earlier notion of science lost its cash value in enlightened circles that the 'molecular' conception of behaviour faded into history. But by then the goal of 'prediction and control' had come to dominate the discipline in any case.

The practical exemplar

During the heyday of behaviourism the transformation of 'behaviour' into an arena also took the very concrete form of the rat learning experiment (pigeons came later). It was in the construction and interpretation of such experiments that fundamental theoretical issues were supposed to be decided. In effect, these experiments functioned as prototypical situations that imposed a very specific meaning on an otherwise almost meaningless term. To a prominent experimentalist the essence of the behaviourist programme seemed to lie in the fact that 'it proposed to take the animal experiment as the model for experiments on human beings' (Woodworth, 1924: 260). That was during the early period of 'classical' behaviourism. But during the subsequent period of neo-behaviourism this aspect of the programme was realized on a scale that Woodworth probably had not foreseen. What consequences did that have for the meaning of 'behaviour'?

Obviously, it would reinforce the association of 'behaviour' with the already existing and pervasive tendency to explain human social conduct in naturalistic terms. But more specifically, the link of 'behaviour' to the prototypical animal learning situation reinforced the understanding of behaviour as something that organisms did as *individuals*. Indeed, the typical animal learning experiment represents a particularly stark depiction of conduct as the affair of independent individuals. What is studied in these experiments is the intercourse of single and isolated animals with their physical environment. These animals represent individuals even more drastically thrown on their own resources than the lone gunmen of the mythical Wild West.

Moreover, such experiments provide an ingenious way of eliminating the element of human communication that is such a troublesome yet absolutely necessary part of experiments with human subjects. In their interpretations of experimental data psychologists had traditionally tried to ignore the fact that all such data were the product of a social interaction (Danziger, 1990a). In animal learning experiments, however, they had managed to construct a situation in which human communication had been eliminated once and for all. The subjects whose behaviour provided the prototype for behaviour in general were speechless subjects. They lacked the means for participating in a language community with their controllers or anyone else. 'Behaviour' was basically an attribute of singular, non-communicating individuals. Applied to humans, anything social or cultural could enter this world only in the form of 'stimuli' external to the individual. No conception of community beyond that of an aggregate of individuals could be formulated on this basis.[8]

'Behaviour' is an extremely abstract category that depends for its meaning on the use of exemplars that function as meaning-conferring prototypes. This is what the animal learning experiments of the neo-behaviourists supplied. It was in these experiments that they sought the key to the principles that governed behaviour in general; here, as nowhere else, behaviour was supposedly manifested in its pure form. So far from that being the case, however, these experimental situations produced exemplars that were pure cultural artefacts.

A cross-cultural comparison will help to illustrate this. European psychologists generally treated behaviourism as a bizarre American fad that was not to be taken seriously. Only their forced emigration obliged some of them to alter that stand. But there was one prominent exception in the 1920s. Karl Bühler, head of the Vienna Psychological Institute and President of the German Psychological Society between 1929 and 1931, agreed that the behaviourist programme was *echt amerikanisch* (Bühler, 1927: 20), but accepted that the study of animal behaviour, or conduct (*Benehmen*), as he called it, provided knowledge that must form part of the foundations of psychology. Accordingly, he tried to incorporate the behavioural aspect in his own synthesis. But what did he take as the prototype of behaviour for this purpose? Not the solitary rat in the maze, not even the problem-solving primate, but the communicating bee! It was the work of von Frisch on the 'language of the bees' that provided Bühler with the exemplars he was looking for. That was because he took it for granted that the kind of animal behaviour that would be most relevant to human behaviour would have to be *communicating* behaviour. For Bühler, humans were fundamentally communicating creatures, and the psychological work of his mature years was mostly devoted to the study of language (Bühler, 1990).[9] The point here is not whether Bühler was right and the rat runners were wrong, but that the choice of the exemplars which give meaning to abstract 'behaviour' depends on culturally determined preconceptions about the fundamental nature of human conduct.

Behaviour and control

Perhaps the deepest and most permanent effect of the behaviourist annexation of the category of behaviour is to be found in the formation of a close association between behaviour and 'control'. That association is already present in the Watsonian concept of behaviour which had embodied the 'engineering ideal' personified by Jacques Loeb in Biology. For Watson, the goal of psychology was not the understanding of the mind, but 'the prediction and control of behaviour': 'If psychology would follow the plan I suggest, the educator, the physician, the jurist, and the business man could utilize our data in a practical way, as soon as we are able, experimentally, to obtain them' (Watson, 1913: 168). The areas of Psychology which were flourishing, according to Watson, were those that had effectively adopted his goal, for example the psychology of advertising, of drugs, and of tests, as well as 'experimental peda-gogy', legal psychology, and psychopathology. These examples illustrate that Watson's category of 'behaviour' was quite broad. Whatever could be reliably predicted and placed under external control could be included. The human engineering perspective, which Watson made explicit, had in fact been prominent in so-called applied psychology for some years. One effect of his campaign was to establish a firm link between that perspective and the category of behaviour.

By the 1920s that link had become unmistakable. This was a time when American Psychology became a significant beneficiary of large scale private funding available for research that might contribute to the control of social problems (Samelson, 1985). There was a clear shift away from the old style of psychological research on the individual mind to research on the distribution of dispositions and on malleability in large groups of subjects (Danziger, 1990a). It now became quite generally accepted that research ought to produce the type of knowledge that would be immediately or potentially useful for purposes of social control. To distinguish this kind of knowledge from the painstaking investigation of consciousness that had characterized an earlier phase of modern psychology, the apostles of the new wave mostly followed Watson's lead and proclaimed their interest in 'behaviour'. The term began to function as a kind of banner under which all those who believed in a science of social control could rally. By 1925, one observer saw a 'Kingdom of Behavior' that had resulted from 'a shift from understanding to control', to 'management, direction, betterment, greater effectiveness' (cited in Samelson, 1985: 42). Those who declared the subject matter of Psychology to be 'behaviour' almost always linked this to the stipulation that its goal was to be the 'prediction and control' of this behaviour.

Behaviourism had been revolutionary in the sense that, although it had sprung out of a discourse about the place of mind in nature, it had transformed that discourse into one about the control of human conduct. As behaviourism matured and its discourse came to dominate the discipline, the polarity of mind and behaviour became more and more peripheral. Eventually, terms like 'cognitive behaviour' and 'cognitive behaviourism' were accepted with hardly a raising of eyebrows. The point was that the discursive context which 'behaviour' signalled had by then changed from questions about mind to questions about techniques for the control of human conduct. 'Behaviour' had come to mean any aspect of human activity that could be predicted and controlled by psychologists.

The neo-behaviourism of the 1930s and 1940s completed this transformation. It marked the formalization of the *positivism* that had always been implicit in behaviourism. Watson had ejected references to brain physiology almost in the same breath with the expulsion of the mind. Behaviourism meant not penetrating beyond the surface of the organism, sticking to what could be directly observed and controlled. Neo-behaviourism formalized the primacy of the observable and manipulable by adopting the language of independent, dependent, and intervening variables. That language is discussed at some length in Chapter 9. It was based on an equation of scientific knowledge with the technical ability to produce specific effects. Psychological constructs now had to be defined in terms of specific operations producing specific effects.[10] But only operations carried out by qualified psychologists in accordance with the prevailing methodological norms of the discipline were recognized for this purpose. Adopting a 'behavioural' approach came to mean that one was committed to these norms and to the controlling role of the scientists who acted in accordance with them.

The older psychology had been obliged to defer to the privileged access to their own conscious experience by subjects in psychological experiments. In 'behavioural science', it was the scientist who was privileged. His/her operations defined the phenomenon under investigation, and they defined it in the service of the goal of 'prediction and control' of the subject's reactions. In this context, 'behaviour' had come to mean an activity defined in such a manner as to make it an object of behavioural science. It referred to that which was predictable and controllable by the specific means in vogue among a particular group of experts.

The abstraction of 'learning'

One of the curious features of the original behaviourist programme was the contrast between the vagueness of its positive proposals and the very specific targets of its critique. Its objections to introspection were backed up by specific examples from the psychology of thinking and imagery, but there was little positive theoretical content, beyond some forcefully expressed philosophical preferences for mechanistic and materialistic explanations.

Soon the concept of 'conditioning' was enthusiastically adopted as an appropriate filler for what looked suspiciously like a theoretical vacuum. This was a concept that had been derived from work that the Russian physiologist, I.P. Pavlov, had done on conditioned reflexes. There was however a world of difference between the meaning that this work had had for Pavlov himself and the significance it acquired in the discourse of American behaviourism. For Pavlov, work on conditioned reflexes was a *means* of generating data from which hypotheses about cerebral processes in intact animals could be derived. For the behaviourists, conditioning became an *explanatory category* that would suffice to account for adaptive behaviour without any reference to brain physiology. Pavlov was well aware of this difference. In an article published in America, entitled 'Reply of a physiologist to psychologists', he expressed himself as follows:

> The psychologist takes conditioning as the principle of learning, and accepting this principle as not subject to further analysis, not requiring ultimate investigation, he endeavours to apply it to everything and to explain all the individual features of learning as one and the same process. . . . The physiologist proceeds in quite the opposite way. . . . Conditioning, association by contiguity in time, conditioned reflexes, even if they serve as the factual point

of departure of our investigations, are nonetheless subject to further analysis. We have before us an important question: What elementary properties of brain-mass form the basis of this fact? (Pavlov, 1932: 91–92)

Conditioning of the Pavlovian, or 'classical', kind became the first of a series of pseudo-explanatory principles introduced to provide the theoretical content that the behaviourist framework in itself could not supply. But what was it that conditioning and its successors were meant to explain? The answer was 'learning'. Prior to the 'theories of learning', which made up the specific theoretical content of neo-behaviourism, there had to be a class of phenomena grouped together in the category of 'learning'. Moreover, there had to be a conviction that this was not a psychologically trivial category, but one of central importance for achieving the goal which the discipline had set itself. Indeed, it was widely believed that the 'laws' of 'learning' represented the fundamental principles of a scientific psychology. But this was a belief that relied on a very recent historical construction, namely, a category of learning phenomena that was sufficiently unified to be explicable in terms of a single set of regularities. In Pavlov's words, basing everything on learning meant 'to represent all the separate sides of learning as one and the same process'.

In the early days of modern psychology such an idea would have seemed preposterous. There was as yet no category of learning-in-general subject to one set of laws. There were a number of contexts in which the term 'learning' cropped up, but, at best, they were linked by only the vaguest analogies. Strangely enough, vague analogies were sufficient for the construction of an abstraction that was to dominate theoretical debate in mid-twentieth-century American Psychology. How did this strange construction originate?

Of course, casual references to children 'learning' such things as walking and talking, or adults 'learning' to play a musical instrument or a foreign language, go back a long way. But such references carried no implication that all examples of learning constituted one natural kind united by common features. On the contrary, in pre-twentieth-century texts of mental philosophy or psychology such casual references to learning were always embedded in discussions of those categories of phenomena that were considered significant, categories like association, habit, imitation, memory, education, training, and so on. It was these latter that provided the discourse with its structure and focus, not any category of 'learning'.[11] That relationship was reversed in twentieth-century psychology, so that these other categories now became mere examples or applications of the more fundamental category of 'learning'. This reversal could not have occurred if 'learning' had not acquired a significance it did not previously possess. How and why did this happen?

At the beginning of the century there were three entirely different contexts in which 'learning' was beginning to be accorded a new significance. One was comparative psychology, the second was the acquisition of skills, and the third was educational psychology. We will consider these in turn.

In evolutionary comparative psychology, the *activity* of learning had been singled out as a crucial 'criterion of mind' (see 'Mind as inference', p. 89ff.). Romanes (1884: 20–21) wrote as follows:

> The criterion of mind, therefore, which I propose . . . is as follows: – Does the organism learn to make new adjustments, or to modify old ones, in accordance with the results of its own individual experience?[12]

His argument was based on the belief that learning from experience must involve 'choice', and choice necessarily implied the presence of 'conscious intelligence'. Be that as it may, studies of the learning of new adjustments became part of evolutionary comparative psychology. Learning had acquired some significance. However, its role was still a secondary one; it was merely a criterion of things like mind and intelligence which were truly fundamental. In this context, 'learning' did not refer to a mechanical, but to a conscious, process.

Subsequently, biologists, such as Loeb and Jennings, who worked with lower organisms, became interested in a basic *modifiability* that seemed to be present in the behaviour of even the simplest animals. But at this level consciousness was effectively out of the picture. One was dealing with automatic adjustments whose physico-chemical basis could sometimes be demonstrated. Sherrington's work on postural adjustments based on unconscious reflex mechanisms pointed in a similar direction. There was a great deal of variety, and even disagreement, regarding the exact nature of the automatic adjustive responses of organisms, but it was clear that a category of such phenomena had to be recognized.

The question was whether this kind of modifiability had much significance for the higher organisms, especially humans, and whether it had much significance for more 'intelligent' levels of response. Biologists differed on this, and the position they took had much to do with their attitude to the theory of evolution. Clearly, the hypothesis that the modifiability of animal behaviour involves the same mechanisms at all levels of evolutionary development restricts the scope of evolutionary theory. On the other hand, the hypothesis that processes of adjustment changed significantly in the course of evolution enhances the domain of evolutionary theory. This was the position of Darwinians like Romanes. Loeb, on the other hand, did not have much time for evolutionism (Pauly, 1987). His goal for biology was as a science providing the principles for the control of life, and in his day evolutionism seemed to have no contribution to make to that. By comparison, the study of primitive adjustive mechanisms seemed much more promising, and Loeb proceeded to push the applicability of these studies to higher forms of life. His claim – really no more than a hope – was that the same fundamental principles of modifiability applied at all levels of animal development.

The second context in which questions about the nature of 'learning' were being raised involved studies in the acquisition of practical skills. American psychologists took an early lead in this area, publishing data on the acquisition of such skills as telegraphy (Bryan and Harter, 1899), shorthand (Swift, 1903), and typewriting (Swift, 1904). Quite remarkably, although these were all instances of learning how to communicate through new media, the process was not conceptualized as social but only as involving changes within a singular individual. These changes were, however, treated as instances of a significant class of intra-individual events. For example, in tracing the acquisition of skills in telegraphy one was supposedly studying something much more significant, namely, 'the acquisition of a hierarchy of habits' (Bryan and Harter, 1899). The concept of 'habit' had an impressive pedigree, having played an important role in empiricist mental philosophy since the days of Hume. In the nineteenth century the motor component of habits had received much attention in the wake of the expansion of the reflex concept.[13] For Carpenter (1874), and for William James who followed him closely, habits were essentially sensori-motor adjustments that also acted as the repository of social custom. Studying 'the telegraphic language' as an instance of habit acquisition (Bryan and Harter, 1899) fitted perfectly into this tradition.

Nevertheless, the transformation of the topic of habits into a label for laboratory studies of practical skills entailed a certain shift of emphasis. The older empiricist discourse on habits had been more concerned with their general structure than with the specific details of their acquisition. Laboratory investigations inspired by a practical interest in what Bryan and Harter called 'the psychology of occupations', however, would necessarily be looking at the details of habit acquisition. They would 'portray the actual typical procedures of men in learning or in failing to learn' (Bryan and Harter, 1899: 349). Quite subtly, the main focus had begun to change from the nature of 'habits' to the nature of 'learning', the process involved in their formation. This quickly becomes more explicit in subsequent investigations of practical skills. They are now identified as contributions to 'the psychology of learning' (Swift, 1903, 1904). In due course, there is talk of something called 'the learning process' (Swift and Schuyler, 1907; Richardson, 1912), whose common features show up in a variety of skills.

Thirdly, 'learning' is something that young scholars and students do in educational settings. But how does one define the psychological issue here? Traditionally, the pupil's learning had been seen as incidental to the real issue, which was that of memory. That was one of the few truly ancient psychological topics, and speculation about the nature of memory had existed for centuries. But modern practices brought a change in the relative status of memory and learning. This was because the most widely adopted programme for the experimental investigation of memory (Ebbinghaus, 1885) defined memory in terms of the *work* of memorizing and not in terms of the *experience* of remembering.[14] In this context 'learning' was used as a synonym for memorizing, and experimental investigations were designed to answer questions about the relative efficiency of different techniques of learning.

That approach furnished an excellent basis for a major programme of applying psychological knowledge in school settings. By the beginning of the twentieth century there was an interest in the rationalization of educational practice in all the rapidly industrializing countries of the northern hemisphere. Traditional methods and goals of education were increasingly being rejected as inappropriate for modern conditions. Schooling ought to prepare individuals to occupy workplaces in an industrial society governed by the goal of maximizing efficiency. It would not be able to do this very effectively, unless the same principles of technical rationalization that were being so impressively employed in industry were also put to work in reforming educational practice. Such was the background for the work of a group of German educators who were committed to putting pedagogics on a scientific footing. That meant conducting experiments to discover the relative effectiveness of different techniques of learning, a procedure for which Ebbinghaus' studies of memory had laid the basis. The central figure in this endeavour was the psychologist Ernst Meumann, whose standard text for the area had gone into a second edition by 1908 under the title 'Economy and Technique of Memory' (Meumann, 1908). The third edition appeared in English as *The Psychology of Learning* (Meumann, 1913). By then, there was an established area of psychological research devoted to the comparison of different techniques of learning from the point of view of efficiency.

The German work in this area evoked considerable interest in America, where similar lines of experimentation were beginning to open up. In many ways, E.L. Thorndike was Meumann's counterpart in America, using his academic position at Teachers' College, Columbia, to promote studies of the effect of various conditions on the learning of school-like tasks. In 1913 his three-volume *Educational Psychology* was published, the second volume of which was entirely devoted to *The Psychology of Learning* (Thorndike, 1913). The third context of learning studies was by now well developed. Thorndike's volume included a nine-page bibliography, though some of the items referred to research on animal learning and on the acquisition of skills.

In this respect there was a striking difference between Thorndike's text and Meumann's text. The latter was exclusively devoted to human memorizing of symbolic material. In Thorndike's case, however, there is an introductory chapter on 'the laws of learning in animals', as well as frequent reference to research on the acquisition of skills. Closer inspection reveals that the meaning of 'learning' is quite different for these two authors. For Meumann, 'learning' was essentially a synonym for 'memorizing'. It was an intentional human activity, involving conscious attention, and studied in the very specific context of school work. Thorndike's 'learning' was a far grander affair. What went on in learning at school was only one manifestation of a biological process that could also be observed in animals – monkeys, cats, chicks and turtles being explicitly mentioned. Moreover, this process obeyed a few simple 'laws', which Thorndike enumerated. The same laws operated in the acquisition of human motor skills and in ideational learning. What had been studied in three very different contexts was now assumed to be all the same process. Clearly, a psychological phenomenon as pervasive as Thorndike's 'learning' would provide a focus for a significant part of the discipline. By contrast, Meumann's 'learning' was merely a technical means employed in a very restricted practical context. Neither he nor any other European psychologist had thought of 'learning' as defining a major area of basic psychological research and theory.

But in America Thorndike was only the most influential contributor to an emerging discourse that took 'learning' in the grand sense as its object.[15] His had not been the first volume to be devoted to the topic. A text on *The Learning Process* (Colvin, 1911) had appeared two years earlier, claiming that the process was similar in animals and children and also including some reference to the acquisition of skills. In the year that Thorndike's text was published, the *Psychological Review* carried an article on 'The laws of learning', based on the proposition that 'the several processes which in various animals are called learning, habit-formation, memory, association, etc. are at bottom one and the same process' (Haggerty, 1913). Soon, it seemed perfectly reasonable to undertake experimental studies that used both rats and humans as subjects in research on the learning process (e.g. Pechstein, 1917; Webb, 1917).[16] Psychologists also adopted the practice of pooling data from a number of subjects to produce 'learning curves' based on averages that need not correspond to the performance of a single living organism. Such statistical abstractions often functioned as the practical counterpart of the conceptual abstraction involved in the category of 'learning'.

During the period of Psychology's involvement with the military in World War I the term 'learning' was used as a vehicle for advancing extravagant claims to professional expertise. It was suggested that psychologists had scientific knowledge of 'learning' which would be applicable in a broad variety of contexts, from 'the learning of complicated military manoeuvres' to 'losing one's temper' (Strong, 1918).

The post-war period saw the firm establishment of 'learning' in the abstract as a major subdivision within American Psychology. Introductory texts, beginning with Woodworth's very successful *Psychology* of 1921, would discuss evidence from animal experiments in conjunction with work on human skills and studies of memory to promote the notion of so-called 'laws of learning' whose domain was universal. Earnest debates about the precise content of these laws merely strengthened belief in their existence. Over the next two decades, 'theories of learning' emerged as the focal area of basic theorizing in American Psychology. Always abreast of current trends, Woodworth (1934: 223) writes in the third edition of his text that 'the work of psychology must consist very largely in the investigation of learning'. Moreover, animal experiments, especially on rats, have moved up to become the favourite vehicle for this kind of work. As the text explains: 'Psychology seeks to unravel the learning process not as a specifically human process – which it is not – but as a process common to many if not all animals. The simpler processes in the rat are instructive just because of their comparative simplicity' (Woodworth, 1934: 225).

The fate of the category of 'learning' was closely intertwined with that of behaviourism. Watson (1914: 45) seems to have anticipated this: 'On account of its bearing upon human training, learning in animals is probably the most important topic in the whole study of behavior.' The laws and the theories of learning provided the content which behaviourism lacked, an assimilation that was based on common presuppositions. First, there was the implicit minimizing of evolutionary change.[17] By contrast with the Darwinians, the 'laws' the behaviourists were interested in were not historical accounts that explained massive natural changes over long periods of time. Their model was much closer to physical engineering than to evolutionary biology. What they were looking for were principles of wide applicability that could be employed in the practical control of conduct. For that they required abstract categories of manipulable short term change (Mills, 1997), and that is what the theories of 'learning' provided. In this perspective, all organisms were seen as potential objects of control, not as the products of a historical process. Organisms were not only 'empty', devoid of fixed species characteristics, they were also lonely, that is, they were studied in isolation from any natural environment. In the case of humans, that converged with the tendency to perform a radical divorce between individual and society. In this usage, 'learning' was always a phenomenon of individual change, never one of co-change among several individuals sharing a social field.

The categories of 'behaviour' and 'learning' undoubtedly represented the purest expression of twentieth-century modernism within the entire domain of psychology. There is considerable irony in the fact that the categories which most stridently proclaimed Psychology's abstract universalism were precisely the ones which were most parochial in a cultural and historical sense.

Notes

1. More recently, the category of 'cognition' has played a similar role. The idea of abstract laws uniting many domains of psychological functioning, irrespective of content, reappeared in the form of the category of 'cognition' just when 'learning' could no longer play this role effectively. But this development falls outside the time period of this book.

2. The qualification 'relevant' is necessary, because, earlier, one can find instances of talk about the 'behaviour' of physical substances. Certainly, this played a role in the choice of the term by biologists and psychologists, because it was seen as establishing the term's value-free, amoral pedigree. But 'behaviour' was never a technical term in the physical sciences; it became one only when it began to be used in a biological and especially a psychological context.

3. In this context the term 'Darwinism' must be understood to refer to doctrines that were not unique to Darwin but owed a great deal to Herbert Spencer. For the historical background, see R.J. Richards (1987).

4. Romanes did not invent the notion of a bodily criterion of mind. It had emerged out of the Pflüger–Lotze controversy mentioned in Chapter 4 and was the subject of considerable discussion in the latter part of the nineteenth century. William James (1890) puts this topic right at the beginning of his *Principles of Psychology*.

5. One of the first texts to define Psychology as 'the science of behaviour', prior to the advent of behaviourism (Pillsbury, 1911), grounded its definition in this belief. For it, behaviour was the most important of 'the evidences of mind'.

6. The point had been made quite forcefully by Wilhelm Wundt in 1892, when he noted 'the unfortunate absence of the critical attitude' in the work of Romanes (Wundt, 1894: 343).

7. For some details of how this manifested itself in practice, see Mackenzie (1977).

8. It is likely that these features of the category of behaviour helped its promotion as an alternative to 'social' during the McCarthyite period. There were political factors involved in the push to replace 'social science' with 'behavioural science' during this period. (Senn, 1966).

9. It took over half a century for this work to be translated into English! Cultural dissonance played a significant role in Bühler's being written out of the (American) history of psychology (see Brock, 1994; Weimer, 1974).

10. For a thorough and up to date discussion of the historical link between neo-behaviourism and operationism, see Mills (1997).

11. William James' famous chapter on 'habit' in his *Principles of Psychology* (1890) provides an example of this.

12. This was actually a self-quotation from his slightly earlier *Animal Intelligence* (1882).

13. See Chapter 4.

14. For further clarification of this fundamental point, see Danziger (1990a).

15. Thorndike had also been the first to use 'learning' as a category for popularizing psychology. In his early work on animal learning he had used the then current expression 'animal intelligence', but in his popular *The Human Nature Club* (Thorndike, 1902), which followed shortly thereafter, he already uses 'learning' as a psychological category.

16. One reason for the early popularity of the maze as a device for the study of learning may have been that it was a task which could be given to both rats and humans, indicating that one was dealing with fundamentally the same phenomenon in both cases. The maze also seemed to require motor learning, making it easy to put maze learning in the same category as the acquisition of a skill. Thus, studies of maze learning became the investigative practice that provided the perfect empirical content for a category of learning that had been derived by abstraction from three very different contexts.

17. Thorndike (1911: 280) had spelled this out at an early stage: 'If my analysis is true, the evolution of behavior is a rather simple matter. Formally the crab, fish, turtle, dog, cat, monkey and baby have very similar intellects and characters. All are systems of connections subject to change by the law of exercize and effect.'

7

MOTIVATION AND PERSONALITY

Nothing attests to the vaulting ambition of American inter-war Psychology quite as well as the invention of two wholly new fields of investigation – motivation and personality. More than any others, these two categories staked the claim of Psychology *as a discipline* to special and privileged knowledge about the *entire* range of human affairs.

One of the first systematic texts in this area begins as follows:

> All behavior is motivated. Getting out of bed when the alarm clock rings, brushing the teeth, shaving, selecting the day's necktie, ordering rolls and coffee or ham and eggs from the menu card, picking up the paper to read the news – these everyday activities are all causally determined. You take them for granted, generally being unconscious of any motive determining what is being done. Nevertheless a definite motivation is invariably present. (Young, 1936: 1)

Scientific psychology promised to unravel the secrets of this invisible but ubiquitous network of causal determination. No human action, no matter how trivial, could now escape its reach. And what was not covered by the general laws of motivation, namely the differences among individuals in carrying out these actions, would be netted by the new field of scientific personality research. Seamlessly, the new Psychology will account, not just for the 'how' but for the 'why' of all human activity.

In its earlier phase the new experimental psychology had had far more modest aims. It would not have occurred to a Wundt or a Titchener that their field ought to provide explanations of everyday conduct. The special problems arising out of the structure and flow of human consciousness, which they investigated, would impinge on ordinary human activity here and there, but there was no pretence that their laboratory studies would yield knowledge that could, in principle, explain why anyone ever did anything. Accordingly, their modest psychology lacked the categories that would have provided a suitable framework for accommodating such claims. They knew neither 'motivation' nor 'personality'. Baldwin's (1901) comprehensive turn of the century dictionary has no entry for 'motivation' at all. It has an entry for 'person', whose content is entirely philosophical, and an entry for 'personality', whose content is entirely medical, but there is no psychology of personality.

Both the psychology of motivation and the psychology of personality were constructions of the inter-war period, the twenties and thirties of the twentieth century. Let us trace each of these constructions, first 'motivation' and then 'personality'.

The interest in motivation

In 1928 the Harvard psychologist, L.T. Troland, published the first general text featuring the word 'motivation' in the main title (Troland, 1928). With the appearance of this text the editors of *Psychological Abstracts* apparently felt that it was time to give 'motivation' its own entry in their index. In the previous year, another text had used 'motivation' in its subtitle (Thomson, 1927), and from now on introductory texts began to add a chapter on this topic to their survey of the discipline (e.g. Dashiell, 1928; Hollingworth, 1928; Perrin, 1932). By 1936, the author of a new authoritative volume on motivation was able to mention its use as a text in a college course devoted to this topic (Young, 1936). Such courses gradually became common. Two years later, that is, ten years after its first recognition of the category, *Psychological Abstracts* carried twenty-six entries under this heading.

What was behind this growth? A first clue is provided by Troland's early reference to a discrepancy between the source of students' interest in psychology and the actual content of the discipline. Laymen were usually drawn to psychology because of their interest in human motives, it was said, yet the older textbooks covering the field offered nothing to satisfy that interest (Troland, 1928: 1). Certainly, the marketing orientation of American college professors, the pressure to keep the lay consumers of their wares interested, was a factor not to be overlooked in this context. But it is necessary to go a little deeper. One must ask why lay persons came to psychology with this particular orientation in the 1920s, when there is no indication of such expectations during the previous century. No doubt, the massive popularization of psychoanalysis in the post-war period played a significant role in establishing a link between the subject of psychology and the exploration of individual motives. In the subsequent academic literature on the topic of motivation Freud is always mentioned as a motivational theorist, if only to repudiate his theories as unscientific. Among other things, the construction of the new field of motivation enabled academic psychology to extend its dominion to topics that psychoanalysis had put on the agenda and threatened to monopolize. The new science of motivation began to act like a superior court that would adjudicate the truth claims of other psychologies.

But psychoanalysis was far from being the only source of contemporary interest in human motivation. The enormous expansion and rationalization of the educational system had created problem situations that could not be entirely mastered by recourse to the doctrine of differential ability or 'intelligence'. That children often lacked interest in their school work was hardly news. What was new was the conviction that this condition was treatable by applying scientific knowledge about 'fatigue' and whatever counteracted it: the will, motives, interests, as the case may be. Reform-minded educators began to propound such ideas early in the twentieth century. The first book to have 'motivation' in its title was not Troland's (as he claimed) but the Wilsons' *The Motivation of School Work* of 1916. Once educationists had come to conceptualize some of their problems in terms of the category of 'classroom motivation', there was a potential market for psychological principles and techniques labelled as pertaining to this category (Knight and Remmers, 1923).

Psychologists were becoming more and more involved in such markets, as various fields of what was called 'applied psychology'[1] were opening up. One such field was vocational guidance, where psychologists had to contend with the influence of humanists and moralists. The very first volume of the *Journal of Applied Psychology* contained an article which pointed out that if psychologists were to be successful in this endeavour they would have to rely less exclusively on 'intellectual tests' and pay more attention to 'the psychology of interests, motives, and character' (Folsom, 1917). In the years that followed they certainly did so.

Another prominent area of early 'applied psychology' was advertising research, a branch of the broader 'psychology of salesmanship'. Here, psychologists became involved with an industry that was switching from an early preoccupation with perceptual effects to the more fundamental issues of inducing new needs and desires among potential consumers. Adopting the language of the industry, psychologists conducted investigations showing that the most effective kind of advertising was aimed at the creation of new 'wants' (Strong, 1925, Strong and Loveless, 1926). As in other fields, psychologists' growing involvement with practical problems was contributing to the greater salience of categories of psychological discourse that had a non-cognitive, non-intellectual content.

In industry, there were several problem areas for which the question of rewards and incentives was beginning to appear particularly relevant. More than the issue of productivity, which was traditionally handled rather mechanically, rising concern about extraordinarily high rates of labour turnover prompted calls for psychological input into questions of 'unwillingness to work' and work satisfaction (Frost, 1920). The steady centralization of hiring and firing decisions in large companies, and increasing faith in the wisdom of scientific experts, had also made the application of relevant psychological knowledge more feasible. Before World War I, psychological knowledge pertaining to rewards and incentives hardly existed; in the 1920s, however, research in this area blossomed. By 1927, the textbook presentation of the sub-discipline of applied psychology included chapters on 'the measurement of character and interest' and 'satisfaction as a product of work', as well as sections devoted to such topics as the 'relative strength of desires', 'consumers' likes and dislikes', and 'the conflict of motives' (Poffenberger, 1927). In addition, there is a discussion of laboratory studies of punishment in the context of the treatment of criminal offenders.

The more popular literature of 'personal efficiency', directed at ambitious and aspiring managers and salesmen, had been using the semantics of motivation and personality for some time. As early as 1917, about half of a book entitled *The Executive and his Control of Men* (Gowin, 1917) was devoted to what was called 'motivating the group'. This included chapters on 'rewards' and on 'personality'. The post-war literature on 'influencing people' popularized the notion that individuals could be readily manipulated by playing on their wants, interests and motives (Overstreet, 1925).

Comparing the psychological and quasi-psychological literature of the second and third decades of the twentieth century with earlier usage, the change in the semantics of 'motive' is quite striking. Traditionally, a 'motive' was a substantive that referred to a specific aspect or entity linked to some human action. The verbal form, 'to motivate', and the abstract form, 'motivation', were quite rare and are not documented as having occurred before the late nineteenth century (*Oxford English Dictionary*, 1989). Even then, we get no more than a reference to the motivation of events in a novel or a principle of ethics (Tufts, 1904). In the twentieth century, however, there occurs a veritable explosion in the use of verbal and abstract derivatives of 'motive'. If dictionary entries are any guide, a large part of this development is directly associated with the literature of Psychology and its derivatives.

What we witness first of all in the early twentieth century is the new popularity and prominence of the verbal form 'to motivate'. This is a form that occurs as part of a rapidly expanding discourse of 'social control'. The specific reference of this term was at that time directed at the growing literature on the improvement of advertising and sales-manship, industrial efficiency, teaching practice, and personal advance-ment. It was recognized that these improvements could not be achieved simply by force or by the manipulation of the environment. One had to play upon what individuals wanted, what they were interested in, what they privately wished for. Everyday terms like desire, want, interest, and also motive, were used to represent what it was one had to influence. But in American social science 'social control' also acquired a more general meaning as a process that provided the basis for any kind of social collaboration or conformity within a society imagined as an aggregate of autonomous individuals. This generalized discourse of social control required a general term to refer to the entire variety of personal direction as a potential object of external influence. In time, 'motivation' came to play that role. The situation was quite clear to those who began arguing for a psychology of motivation in the 1920s. An early contribution to this argument, published in the *Psychological Review*, begins as follows:

> A rather insistent demand for an adequate psychology of motivation has always been made by those who are interested in the control of human nature. It has come from economists, sociologists, educators, advertisers, scout masters, and investigators of crime; more recently it has been voiced by certain psychologists, particularly those interested in personality and character, and in the various applied phases of the science. (Perrin, 1923)

Early textbooks of motivation continued to show awareness of these roots in introducing their topic. Troland (1928: 1) begins his pioneering treatise by referring to the businessman who 'wishes to know how to play on the motives of other men so that they will purchase his goods and services'. Young (1936: 2) says disarmingly: 'We all desire to influence and control human behavior – our own and that of others', and follows this with a tale about a student who applied 'scientific motivational principles' to his work as a salesman 'and before the semester was over had won a national prize in salesmanship'. (Surely the author of this text on motivation also deserved such a prize.)

The way in which the new concept of motivation is contextualized by its psychologist advocates signals a profound change in the understanding of human subjectivity. There had always been words referring to different facets of human intentionality, wish, desire, want, will, motive, and so on. These were usually invoked when it was a matter of accounting for one's own, or others', deviation from the automatic, habitual patterns of action that characterize everyday life. 'Motivation', however, departs from this usage in setting up an abstract category that groups all the older referents together, implying that they all have something important in common. *All* action, no matter how trivial or habitual, is motivated, according to those who were selling motivation.

In its abstractness 'motivation' has some similarity to the nineteenth-century term 'conation' (Hamilton, 1863). Why then was it necessary to invent a new term? Why did conation disappear, just when it might have taken on new life? Conation certainly suffered from the company it kept. It was a term invented by philosophers and used by philosophical psychologists that had never become part of the common language. In the twentieth century, conation was used by William McDougall, whose insistence on its instinctive basis did nothing to advance its cause among American psychologists of the 1920s. Traditionally, conation had referred to an assumed active principle in consciousness. Its reference was to the inner life of the individual; the evidence for its existence was largely introspective.

By contrast, 'motivation' did not abstract from a variety of terms referring to inner experience but from a variety of terms used in the context of influencing people. The actual words – want, wish, motive, etc. – might be the same, but the context of their use was different.

'Conation' abstracted something that, for example, will and desire had in common *insofar as they were objects of inner experience*. However, 'motivation' abstracted something that, for example, wants and motives had in common, *insofar as they were potential objects of manipulation and influence*. The qualities of consciousness that were important in nineteenth-century discussions of conation were irrelevant for the twentieth-century discourse on 'social control'.

Nevertheless, the older meanings did not disappear from ordinary usage. 'Conation' may have gone, but the lower order terms that it sought to unify are still with us. Everyday language still uses many terms that are taken to refer to an inner experience of intentionality or agency. The discipline of Psychology had to come to terms with the duality in the use of the terms that the concept of 'motivation' was intended to unify. Desires and motives may be objects for the exercise of influence and control, but they also remain anchored in a discourse of subjective purposes and intentions. Bridging this duality was the fundamental theoretical task faced by the new psychology of motivation. What resources were available for accomplishing this task?

First, there was a legacy of nineteenth-century speculation about the relationship between consciousness and bodily movement. This had resulted in a reduction of intentional consciousness to a matter of habit mechanisms that were subject to external influence through training. From Alexander Bain to William James there had developed a literature on 'the education of the will' in which conscious intentionality had already been transformed into an object of control. Motives were smoothly substituted for the will.

But there was another resource that was readily available for bridging the gap between the subjective experience of striving and 'motivation' as an object of control. This was the powerful metaphor of 'energy'. The same popular and textbook literature which posited 'motivation' as an object of influence generally also employed the energy metaphor to take care of the subjective side of its topic. This metaphor had emerged in the nineteenth century and promoted the naturalization of the will. By the beginning of the twentieth century, it had become highly popular as a vehicle of self-understanding. What would once have been described in voluntaristic terms as an action of the will is now more often represented as a mobilization of energy. In the more up-to-date advice literature, success for business executives is not presented as depending on exerting one's will power, but in being an energetic personality and controlling 'the energizing level' of one's subordinates (Gowin, 1917). There is widespread interest in what is called 'mobilizing one's hidden reserves of energy', or getting one's 'second wind', and widespread concern, not about weakness of will, but about depletion of one's stock of energy (Kugelmann, 1992).

William James was an early contributor to this literature. In his 1906 lecture on 'The energies of men' he claimed that 'the human individual

. . . energizes below his maximum' (James, 1911: 12). Pointing the way
to the psychology of motivation that was to develop some years later, he
presents the problem as follows:

> In rough terms we may say that a man who energizes below his normal
> maximum fails by just so much to profit by his chances in life; and that a
> nation filled with such men is inferior to a nation run at higher pressure. The
> problem is, then, how can men be trained up to their most useful pitch of
> energy? And how can nations make such training most accessible to all their
> sons and daughters. This, after all, is only the general problem of education,
> formulated in slightly different terms. (James, 1911: 8)

Note how James' skilful deployment of the energy metaphor allows him
to slide smoothly between the engineering language of things being run
at high pressure and the language of social policy. This facile mixture of
the moral and the physical characterizes his entire presentation of the
topic and sets the tone for the psychological discourse on motivation
that was to follow. James (1911: 32) tells us that 'the idea of one's honor,
for example, unlocks energy', and generalizes as follows: 'The physiologists call a stimulus 'dynamogenic' when it increases the muscular
contractions of men to whom it is applied; but appeals can be dynamogenic morally as well as muscularly' (James, 1911: 15). This ambiguity of
the 'dynamic' language of psychological energy, this sliding between the
moral and the muscular, was to provide the magic formula that brought
the psychology of motivation into existence.

Around the time of James' address, subjects in a psychological study
were already supplying introspective reports that referred to the 'force'
of a motive (Barrett, 1911), while the psychological theories of Janet and
Freud operated with concepts of mental force. What the subsequent
literature on 'motivation' added was the metaphorical framework that
would permit the domestication of this discourse of forceful subjectivity
by the imperatives of social control and social engineering. 'Energy',
which could be mental, yet engineered like physical energy, was the key
to that framework.

Emergence of the concept of drive

Practical interest in 'motivation' and human energetics had created an
area of discourse that appeared ripe for theoretical unification. If this
area was to be successfully annexed by the discipline of Psychology, the
latter would have to show that it possessed concepts and practices that
could provide it with a scientific foundation.

Unfortunately, the discipline was not well equipped for this task. Its
experimental core, preoccupied with laboratory studies of cognitive
problems, was quite remote from such concerns. More recent, biologically inspired, inquiries offered more hope, especially on the level of

practice. As we saw in the previous chapter, a sub-discipline of animal behaviour studies had grown up within American Psychology. Unlike its European counterpart, this field had adopted a distinctly interventionist stance towards its subject matter. Animals were confronted with strange environments and alien problems. The creature that American experimentalists were interested in was the animal *at work*. Now, working animals, like working people, required incentives to keep them going. These could be either positive, like food and sex, or negative, like escape from punishment through electric shock or confinement. At first, the use of such incentives was incidental to the main interest of the experimenter in the way the animal solved the tasks on which it had been put to work. But gradually, the incentives themselves became the focus of attention, so that experiments were designed so as to explore their relative effectiveness. By the early 1920s there was a considerable literature on this topic (Simmons, 1924).

This was a psychologically oriented, not a zoological, literature. It was not intended to contribute to the more efficient training of circus animals but to the development of fundamental principles that would also apply to the relative effectiveness of different incentives in humans. Potentially, such work might supply basic scientific insights that could then be applied by those concerned with the working of incentives in industry, in the classroom, in the administration of justice, and so on. But one could only have faith in that promise if one uncritically accepted the analogy between working laboratory animals and humans in institutional settings. To a large extent, this analogy depended on a highly elastic use of certain key terms. It had to be assumed that what was classified under the category of 'incentives' in factories, schools, prisons, etc., was *essentially* similar to what was called an incentive in the animal laboratory. Otherwise, there would be no foundation for the belief that investigation of the one would lead to knowledge about the other. Behind the trappings of scientific procedure there lurked a naive verbal realism: because something was *called* a reward in one situation it had to be similar, at some profound level, to something else that was called a reward in a very different setting. What propelled such vaults of reason was an ideology of biological essentialism, the belief that human conduct was *directly* governed by universal biological principles, irrespective of its context.

Nevertheless, there were obvious limits to the range of problems for which studies of incentives among laboratory animals might be considered relevant. Huge areas of human experience, hitherto accounted for by invoking such concepts as will, motive and attitude, were left untouched by such studies. If a biological psychology was to extend its sway over these content areas, something more than studies of animal incentives would be needed. It was necessary to come up with new theoretical categories that would cement the biological anchoring of these areas of human experience.

But first one had to decide which form of biology one was to espouse, for there were still two forms extant, the vitalistic and the mechanistic kind. The former was represented psychologically by William McDougall, a tireless propagandist for the idea that all human behaviour was driven by a finite number of fixed instincts. The category of instinct had enjoyed a period of great popularity among those who felt that Darwin had unlocked the door through which psychology had to pass to become a true science. William James enthused about instincts, as did many of his contemporaries. But McDougall's version was hard to swallow, at least in an American setting (Krantz and Allen, 1967). It was too closely linked to an explicit purposivism that offended the mechanistic sensibilities of its audience. Moreover, its way of making room for environmental influences, through its author's rather old-fashioned belief in the inheritance of acquired characteristics, made it unappealing to a generation that was pinning its hopes on the quick environmental fix.[2]

If a category of instincts grounded in purposivism was a non-starter, as far as unifying the psychology of motivation was concerned, perhaps mechanistic biology held the answer? Attempts in this direction were not lacking. Their common feature was the reduction of the category of 'motive' to that of 'reflex'. All behaviour, animal or human, simple or complex, was a matter of specific stimuli eliciting specific responses. Like all would-be scientific accounts of motivation, this one was based on the ambiguous notion of 'energy', but in this case the source of the energy that directed action was located in the environment rather than the organism. Doing one thing rather than another meant coming under the influence of one specific set of stimuli rather than another. This view, rooted in the tropistic ideas of late nineteenth-century mechanistic biology (Pauly, 1987), implied an energetic interpretation of the category of stimulation. Power to provoke movement ultimately resided in stimuli, not in organisms, and questions of motivation were therefore reducible to questions of competition among stimuli as to which of them would become prepotent at any particular time. Early behaviourists opted for such an approach, but one did not need to identify with all aspects of their programme to do so. Troland, whose early text on motivation has already been mentioned, also favoured this kind of theorizing. However, in the long run, the enormous theoretical load placed on the vague notion of stimulation proved too much even for this supremely elastic category. Something more distinctive was needed to pull together all the bits and pieces that constituted the new field of 'motivation'.

The task was accomplished by the concept of 'drive', which was invented towards the end of World War I, and achieved theoretical dominance of the field by the 1930s.[3] Its inventor was Robert Sessions Woodworth, a prominent experimentalist located at Columbia University, whom we will encounter again in Chapter 9. His own account of his invention of 'drive' is not without interest:

I am sure I did not derive the word from any previous psychologist. I got it from mechanics. A machine has a mechanism, such that if it is put in motion it operates in a certain way; but it must be driven in order to move. The 'drive' of a machine is the supply of energy that puts it in motion. (Young, 1936: 71)

Woodworth introduced 'drive' to the psychological world in a 1918 monograph, entitled *Dynamic Psychology*.[4] Likening the living organism to a loaded gun with stored energy, he noted that a stimulus acted as a 'drive' to release this energy. Recognizing that this could hardly be equated with the operation of a motive, he then posed the question of 'whether we can work our way up from the drive as external stimulus to the drive as inner motive' (Woodworth, 1918: 38).

He thought he could accomplish this transformation by drawing on ideas about nervous activity that had been developed by the neuro-physiologist, Sir Charles Sherrington, with whom he had worked (Woodworth, 1961). As we saw in Chapter 4, Sherrington stood in a line of development that had resulted in a convergence of empiricist mental philosophy and bioenergetics. Woodworth relied on the following Sherringtonian notions in his construction of the concept of 'drive': (1) the nervous system was organized into (reflex) sub-systems that stored and released energy; (2) the release of energy by a nervous segment could take place over a period of time, especially if direct release was not possible; (3) the release of energy in one nervous segment could trigger the release of energy in other segments; (4) the above mechanisms underlie two distinct classes of organismic reactions, *consummatory* and *anticipatory*. Consummatory reactions are those which constitute the natural end or final term in a sequence of movements by the organism, such as swallowing the meat of prey that has been hunted down, killed and ingested. Anticipatory actions are all those that lead up to consummatory ones (Sherrington, 1961: ch. 9).

Woodworth simply generalized these notions so as to produce a framework for the explanation of any kind of human conduct. The hypothetical action of one segment on another (no. 3 above) he called 'drive', evoking the machine analogy he had in mind. A case of drive action that had particular biological importance would occur when the nervous segments serving consummatory actions were energized but could not discharge (when there was no food to swallow), so that they would trigger the activity of other segments serving 'preparatory' actions (Sherrington's 'anticipatory' actions). That made it possible, for example, to speak of the 'hunger drive' as 'motivating' all sorts of actions leading up to the act of eating. Drive action attributable to biological consummatory activity came to be called 'primary', but Woodworth (1918: 42) was quite clear about the fact that 'any mechanism might be a drive'.

Although the Sherringtonian derivation was soon forgotten, the concept of 'drive' quickly became popular. Its equation of animal drive and mechanical drive led to concerted attempts at measuring the strength of the former in the same way as one would measure the latter, by pitting it against an opposed force of known strength. Thus, Moss (1924) measured drive in terms of the strength of electric shock animals were prepared to undergo in order to reach a goal object. Other psychologists (Dashiell, 1925; Warden, 1931) soon joined in this endeavour. Richter (1927), a biologist, pursued a long term programme of research into the physiological conditions of 'animal drive'. For some time, these were mainly looked for in the blood and digestive systems, rather than in the brain. That allowed recourse to physiological notions of 'homeostasis' (Cannon, 1929) in explaining the action of drives. Only in the post-Second World War period was there a return to neurophysiological speculation regarding the physical basis of motivation (Hebb, 1949).

The term soon found its way into psychology textbooks, providing the unifying concept for their treatment of motivation. Human motives were supposed to be reducible to 'primary' drives, equated with the 'animal drives' manipulated in laboratory studies. At this point, the drive concept played much the same role as the concept of instinct had done a generation earlier. It was the vehicle for a radical biological reductionism in psychology, though the biology that was now favoured was starkly mechanistic in character.

In the 1930s, the concept of 'drive' took on the form in which it was to survive for the rest of the century. It was taken up by both major versions of neo-behaviourist doctrine, that of Tolman, and that of Hull. Like much else characteristic of neo-behaviourism, the drive concept survived the demise of the more idiosyncratic features of these theoretical systems (Smith, 1984). In both systems the notion of 'drive' was a crucial component of the structure of mechanistic instrumentalism that they imposed on all activity, human as well as animal. Tolman (1932), who had made a comfortable switch from instincts to drives, took over, from the biologist Craig, a distinction between 'consummatory' reactions and a state of 'appetite' which precedes them. This was similar to the Sherringtonian distinction between consummatory and 'anticipatory' activity earlier adopted by Woodworth. In both cases, there was a strict separation of directional and energetic components. The state referred to as 'appetitive', 'anticipatory', 'preparatory', or simply as 'drive', is a 'state of agitation' (Tolman, 1932: 273) whose role is the energizing of behaviour. The directional component is supplied by a different feature, which Tolman calls 'expectancy' or 'means-end-readiness'. In Hull's (1943b) version, behaviour is also energized by 'drive', but the directional component consists of chained stimulus–response connections called 'habit'. The theoretical differences involved here should not be allowed to obscure the fundamental similarity: both systems were built on a basic distinction between energizing and directing components, universally applicable to *all* behaviour, human and animal.

Motivational psychology as normative

The energy vs. direction distinction provided the basis for interpreting all behaviour in instrumentalist terms (Koch, 1956). Only a few actions, such as eating and copulating, were classified as 'consummatory'. For the rest, 'consummation' was extrinsic to the action itself, though the 'need' for such consummation was supposed to supply the energy without which no action would take place. For the discipline of Psychology, the advantage of this model was that it made possible the integration of practical and scientific imperatives. The burgeoning practical interest in 'motivation' as a means of social control, discussed in the previous section, had presupposed instrumentalism. One could influence people's actions as producers and consumers by playing on the motives they had for working or for purchasing products. These motives were thought of as extrinsic to the actions themselves. One could induce individuals to work more intensively or more consistently by exciting personal ambitions; one could induce them to purchase one's brand of drugs or cosmetics by exciting fear and envy. Implicitly, there was a notable lack of faith in the intrinsic attractions of work, of many consumer products, and more generally, of socially valuable activity. What a science of 'motivation' might supply were principles to guide attempts at influencing people's actions by controlling the extrinsic motives that governed those actions.

Such hopes jibed comfortably with the prevailing engineering model of science. The principles to be looked for took the form of linear sequences of efficient causality. In the paradigmatic experimental situation, starving the rat was conceived as being analogous to pulling a control lever on a piece of machinery that would set in motion a chain of causes and effects. Conceptually, this was represented, both by Tolman and by Hull, in terms of a series of links between antecedent, intervening and consequent variables.[5]

An important feature of the neo-behaviourist use of the drive concept was its *stipulative* nature. The basic separation of energizing and directing components, the ubiquity of extrinsic motivation, the notion that motives must act like the efficient causes of mechanics, these were all non-empirical principles built into a conceptual framework for interpreting the behaviour of both laboratory rats and humans. There was no way in which any of these principles could be refuted without abandoning this framework. Adhering to the framework meant stipulating the universal validity of these principles. That could easily have normative implications. The deeply buried, culturally rooted, taken for granted quality of the principles meant that, for many, alternative interpretations became literally unthinkable.

Perhaps this accounts for the continued popularity of the drive concept and its analogues during the post-Second World War period, in spite of the fact that by 1950 their inadequacy was apparent, even in the closed world of animal experimentation (Koch, 1951). During the decades that followed, 'drive' continued to function as 'the main motivational construct all across the wide spectrum of psychological studies', though admittedly, its use had 'become increasingly vague' (Bindra, 1985: 347). In part, that vagueness was due to a practice which had led to the worst excesses of instinct theory and was increasingly affecting the drive concept: a collection of particular goal-directed activities was given a general name which was then used as the name of some hypothetical internal force, variously called instinct, drive, need or motive, that was supposed to be the cause of all the particular activities. In this way, psychologists like William James (1890) had posited instincts of rivalry, acquisitiveness, secretiveness and cleanliness. More than half a century later, we encounter talk about innate drives responsible for general cognitive processes, like knowing, learning and comprehending (Nissen, 1954). The circularity of such 'explanations' is obvious, for the facts which these drives or instincts are supposed to explain are identical with the facts adduced to establish their existence.

But if the logical deficiencies of such 'explanations' are so glaring, what accounts for their apparently inextinguishable popularity? To answer that question we have to look at some further developments of the drive concept that are even closer to the Jamesian listing of instincts than Nissen's cognitive drives. Shortly before World War II, H.A. Murray, the head of the Harvard Psychological Clinic, had compiled a list of human 'needs', like those for acquisition, for superiority, for autonomy, and for achievement (Murray, 1938). The difference between this concept of 'need' and the prevailing drive concept was that the foundation in mechanistic biology was dropped. The psychology of human motivation had become autonomous, and animal experimentation had lost its privileged status as a source of basic knowledge about motivation in general. In the post-war period, this approach was popularized by psychologists like McClelland (McClelland et al., 1953), who established a minor industry devoted to 'achievement motivation', and Maslow (1954), for whom the concept of human needs provided a crucial component in an approach that came to be known as 'humanistic' psychology.

Hypothetical biological mechanisms no longer played any significant role in the construction of any of these motivational concepts. Their place was taken by cultural conventions employed in the everyday justification of actions. Such everyday accounts of the reasons for a person's actions may simply refer to a specific goal pursued by the person, but sometimes the explanation is in terms of a general personal quality, such as the individual's ambition or greed. In that case, a certain class of actions is distinguished from others on the basis of certain features that all members of the class are perceived to share. These features are then attributed to the person carrying out the actions. But in the making of such distinctions cultural-linguistic conventions play a crucial role. In picking out common features among different actions performed in different contexts one makes use of named categories that are current in one's culture and that provide an acceptable account of individuals' actions. Societies differ greatly in the categories that are available and recognized for this purpose. They also differ historically in the categories that are available and recognized at any particular time. What the psychology of so-called human needs did was to take categories that were in vogue in a particular society at a particular period and to reify them by using them as names for hypothetical forces within the person that were supposedly responsible for producing all the actions that could be given the corresponding label.

The role of this form of the psychology of motivation as a kind of *cultural apologetics* is unmistakable. Elevating one set of historically contingent conventions to the status of universal human needs not only emphasized their importance for the society in which they originated but provided a rationale for proselytizing efforts elsewhere. This was especially evident in the case of the most popular of these supposed needs, those for 'achievement' and for 'self-realization'. Being so closely tied to culturally sanctified values and to unexamined conventions, this version of the psychology of motivation was reassuring and lacked the potentially subversive implications that the Freudian alternative had once harboured (Marcuse, 1956). Moreover, the psychology of human needs perpetuated the more general, and historically more deeply rooted, belief that the reasons for human conduct were to be looked for, not in particular social situations, but in hypothetical forces that inhabited individuals, 'springs of action', as they had been so vividly called in an earlier age (Bentham, 1969).

That kind of appeal was undoubtedly of benefit to the science of psychology. But more specifically, it allowed 'motivation' to continue in being as a recognized sub-field of that science. Although the field took on the appearance of a hotchpotch of topics without a common structure (see for example Weiner, 1992), the belief that 'motivation' constituted a psychological 'natural kind', potentially unified by one set of principles, continued unshaken. From the beginning, psychological writers on motivation claimed that their topic was meant to provide answers to the question of the 'why' of human behaviour. In fact, they were interested in only one kind of answer, the kind that posited intra-individual impulsions. It was this foundational commitment that created the field. Yet, even in the heyday of motivational psychology, there were those who pointed out that answers to the 'why' question could be of many kinds (Peters, 1958), and that the great defect of prevalent psychological accounts was that they universalized one kind of answer as the only acceptable kind. Had the implications of this critique not been ignored, there would have been nothing to hold the field together, even in its later highly tenuous form.

The category of personality: historical

Historically, the big question about the category of 'personality' is how it ended up as a *psychological* category. It certainly did not start out that way. Prior to the nineteenth century it had been used primarily in theological, legal and ethical contexts. The theological context is the oldest, going back to mediaeval debates about the attributes of God and other spiritual beings.[6] Here, 'personality' tends to be used mostly in the sense of a quality of personhood. Transfer to a legal context followed during the Renaissance. This was important for subsequent developments in that the category was now definitely humanized. In due course, natural right theorists were able to speak of a 'right to personality', and by the late eighteenth century the category had become established in the discourse of Continental European moral philosophy. Kant introduced a clear distinction between 'person' and 'personality', reserving the latter for the autonomous ethical subject. In the course of the nineteenth century, however, the tendency was to apply the term to the concrete individual, though often still in an ethical, not a psychological, context. 'Personality' was beginning to come down to earth.[7] For example, the French philosopher, Renouvier, for whom William James had a high regard, used the category to refer to the embodied, empirically knowable individual (Collins, 1985). By 1895 James (1983) had imported that usage into America.[8]

It is unlikely that this would have been a matter of great consequence had it not been for another development that had occurred in France in the late nineteenth century. This was the *medicalization* of the category of 'personality'. The philosophical doctrines with which the term had become enmeshed were much despised by certain French doctors strongly committed to a naturalistic approach to human problems. For them, an individual's personality was no spiritual principle but a natural, embodied entity as much prone to disease as other such entities. Of course, insofar as it was subject to disease personality became an appropriate object for medical, rather than philosophical, attention. By 1885 Ribot had published the first authoritative text on 'The Diseases of the Personality'.[9] Cases of what had previously been known as 'alternating consciousness' played a key role in these developments. They now became cases of 'alternating personality', a reformulation adopted by William James in his widely read *Principles of Psychology* of 1890. A warrant for this transformation could be obtained from the Lockean tradition of equating the individual self with consciousness of self (see Chapter 3). Another prominent figure who played a role in bringing the French medical usage of 'personality' to America was Morton Prince (1905) whose early studies of multiple personality were disseminated very widely.[10]

By the early years of the twentieth century public fascination with the medical features, the abnormalities, of personality had become quite unmistakable. The category, which had not been widely used in the nineteenth century, was beginning to appear with increasing frequency in popular literature. In America this was particularly evident in self-improvement literature. For the older examples of this genre the category of 'character', with its moral overtones, had usually been central, but now a series of books and articles addressed to the development of 'personality' began to appear. Whereas guides to character improvement had primarily traded in such concepts as 'duty', 'citizenship', 'integrity' and 'manhood', the newer personality development guides emphasized adjectives like 'attractive', 'creative' and 'dominant' (Susman, 1979). Not only had 'personality' become a part of the individual that had to be watched anxiously for signs of disease, it had also become a universal possession capable of degrees of perfection defined in terms of a vocabulary of social effectiveness.

It took some time for these developments to be assimilated by the new discipline of Psychology. In Continental Europe there were some, ultimately abortive, attempts to extend the objective study of individuals from the abnormal to the normal. The prominent German psychiatrist, Kraepelin, who had studied with Wundt, launched a programme of investigating differences in individual functioning experimentally, but even Kraepelin's considerable prestige could not generate any general interest in its results.[11] In France Alfred Binet, who had been directly involved with some of the work on abnormal personality, collaborated with Victor Henri in launching a programme of studies in what they called 'Individual Psychology' (Binet and Henri, 1895). This involved an intensive investigation and comparison of individuals to discover characteristic relationships among psychological processes in particular persons. Binet's study of his own daughters, Alice and Madeleine, is probably the best-known example of this approach.[12] But, apart from the important suggestion that normal individuals *as individuals* were to form appropriate objects for psychological investigation, this work also remained without consequence.

In America the intensive psychological study of individuals remained very largely a psychiatric preserve founded on the clinical methodology of the case history. The object of study was therefore defined as the 'case', rather than as 'personality'. American psychologists had shown little interest in the study of individuals but had manifested an early fascination with the collection of masses of information on large numbers of individuals, a kind of psychological census taking.[13] Galton's 'anthropometry' had been adapted to the study of what came to be called 'individual differences' in the form of so-called 'mental tests'. Eventually, this led to the institutionalized practice of mass intelligence testing, as discussed in Chapter 5. But there was no claim that this amounted to a study of 'personality'. Until the 1920s such an object of investigation lay quite beyond the horizon of American psychology.

What seem to have provided the major impetus for change were the practical shortcomings of intelligence testing. The historical tie of test content and form to educational settings had produced an instrument that correlated with academic success but was of very limited usefulness in non-academic settings where it would do little more than eliminate some obviously unsuitable candidates. Therefore, from the earliest days of the application of mental testing in non-academic settings, there had been attempts to supplement intelligence testing with a rough assessment of non-intellectual qualities.[14] The problem surfaced again during World War I, when such assessments appear to have been more useful to the US Army than its vast programme of intelligence testing (Mayrhauser, 1987; Samelson, 1979).

With the huge expansion of intelligence testing in American schools after the war it became apparent that the excessive hopes which had been pinned on this technology were not to be fulfilled even on its home ground. There was a growing feeling that the value of these tests for predicting school success had been overrated and that they needed to be supplemented by an assessment of 'non-intellectual traits'. A similar recognition of the limitations of intelligence testing gained ground in connection with vocational selection, the prediction of criminal and delinquent behaviour, and the prognostic testing of psychiatric patients.[15] But the institutional demand for rationalized, impersonal methods of social selection on a mass scale continued undiminished. The result was a scramble to invent and apply techniques for the assessment of 'non-intellectual traits'. Many of the new instruments did not survive for long, but gradually a few came to dominate the field. In any case, a mass of data accumulated that could not easily be accommodated within any of the existing subdivisions of the discipline. The need for a label that would be less cumbersome than 'non-intellectual trait testing' became obvious.

Three candidates immediately presented themselves and were all used more or less interchangeably for a time. The first, 'temperament', had a long history in a medical context but was not in current use in scientific medicine. It originated long before the rigid mind–body distinction of the modern period had come into vogue, and, once that distinction had been imposed on it, it was too easily identified with some sort of physiological reductionism. That was not what most psychologists wanted. The second candidate, 'character', certainly enjoyed widespread lay use, not least in business and industry, but had certain moralistic connotations that seemed to be incompatible with its employment as a supposedly scientific category. In particular, character was tainted by its historical association with the concept of will, a concept that had become anathema to scientifically minded American psychologists.[16]

The third candidate, 'personality', had several things in its favour which have already been mentioned. It had recently become a popular category of folk psychology that professional psychologists were expected to know something about. In its new popular meaning 'personality' was no longer the property of the few, but referred to everybody's capacity for being different from others (Susman, 1979). This change in the semantics of 'personality', together with its lack of moralistic connotations, certainly provided a better fit with the aspirations of many American psychologists than its potential competitors, character and temperament.

But the decisive factor favouring the emergence of 'personality' as the description of a twentieth-century psychological object was probably its preceding medicalization. That meant that it had already been constituted as a potential object of scientific investigation, not only in the basic sense of being a natural object subject to disease, but also in the more special sense of being what Ribot (1885: 3) called *un tout de coalition*, 'an associated whole'. Unlike 'character', whose reference was to something considered essentially unitary, 'personality' was essentially diverse, an assembly of various tendencies. Its health depended on the relationship among its components. This componential model provided a far more promising starting point for quantitative empirical research than the unitary model implied by current usage of the term 'character'.[17]

It is true that the earlier medical interest was limited to the aberrations of personality, but the step from that to the inclusion of all individual proclivities in the medical gaze was soon taken. In North America a major location for this process was the mental hygiene movement. At the height of its influence during the period of the emergence of 'personality' as a distinct object of psychological investigation, it was dedicated to the identification of *potential* cases of individual maladjustment and their timely treatment. That meant that everyone's personality, not just that of people already classified as disturbed, was now an object of medical interest because it might carry the seeds of future disturbance.[18] Had mental hygiene limited itself to a concern with the major psychiatric disorders its influence might have been relatively restricted. However, it became a powerful expositor of a pervasive social philosophy that attributed the causes of virtually all social problems to the personal 'maladjustment' of individuals.[19] The 'personality' which everyone possessed was now seen as the site where the seeds of future individual and social problems were sown and germinated.

That not only demanded energetic programmes of shaping and intervention for which teachers, social workers and others were recruited, it also provided a niche that could best be filled by the up and coming discipline of Psychology. The specific features of this 'personality', now seen as the fountainhead, not only of human achievements, but of so many human problems, had to be identified, classified and measured, if the practical measures inspired by the hopes of mental hygiene were to be placed on a scientific footing. No one was in a better position than psychologists to perform this task. Had they not already accomplished something similar with regard to the most important of all individual attributes, namely, intelligence? Why should the methods which had proved so effective in making intelligence an object of scientific social selection not provide the model for how other personal attributes might be subjected to the same process?

Indeed, psychologists proceeded to make their contribution by using the experience gained in intelligence testing to construct techniques of what was called 'personality measurement'. These techniques were based on standard sets of questions about personal attributes to be answered by the person herself or by some other individual who had some acquaintance with the person. Various other personality tests went into and out of fashion from time to time, but rating the attributes of others or of oneself formed the bedrock of personality measurement from the beginning and remained so. The appeal of this technique depended not on the flimsy instruments that formed its basis but on the interpretation that was placed on its results.

The instruments deployed by psychologists were of two kinds, verbal and statistical. The former employed labels that might be applied to individuals in ordinary language, such as sociable, submissive, emotional, and so on. The latter employed statistical correlations, almost always performed on data collected from large numbers of individuals, and in due course, the mathematical description of matrices of such correlations. This resulted in the production of 'scales' for the 'measurement' of various features of 'personality' that were of potential interest to clinicians, personnel managers, school principals and anyone else who had to make decisions about the fate of individuals on the basis of their supposed ability to perform effectively in various social settings. Later on, as personality measurement became a flourishing enterprise within academic psychology, it lost its earlier link to social practice and developed loftier ambitions.[20] The goal was now the development of a short list of basic and universal attributes that would account for the maximum amount of individual variation on the entire universe of traits constituting human personality.

Personality psychology and cultural conservatism

In their pursuit of the project of personality measurement psychologists worked within a framework of assumptions that never had to be questioned because they were so widely held in the societies in which they operated. Among these assumptions two deserve at least a passing mention here. One concerns the belief that human conduct is the expression of some essence within the individual, an essence that remains the same irrespective of the conditions under which the conduct occurs and is observed (Kagan, 1988). The psychology of personality measurement added the refinement that variations in intra-individual essence between individuals were purely quantitative, so that all individuals could be assigned a position on the same universal set of attributes.[21] This refinement had played a crucial role in the first constitution of a human quality as a measurable, universal attribute, namely, intelligence. It was now extended to all individual attributes in principle. 'Personality' was now constituted as the sum of these universally present, measurable intra-individual essences.

The second major assumption that was indispensable for the constitution of personality as the object for a certain kind of measurement concerned the role of language. 'Personality' was posited as a real natural entity existing quite independently of anyone's description of it. Yet the favoured method for the investigation of this entity depended entirely on verbal description! On the one hand, 'personality' was to be treated as an object not fundamentally different from any other object of natural science, but on the other hand, scientific access to this object was to be gained primarily through its description in everyday language. One has to wonder how the older natural sciences would have fared, had they adopted this approach to knowledge. So personality research based on questionnaires, rating scales, adjectival checklists and so on would seem to have faced a fundamental problem. How could it be claimed that it provided knowledge of anything beyond the semantic space of personality description?[22]

Yet this problem hardly seems to have disturbed the busy work of personality research. One probable reason for that was the predominance of purely practical goals in the early days of this research. But as the scientific pretensions of the domain grew, it became clear that they depended on certain articles of faith pertaining to the role of language. In the first place, it was never questioned that language *represented* reality, and more specifically, that it *reflected* the natural contours of an objective world existing outside and independently of it. So there was no problem about investigating personality via its verbal description – it was like observing something in a mirror. Such ideas about the role of language had a long tradition behind them and were deeply ingrained in the culture that nurtured personality psychology (Crapanzano, 1990).

Almost equally ingrained was the belief in a timeless 'human nature', independent of culture and history. That made it possible to turn undeniable historical variations in language into an advantage. If 'personality' (i.e. 'human nature') never changes, and if the verbal descriptions that are its reflection change over time, then it is easy to conclude that these changes represent an ever better reflection of what was really there all the time. But then, why not go all the way and say that this process is already complete, that the words in the language already provide, not just a reflection, but a *perfect* reflection of 'personality'? Some of the most influential personality researchers did in fact mount such an argument. R.B. Cattell, to cite only one prominent example, said that he was 'making only the one assumption that all aspects of human personality which are or have been of importance, interest, or utility have already been recorded in the substance of language' (Cattell, 1943: 483). Such a statement would not have been remarkable had it been made a century earlier. What makes it remarkable is its historical location. It epitomizes a striking feature of the construction of 'personality' as an object of psychological research in the twentieth century, namely its cultural conservatism. This enterprise could only flourish by appealing to rather venerable folk beliefs about human nature and language and steadfastly ignoring relevant contemporary developments in philosophy and social science.

That cultural conservatism is also in evidence when one considers a further aspect of the historical construction of 'personality' within the discipline of Psychology – its role in warding off the radical threat of so-called 'depth psychology'. The period during which 'personality' took its place as a recognized academic domain within Psychology was also the period during which that discipline faced a serious threat to its continued popular success from a competitor that could not simply be ignored. That competitor was psychoanalysis, or more accurately, depth psychology. The latter term is to be preferred because Freudian psychoanalysis was only the most visible, the most successful, representative of a set of approaches which included that of Jung and some of the neo-Freudians, all of which had a family resemblance to each other. The basis of this resemblance constituted an indirect threat to much of academic psychology and a direct threat to the foundations of American personality psychology.

All versions of depth psychology were founded on a basic disjunction between appearance and reality in matters psychological. Whatever seemed to be unproblematically observable and reportable was suspect. It was likely to be but a screen, a camouflage whose function was to mislead. Behind this screen there existed the real psychological world, very different from what was displayed for all to see. That disjunction extended to everyday language. So far from being a reflection of reality it was more likely to be an instrument for its disguise. All this was expressed in the central metaphor of this psychology, the metaphor of surface and depth.

That represented a radical challenge to the naive empiricism of much academic psychology, particularly the emerging psychology of motivation and personality. The methods of the latter, especially, depended on taking verbal description at face value, treating it as a trustworthy reflection of what was actually there to be known. From the point of view of depth psychology, however, the investigations of empiricist personality psychology were about as likely to lead to scientific insights into the functioning of human individuals as the printing of pretty flower postcards was to lead to breakthroughs in scientific biology. Yet depth psychology in its Freudian version was experiencing an astounding wave of popularity, particularly in the United States. This popularity affected many of those whose opinion mattered to American psychologists – psychiatrists, advertising executives and educationists among others. It even led to stirrings of self-doubt in the ranks of the psychologists. It could not be ignored.

Some psychologists continued to dismiss psychoanalysis and the rest as unscientific. There was a certain honesty about this, for the notions of science of most academic psychologists and most depth psychologists were indeed incompatible. But in the long run another solution to the problem proved more viable. Depth psychology was domesticated, a process in which the category of 'personality' played a key role. What happened was that some of the doctrines of depth psychology, in suitably watered-down form, were presented as 'theories of personality'. Courses began to be taught on this topic and textbooks written. 'Personality' became an umbrella term to cover both what depth psychology was after and what those who relied on questionnaires and rating scales were after. The insinuation that this was ultimately the same thing was however false and misleading. Freud was not a 'personality theorist'. Whatever the objects he was theorizing about, they were not 'personality' as it had been constructed within American psychology. Indeed, there developed the extraordinary situation where the teaching of 'personality theory' and research on 'personality' went their separate ways. The exception was formed by sporadic attempts to test psychoanalytic theories by means of the standard methods of academic psychology. These signalled that 'personality' hardly functioned as a neutral term accommodating all constructions of the psychological object without bias. There was always a strong tendency to treat the empiricist construction as the metaphysically real one. Attempts to 'test' psychoanalytic theories by methods based on the assumptions of naive empiricism were never matched by attempts to test these assumptions by methods that assumed the truth of psychoanalytic theory.

All the psychological categories discussed in this book present a Janus face. In intra-disciplinary discourse they acquired a rather specific meaning based on shared methodological commitments, but in psychologists' contacts with extra-disciplinary institutions they retained a much broader and varied meaning. The category of 'personality', however, acquired, not just these two faces, but a plethora of meanings that had only the most tenuous connection with each other. Among these meanings the following are particularly worthy of note: (1) personality as the object posited by the project of building a body of universally valid knowledge about socially decontextualized human individuals; (2) personality as a quasi-medical entity subject to disease, disorder and symptomatology and therefore the target of measures to ensure 'normality' or 'health'; (3) personality as an aggregate of traits reflected in verbal descriptions; (4) personality as the supposedly common object of interest among incommensurable approaches to human psychology; (5) personality as a container for a variety of psychological investigations and questions that did not fit into the other recognized subdivisions of the discipline.

Historically, the use of the same term to denote all these things removed the need of proving that they were ultimately all one thing. This process of 'unification by naming' certainly helped to keep the work of the discipline going without being slowed down or interrupted by awkward questions. The significance of this work was another issue entirely.

Notes

1. The inverted commas around 'applied psychology' are intended to indicate that the term was misleading. At that time, there was very little 'pure' psychology to apply to anything, and for the most part, applied psychologists made up their psychology as they grappled with specific problems. Often, their innovations would then lead to new questions and procedures in 'basic' psychology. This tail was capable of wagging the dog.

2. The contrast between the poor reception McDougall's ideas received in America and their much greater success in Britain (the first edition of his *Introduction to Social Psychology* was published there in 1908 – the 33rd edition in 1950) provides a rather vivid little example of the cultural embeddedness of psychological theory.

3. One occasionally meets the grotesque suggestion that 'drive' might have been derived from the German *Trieb*, which Anglo-Saxon psychologists had come across in the writings of Freud. Apart from the fact that the German equivalent of 'drive', *as used in American Psychology*, is not *Trieb* but *Antrieb*, the meaning and antecedents of 'drive' and *Trieb* are utterly different. The modern derivation of 'drive' from the world of machinery is well documented. *Trieb*, however, has a long pedigree in German philosophy and philosophical psychology. It played a role in Kant's version of faculty psychology, represented the pure activity of the ego in the philosophy of Fichte, and became the basis for the self-realization of living subjects in Hegelian psychology. It was a basic concept in most versions of German nineteenth-century philosophical psychology and was taken up by Wilhelm Wundt, who regarded it as providing the basis of mental activity. In the late nineteenth century *Trieb* began to acquire a more biological hue, but its connotations continued to be very different from the English *instinct*. The task of Freud's translators was an impossible one, because there simply is no English equivalent for *Trieb*. The term epitomizes the very different paths taken by Anglo-Saxon and by German psychology during the nineteenth century.

4. 'Dynamic' became a psychological catchword that usually indicated employment of some variant of the energy metaphor, but eventually became almost meaningless from overuse.

5. This scheme was not limited to the explanation of motivation. Its more general significance is discussed in Chapter 9.

6. The best overview of the historical vicissitudes of the categories 'person' and 'personality' (not always clearly distinguished in the past) is to be found in Ritter and Gründer 1989: 270–338, 346–354).

7. Romanticism, with its admiration for the singular, the outstanding, individual was part of this process. As a result, it now became possible to ascribe an 'overpowering personality' to an individual like Napoleon, or to associate an attribute like 'charm' with an individual's personality (see *Oxford English Dictionary*, 1989, XI: 602).

8. See also Leary (1990).

9. Two features of Ribot's *personalité* are particularly worthy of note: it is not regarded as a unity but as 'an associated whole' (p. 3), and it has a biological basis – even animals are considered to have a form of it.

10. These developments, all too briefly summarized here, are discussed at much greater length in Hacking (1995).

11. Kraepelin even launched a journal, *Psychologische Arbeiten*, that would publish work conducted under this programme. Only nine volumes ever appeared, and it ceased publication upon Kraepelin's death. This work remained largely unknown to American psychologists.

12. See Binet (1903). Good secondary accounts are to be found in Wolf (1973) and Fancher (1990). Sharp (1899) provides an interesting review during the heyday of Individual Psychology.

13. For further details, see Danziger (1990a), Chapter 5.

14. Historically, the most important of these attempts was made by Walter Dill Scott, appointed professor of advertising in 1909 and of applied psychology in 1916 (Mayrhauser, 1987), who developed a system for the selection of salesmen.

15. The list of relevant publications is too long to be reproduced here. Some examples are given in Danziger (1990a); for further details, see Parker (1991).

16. For an extensive discussion of the history of temperament and character, see Roback (1927). On the international ramifications of 'character' vs. 'personality', see McDougall (1932). Both of these authors were outside the mainstream of American psychology. The insider who helped most to establish 'personality' rather than 'character' as the 'scientific' term of choice was G.W. Allport (1927). He did this by adopting J.B. Watson's (1919) distinction between 'personality evaluated', which was 'character', and 'personality' taken as a morally neutral scientific object. For these psychologists the avoidance of moral connotations always went hand in hand with the denial of the essentially social nature of personality. Social factors could 'influence' personality from the outside, but were not part of its 'actual nature', its psychological essence. On Allport's historical role and psychological essentialism, see Nicholson (1996).

17. In Germany there was a concerted attempt to subject 'character' to empirical investigation (Geuter, 1992). This failed for a number of reasons, one of which was the inapplicability of quantitative models. See Vernon (1933) for an early description of the contrast between the German and the American approach, and Danziger (1990a) for further analysis.

18. The psychiatrist Adolf Meyer played a key role here. See Leys (1990b).

19. See Shea (1980); Cohen (1983).

20. The codification of 'personality' as a recognized domain within academic psychology was marked by the almost simultaneous appearance of three texts defining the field for many years to come: Allport (1937); Murray (1938); and, much less influential, Stagner (1937). On Allport's trajectory from early behaviouristically inspired and practically oriented research to personalistic essentialism, see Nicholson (1996).

21. See Danziger (1990a) and Rose (1988) for more extended discussions.

22. For a review of this problem, see Semin (1990).

8

ATTITUDES

Social Psychology has been more affected by passing fads and fashions than almost any other major branch of the discipline. Yet, through all the changes in briefly 'hot' research topics, one concept has maintained its commanding position at the core of this sub-discipline. It is the concept of 'social attitudes', more often simply referred to as 'attitudes'. Psychological social psychology's first modern textbook[1] already devotes a section to this topic (F.H. Allport, 1924), and seventy years later, it is reported that during the most recent twenty-year period over 34,000 published studies addressed attitudes in some way (Kraus, 1995).

Popular and convenient as the notion of 'attitudes' may have turned out to be, it is nevertheless a rather recent addition to the conceptual inventory of psychology. Although the *word* 'attitude' occurs in some psychological literature dating back to the first two decades of the twentieth century, the *category* of 'social attitudes' (note the plural) only makes its decisive entry into social psychological discourse in the period beginning at the end of World War I. The history of modern usage might well be regarded as beginning at this point. However, because earlier technical uses of 'attitude' throw an interesting light on more recent usage, it is worth taking a brief look at this bit of 'pre-history'.

An unpromising beginning

Technical, as distinct from everyday, uses of 'attitude' first occur in discourse about art, especially visual art and the theatre. Both of these art forms were very much concerned with making inner states visible, presenting outwardly visible forms as the *expression* of an inner reality. The *posture* of a figure depicted by an actor, a painter or a sculptor was never understood merely as a physical disposition of bodily parts in space but always carried a meaning due to its expressive function. The 'attitude' of the figure was the visible arrangement of its parts into a meaningful pattern, as in 'an attitude of waiting', or of devotion, or of nonchalance, for example. It should be noted that here there is no question of a causal link between an inner and an outer aspect. Rather, the 'attitude' of the figure refers to an inherent unity of inner and outer which endows certain physical appearances with expressive meaning (Hoff, 1990).

But once 'attitude' had been given a home in the arts, it acquired connotations of artificiality which were probably decisive for its subsequent history. For the attitudes depicted on stage and on canvas were of course deliberate creations and not spontaneous expressions. Certainly, by the nineteenth century people could be accused of 'striking an attitude', though this usage was clearly parasitic on the earlier understanding of attitude as 'the unstudied expression of action or passion' (Oxford English Dictionary, 1989 I: 771).

Attitudes were rescued from the taint of artificiality by their appearance in the biological discourse of the late nineteenth century. No small role was played in this by the appearance of Charles Darwin's The Expression of the Emotions in Man and Animals in 1872. Although Darwin did not explicitly define 'attitude' as a technical term, he did make quite frequent use of it as referring to the pattern of motor activity which constitutes the overt expression of an emotion. Not only did this establish 'attitude' as a category of nature rather than of art, it also suggested deep biological roots. No longer was the term limited to humans in its application. Rather, humans displayed attitudes because of their biological heritage. Darwin's use established 'attitude' as a category of natural phenomena that clearly fell within the domain of a biologically oriented psychology. Accordingly, we find 'emotional attitudes' being addressed by the Chicago functionalists, Dewey (1894) and Angell (1904). The link between attitude and the relatively specific topic of emotional expression was however becoming fragile. James Mark Baldwin was already devoting considerable attention to so-called 'motor attitudes', a much broader category that included all kinds of habitual response in addition to emotional expression (Baldwin, 1894).

The notion of 'motor attitudes' was soon to acquire a certain aura of scientific respectability through the work of Sir Charles Sherrington, the British neurophysiologist, who spoke of attitudes in the context of reflex postural adjustments on the part of animal organisms (Sherrington, 1961). In this case, attitude had been shorn of its mental, experiential, aspect and could be employed as a purely physiological category. This made the term acceptable to behaviourists like J.B. Watson (1919) who wanted to establish Psychology as a purely biological science concerned with the reactive movements of organisms.

While the biological and physiological appropriation of attitude showed an increasingly physicalistic slant, its everyday use seems to have taken the opposite tack of taking it to refer to purely mental events. The phrase 'attitude of mind' is to be found in quite a number of nineteenth-century works, including that of Herbert Spencer (1871). However, this phrase is used colloquially and never takes on scientific pretensions. Alexander Bain, the major defender of nineteenth-century associationism, takes a small step in this direction when he speaks of 'the forces of the mind' getting into 'a set track or attitude' (Bain, 1868: 158). But 'attitude' never becomes a significant category of nineteenth-century psychology in any way comparable to 'attention' or 'habit'.

The fact that American psychological texts of the early 1920s (Pillsbury, 1921; Warren, 1922; Woodworth, 1921) generally do contain some treatment of attitude as a psychological topic is due, primarily, to the physiological grounding of the term, as discussed earlier, and secondarily, to a peculiar accident of translation that had occurred a few years earlier. At the beginning of the twentieth century, a number of investigators at the University of Würzburg in Germany began a series of systematic introspective studies on the conscious processes that could be observed while one was engaged in trying to solve a task set by an experimenter. Traditionally, conscious experiences were categorized as either ideational or volitional (a division which has its roots in an Aristotelian distinction), but the Würzburg investigators believed they could detect a third variety of conscious event, to which they gave the name of *Bewusstseinslagen* (Mayer and Orth, 1901). The German language allows one to combine words to form compound words with a new meaning. So in this case we have *Bewusstsein*, which means consciousness, and the plural of *Lage*, which means position. Thus, *Bewusstseinslagen* refers to the positions assumed by consciousness under different conditions. But 'positions of consciousness' is an awkward and not very illuminating term in English. Perhaps there is a more effective translation?

E.B. Titchener, the major representative of an introspective psychology of consciousness in the US, thought so. He decided that *Bewusstseinslage* meant 'something like posture or attitude of consciousness' (Titchener, 1909: 100), ignoring the fact that both posture and attitude have quite straightforward German equivalents (*Haltung* and *Einstellung*) which had *not* been used by the Würzburg investigators. No matter, Titchener's 'something like' was good enough to establish 'conscious attitudes' as an important category for English-language introspective psychology.

Interestingly, the category survived the demise of this branch of the discipline which followed within little more than a decade. That survival is presumably due to the possibility of fusing a physicalistic meaning, expressed in the term 'motor attitudes', with a metaphorical extension of that meaning to what were now called 'conscious attitudes'. The mind was now supposed to be capable of taking up a mental posture towards some presented content, much as an animal organism takes up an emotional posture *vis-à-vis* a predator or rival. For Margaret Washburn, who had studied with Titchener, the literal interpretation still predominated. She claimed that all cognitive events were accompanied by motor reactions. Even though these might be very slight, they were crucially implicated in the maintenance of 'conscious attitudes' (Washburn, 1916). As the existence of these hypothetical motor reactions proved to be unconfirmable by means of objective observation, later

authors paid less and less attention to them, relying more on a metaphorical extension of the concept of posture from the physical to the
mental level.

One can identify three features of the early history of the attitude
concept that were particularly important for later developments.

First, there was a gradual transformation of 'attitude' from a category
whose members consisted of observables to a purely *dispositional* concept
involving inferred entities. Certainly, the earlier 'expressive' attitudes
referred to things that were visually observed: the inclination of the
head in a painted figure, the gait and bearing of a dramatic actor. This
remains true of Darwin's expressive emotional attitudes and Sherrington's postural reflexes. In these cases there is however also an implication that certain attitudes are based on the hard wiring of the organism.
American psychologists took up the notion that attitudes involved a
disposition to react in specific ways, though they tended to reject the
inborn nature of such dispositions. As stimulus–response psychology
became fashionable during the 1920s, there was an increasingly obvious
need for dispositional concepts that could account for the extreme
variability of stimulus–response relationships. John Dewey, who had
become aware of the limitations of stimulus–response psychology two
decades earlier (Dewey, 1896), favoured 'habit' as the major dispositional
concept and used 'attitude' as a synonym for it (Dewey, 1922).

Broad though Dewey's conception of attitude was, it appears almost
pedantic next to the promiscuous use of the term by psychologists
around 1930. 'Attitude' was now in general currency, as an all-purpose
dispositional term that no longer needed to be qualified by adjectives
like 'motor' or 'conscious'. Instead, it was used indiscriminately as a
synonym for virtually any other psychological dispositional term in
current use. For example, a 1932 article with the general title 'Theories
and measurement of attitudes' is entirely concerned with the assessment
of what was then called 'character', i.e. 'personality' in modern parlance
(Sherman, 1932). A review article with much the same title, published
two years earlier, declares that 'it must be confessed that most writers
use such terms as attitude, trait, opinion, wish, interest, disposition,
desire, bias, preference, prejudice, will, sentiment, motive, objective,
goal, idea, ideal, emotion, and even instinct and reflex, loosely, indefi-
nitely, and often interchangeably' (Bain, 1930: 359). The common
denominator of all these terms is said to be their reference to 'acquired
and conditioned action-patterns that motivate human social behavior',
where 'conditioned action-pattern' is used as a synonym for 'drive'. Not
only had 'attitude' lost any precise empirical reference, it had been shorn
of any distinctive conceptual characteristics as well.

The second feature to be noted in connection with the early twentieth-
century development of the attitude concept concerns the nature of the
link between the 'inner' and the 'outer'. Both in classical and in latter-
day usage 'attitude' was deployed so as to establish a link between

something visible on the surface and something going on under the surface. Classically, that link was characterized as 'expression'. Particular facial expressions or bodily postures 'expressed' particular emotions or feeling states. The link of inner and outer through expression definitely did not imply that the inner *caused* the outer. Actors were usually advised not to attempt experiencing the emotions which their actions on stage depicted. Visible actions and postures were assumed to have an intrinsic inner meaning which they made manifest to the observer.

By the time we get to twentieth-century psychology the idea of an expressive link between inner and outer has been lost.[2] Instead, we get two entirely distinct domains constituted, on the one hand, by so-called 'motor attitudes', which are purely physical events without intrinsic meaning, and on the other hand, 'conscious attitudes', which have no connection with overt action. In the behaviourist realignment that is characteristic of the post-World War II period, motor attitudes are submerged in the all-inclusive category of 'behaviour', and conscious attitudes are replaced by a mishmash of dispositions, as illustrated above. The link between the two domains is causal. Dispositions like motives, attitudes and personality characteristics are conceived of as causing 'behaviour', much as a gas under pressure might cause the movement of a cylinder.

That conception brings us to a third important feature in the development of 'attitude' as a psychological concept, a development that had its basis in certain characteristics of psychological research practice. Psychological experiments with human subjects are of course social situations. Psychological data are the products of a social interaction between the participants in such situations (Danziger, 1990a). Typically, an experimenter presents a subject with certain instructions as well as specific questions, to which a subject responds, verbally or otherwise. Traditionally, however, the data gathered by these means were never interpreted as products of a social interaction; at best, the social aspects of psychological experimentation were regarded as a source of error, to be controlled as far as possible. What makes a psychological experiment a psychological experiment is the unwritten rule that the conduct of the experimental subject is to be interpreted as a response to impersonal, asocial 'stimuli', mediated by psychological processes inside the subject. Working within this taken for granted framework psychologists naturally developed an insatiable appetite for all manner of intra-subjective states that would account for the wide variety of behaviour encountered under experimental conditions.

We can see this imperative at work among the investigators who came up with the idea of what Titchener called 'conscious attitudes'. As was the custom at the time, these investigators served in the role of experimental subject for each other. In the experimental situation, the individual who happened to be taking the role of experimenter would set the person in the subject role various tasks, such as defining a given word, expressing a personal preference between two famous men whose names were presented to the subject, giving free associations to pictures that were shown, answering questions like 'Does monism really mean the negation of personality?'[3] Now, we may ask ourselves, what would constitute an adequate account or explanation of how the subjects in these experiments arrived at their solutions to these tasks? To the introspective psychologists of the Würzburg School the answer to such a question could be taken for granted: one had to identify the mental processes or events that intervened between the presentation of the task and the solution offered by the subject. Accordingly, the experimental subjects were required to supply introspective reports on their mental processes while carrying out such tasks. It was then that the previously mentioned *Bewusstseinslagen* or 'conscious attitudes' turned up. Vague though the reports on them were, they had to be accepted as the answer to the implicit question motivating these investigations: how to account for subjects' response to the experimental situation in terms of their observable mental processes? The possibility of an alternative account that took the experimental subject to be a social agent making the best of a tricky social situation would not have been available to these investigators.

An alternative account was however soon to appear, though it was no more open to the social realities of psychological experimentation than the Würzburg account had been. Having become quite pessimistic about the likely practical yield from the practice of introspection, American psychologists dropped the (Wundtian) requirement that psychological processes had to be *observed* to occur before they could be postulated as mediating between experimental task and response. It now became acceptable simply to hypothesize the existence of such processes located within the individual. No longer did one rely on experimental subjects to identify these processes; instead, it was up to the experimenter to stipulate what they were. The result was total conceptual anarchy. So in the literature of the 1920s the number of different definitions of attitude exceeds the number of investigators working in the field, for some of them used more than one definition at various times. Only one unwritten rule was universally respected: whatever this thing was, it was real and lurked somewhere within the individual. Breaking this rule would have meant abandoning the common understanding of what psychological investigation was all about.

That attitude research grew into a flourishing little industry in spite of this unpromising start was due to two factors which we must examine next. The first of these impinged on the discipline from outside in the form of unprecedented public interest in what were popularly known as 'social attitudes'. The second factor was internal to the discipline and involved the proposal of a credible solution to the task of 'attitude measurement'.

How attitudes became 'social'

Although attitudes were not unknown to Psychology before the 1920s, their theoretical status was that of auxiliary concepts rather than that of a core concept capable of integrating an entire field of research. Titchener's 'conscious attitudes' came close, but when the entire enterprise of 'systematic introspective psychology', never of much importance in the North American context, was abandoned altogether in the years after World War I, the term 'attitude' would seem to have had a very limited psychological future, at best. Indeed, at least one influential writer suggested it be discarded (Symonds, 1927).

What saved 'attitude' from oblivion was its novel coupling with the attribute 'social'. In psychological usage the term 'attitude' had always been qualified in some way or other; in addition to conscious attitudes there were emotional and motor attitudes, as we have seen. Then, in the 1920s, a few psychologists, notably the brothers Floyd and Gordon Allport, began coupling 'attitude' with 'social' and opened an altogether new chapter in the psychology of attitudes. The topic of 'social attitudes' made it possible for psychologists to lay claim to an area of popular concern that had previously been the preserve of sociologists. On the surface, however, there was little to connect the notion of 'social attitudes' with the attitude concepts of the older psychology. In Floyd Allport's social psychological text (Allport, 1924), the first in the psychological literature to pay attention to 'social attitudes', that topic had indeed been treated entirely separately from the psychology of attitudes, discussed in more traditional terms. As late as 1939, a general review of the literature appeared in two parts, one devoted to the 'nature and development' of attitudes, the other to 'social attitudes' (Nelson, 1939).

The category of 'social attitudes' was not based on any conceptual development within Psychology but constituted an importation from outside the discipline. Six years prior to the appearance of Floyd Allport's text the prominent sociologist, W.I. Thomas, had given considerable theoretical significance to the concept in his classic study of Polish immigrants, which he co-authored with the young Polish sociologist, Florian Znaniecki (Thomas and Znaniecki, 1918). In the lengthy 'methodological note' which formed the introduction to that volume, attitudes had been given the role of a core concept in a discipline which scarcely existed at the time, namely, social psychology. This was clearly distinguished from both sociology, which was concerned with the principles of social organization, and psychology, which was focused on the states of individuals. Social psychology had the task of dealing with the evident interdependence of these two levels, and for this purpose it required its own distinguishing concepts. The category of 'attitude' was deployed to satisfy this requirement.

But the term was now given a meaning which ran counter to earlier psychological usage. Certainly, attitudes involved conscious processes, but to treat them simply *as* facts of individual consciousness was to abstract from their social nature and turn them into the objects of a science of asocial individuals. Thomas clearly recognized the role of psychological research practice in this process of abstraction:

> Concretely speaking, any method of research which takes the individual as a distinct entity and isolates him from his social environment, whether in order to determine by introspective analysis the content and form of his conscious processes, or in order to investigate the organic facts accompanying these processes, or, finally, in order to study experimentally his behavior as reaction to certain stimuli, finds necessarily only psychical, physical or biological facts essentially and indissolubly connected with the individual as a psychical, physical, or generally biological reality. (Thomas and Znaniecki, 1918: 26)

Individual psychology necessarily isolates attitude as 'an object in itself' and studies it in relation to other states of the same individual. Social psychology, however, would treat attitude 'as primarily manifested in its reference to the social world and taken first of all in connection with some social value. . . . The psychological process remains always fundamentally a *state of somebody*; the attitude remains always fundamentally an attitude *toward something*' (Thomas and Znaniecki, 1918: 22–23; original italics). The social psychological attitude concept then was to be deployed to study the co-ordination, the interdependence, of individual consciousness and cultural values.

The kind of social psychology envisaged by Floyd Allport was however very different from what Thomas and Znaniecki had had in mind. It was to be a *psychological*, not a *sociological*, social psychology. To Allport, this meant a reduction of all social phenomena to the behaviour of individuals. There was nothing in human social life, except *separate individuals* (the italics are Allport's) and their reaction to each other as external stimuli (Allport, 1924: 3–6). In a later work, the distinctly ideological basis of Allport's position emerged more explicitly (Allport, 1933). Assigning some kind of reality to social institutions was to indulge in dangerous collectivistic illusions. Only individuals and the sum total of their reactions to each other were real, and psychology was the science to study them (Graumann, 1986; Paicheler, 1988). For Allport, there was a gratifying convergence of a general political agenda and the specific disciplinary project which he represented. His psychological social psychology was to be 'experimental', which meant that, rather than studying humans in institutional or cultural contexts, as the social sciences did, the basic data would consist of the responses of separate individuals to artificially constructed situations (Danziger, 1992a).

When F.H. Allport, and the psychologists who followed along his path, used the category 'social attitudes', therefore, they did not mean the subjective side of collective values in the manner of sociologists like W.I. Thomas. Collective or cultural values had no existence apart from the reactions and dispositions of separate individuals. Attitudes were simply individual attributes, to be studied in terms of their intra-psychic organization, their relation to other individual attributes like intelligence and personality traits, and their susceptibility to controlled manipulation. As Gordon Allport put it, 'the political nature of man is indistinguishable from his personality as a whole' (Allport, 1929: 238). Whether individual psychologists were aware of this or not, this sort of belief was itself political and also congruent with political values that were deeply entrenched in American culture.

The excursion of American psychologists into the field of 'social attitudes' took place at a time when this term had acquired considerable currency in public discourse. In 1929, President Hoover appointed a high level Committee to investigate 'social trends in the United States'. This resulted in a number of reports on such matters as population trends, rural social trends, and 'political, social and economic activities of women', but, significantly, it also included a report on 'changing social attitudes and interests' (Hart, 1933). The category of 'social attitudes' had come to be widely accepted as providing a framework for discussing a broad range of social concerns. The report of the Hoover Commission was mainly concerned with such topics as 'declining approval of organized Christianity', 'antagonism toward traditional sex attitudes', 'declining approval of religious sanctions for sex conduct', 'prohibition sentiment', 'radicalism', 'labor relations', and 'international attitudes' (Hart, 1933). Other areas of social concern for which the concept of 'social attitudes' provided an interpretive umbrella were social stratification, delinquency, and immigration (Young, 1931), as well as the influence of propaganda (Chen, 1933) and of motion pictures (Thurstone, 1930). The areas of race relations (Katz and Braly, 1933) and of industrial management (Uhrbrock, 1933) were not far behind. Quite early, the term 'social attitudes' had been used as a synonym for 'opinions', especially political opinions. That made it easy for research on attitudes to merge with existing concerns about political radicalism and the conviction that it had a psychological basis (see Vetter, 1930 for examples). By the mid-1930s 'attitude' had become an all-purpose tool for tracing social problems to their supposed source in individual minds.

The need for such a tool had been anticipated a decade earlier by the highly respected writer and journalist, Walter Lippmann. His widely read *Public Opinion* (Lippmann, 1922) gave expression to current concerns about the magical effectiveness of propaganda and the manipulation of voters by emphasizing the subjective aspects of social behaviour. What people do, even what they think and feel, is determined by what Lippmann variously referred to as 'interior representations of the world' and 'pseudo-environments' (Lippmann, 1922: 27), or, more famously, as 'fictions', 'pictures in our heads', and 'stereotypes'. Expressing a faith in scientific expertise that was characteristic of his age, Lippmann suggested that his analysis showed the need for a body of social scientists who would systematically study public opinion with the purpose of advising policy makers. Arguments such as these would provide effective support for the increasing tendency, in American social science, to ascribe a causal role to desirable and undesirable 'social attitudes'.

The attachment of the term 'social' to the older category of 'attitude' signalled its new deployment as the quasi-scientific equivalent of Lippmann's 'pictures in our heads'. American social scientists gladly responded to the call for expertise sounded by publicists like Lippmann. Whereas the use of the term 'attitude' had been unusual in sociological, psychological and social psychological textbooks prior to 1920, it occurs in half of the texts published between 1920 and 1925; between 1925 and the beginning of the 1930s that figure rises to 80 per cent (Droba, 1933). The surging popularity of 'attitude' was not accompanied by any consensus on what exactly this term referred to. There were many attempted definitions of attitude in circulation. One participant observed: '"Attitude" is a term which has currently come into very general use among sociologists, social psychologists, and writers on education. It is a good example of an ill-defined, or undefined, concept used in a loose, pseudo-scientific manner. The result is a confusion many times confounded' (Bain, 1928: 942). Similarly, a psychological dictionary of that time warned its readers that 'attitude' was a 'loosely used term' (English, 1928). There was little to distinguish the use of the term in the empirical literature of the social sciences from its use in everyday lay discourse. D. Fleming, author of an extensive historical study of the attitude concept, speaks of 'a rampant cross-infection that spread both ways, from popular usage to scientific and back again' (Fleming, 1967: 360).

To a psychologist critic like William McDougall, whose ideas hailed from another age and another culture, the whole situation seemed absurd:

> American social psychologists and sociologists have recently produced a voluminous literature concerning what they call 'social attitudes'; the term is used to cover a multitude of facts of many kinds, including almost every variety of opinion and belief and all the abstract qualities of personality . . . as well as the units of affective organization. . . . I cannot see how progress in social psychology can be made without a more discriminating terminology. (McDougall, 1933: 219)

However, McDougall's gloomy prognosis turned out to be quite wrong, at least on external criteria of 'progress'. There were several reasons for this, one of which was the development of a technology of 'attitude measurement', which will be discussed in the next section. Another reason was that the lack of conceptual rigour was actually an advantage.

if one wanted to advance bold claims for the broad applicability of the attitude concept. For psychologists, it provided a basis for giving a new social relevance to their field. Much of academic psychology had remained quite remote from everyday concerns, but the topic of social attitudes created a new branch of the subject which was relevant for an extraordinary range of immediate public concerns: 'The whims of fashion, the success and the failure of propaganda, the swing of public opinion, the depredations of a mob, and a change in moral standards, are alike unintelligible excepting in terms of the attitudes of individual men and women', wrote Gordon Allport in an authoritative review that was in part a reply to McDougall (Allport, 1935: 806).

In order to succeed, such a claim would have to rely on a certain convergence in the implicit meaning of 'attitude' for the specialist and for the lay public. A core of implicit meaning would also provide a basis for the experts' belief that, in spite of the differences in their formal definitions of 'attitude', they were still talking about the same thing. In spite of surface disagreement, a number of widely shared assumptions characterized the discursive deployment of 'attitude'.

The first, and simplest, of these assumptions touched directly on the quarrel between McDougall and American social scientists. McDougall was an instinct theorist of the old school, who accounted for quite a number of what were now regarded as attitudinal phenomena by invoking the category of 'sentiment'. But McDougall's sentiments were rooted in the instincts, and this was now anathema to American social scientists. One thing on which they did broadly agree was the *acquired* nature of attitudes. Whatever else they might be, they were essentially learned and therefore infinitely modifiable. In the ongoing debate about the plasticity of human nature, the users of the attitude concept were not to be found among the innatists.

A second assumption, almost universally shared by the psychologist friends of 'attitude', has already been discussed in the context of Floyd Allport's launch of a psychological social psychology. For psychologists, attitudes were strictly *individual* attributes, where individuals were understood as separate entities and not as the parts of a social or cultural collectivity. In psychological usage there was no place for Thomas' original conception of attitudes as the subjective side of culture, as necessarily linked to social values. Psychological individuals could come to hold attitudes in common through having been exposed to similar learning experiences, but on this view culture remained an external influence and collectivities were a 'fiction'. An echo of the battle against the sociologists can still be detected in Gordon Allport's insistence that a range of social phenomena could only be made intelligible in terms of 'the attitudes of *individual* men and women' (see above). One reason why the psychological version of the attitude concept proved more enduring than the sociological one is its perfect fit with the traditional beliefs of an individualistic culture.

Thirdly, it is worth noting that psychological definitions of attitude tended to agree in defining it as a *'state* of readiness' of some kind (G.W. Allport, 1935). In other words, 'attitude' is more than simply a dispositional term. It is taken as referring to an actually existing state of affairs inside the individual. Because attitudes always relate to specific objects or situations, an individual necessarily has many attitudes inhabiting him or her, each one having an identifiable and distinct existence. Once formed, they are carried around by the individual on a more or less long term basis. And they are states that have effects. Attitudes have *causal* properties, 'exerting a directive or dynamic influence upon the individual's response to all objects and situations with which it is related,' as Allport (1935: 810) puts it. It is quite possible to think of attitudes as simply a form of attribution that has its place in the discursive practices that people use to make sense of each other's conduct. The use of the attitude concept in Psychology, however, always implied much more than that. Underpinning its use, there is a whole metaphysic of unobservable but nevertheless real and distinct entities that push and direct the person from within. It is this image that gives plausibility to the idea that attitudes can be *measured*.

Before we consider this crucial development, there is one more taken for granted feature of the psychological attitude concept that should be mentioned. When discussing the change from the original, expressive use of 'attitude' to its psychological use, we noted that this involved a splitting of the older unity between an inner state and its outward expression. The disjunction between the inner and the outer aspects of human action reached its most extreme form in early twentieth-century psychology, spawning, first, a 'systematic' introspective psychology of consciousness, and then, in almost immediate reaction, a radical behaviourism that equated action with observable movement. Whatever the stance of individual psychologists towards the more extravagant claims of radical behaviourism, the adoption of the category of 'behaviour' as the centrepiece of a generally accepted disciplinary language entailed the acceptance of a dualistic metaphysic that distinguished sharply between observable, external 'behaviour' and its inferred, internal, causes. When the concept of 'attitude' was assimilated within this framework it came to refer to some inner state that was, by definition, distinct from what was seen on the outside. This provided a basis for endless research and discussion about the degree to which attitude and behaviour were correlated (Kraus, 1995).[4]

Although there was some sociological participation in this debate, sociologically oriented theorists tended to reject the extreme dualism implied in the psychological usage of key terms, thus introducing a further difference in the psychological and the sociological understanding of 'attitude'. Sociologists often spoke of 'acts' or 'action', rather than 'behaviour', emphasizing that the 'inner' intentional or dispositional aspects of an act were part of the act and not to be arbitrarily distinguished from its 'outer', or 'behavioural' aspects (Faris, 1928; Mead, 1934). From this point of view, attitudes could be seen, not simply as intra-individual states, but as part of an inter-individual reality involving individuals 'taking the attitudes of the others' (Mead, 1924–25). This difference in the psychological and the sociological understanding of 'attitude' is intimately tied up with a difference in the meaning of 'social'. In the psychological literature, attitudes were 'social' insofar as they referred to individual reactions to 'social stimuli'. These were simply a sub-category of stimuli in general and were interpreted in terms of a biological metaphor of organisms responding to features of the physical environment. For many sociologists, however, this was to miss the essential character of the 'social'. Social actions, like those of co-operation, competition or exchange, were only intelligible as actions involving several individuals, each playing a part in the completion of the whole action. From this point of view, it was possible to speak of a 'conversation of attitudes' (Mead, 1912), a notion that made little sense in terms of a purely psychological conception of attitude.

The smell of success: attitudes are measured

Had the attitude concept continued simply as an elastic vehicle for psychological claims to have something to say about social issues, it would have commanded little respect in the long run. It might even have been 'exorcized as a metaphysical ghost, pale and wanly qualitative' (Fleming, 1967: 340). What saved the concept's scientific respectability was the development of a technology for *measuring* attitudes. This occurred towards the end of the 1920s and provided the basis for virtually all future research on attitudes, at least within the discipline of Psychology. Agreement on the appropriate technology made it possible to ignore fundamental questions about the nature of attitudes and concentrate on such empirical questions as could be asked and answered within the framework established by this technology. It was clear to many of the participants that this created a situation quite analogous to that in the field of intelligence testing, where the successful application of a technology had not been impeded by theoretical disagreement (G.W. Allport, 1935: 828).

Attitude measurement greatly strengthened claims for the social utility of attitude research. In fact, the realization that this would be the case helped to launch the enterprise of attitude measurement in the first place. By 1925, there had been attempts by prominent figures, both in Psychology and in Sociology, to develop a plausible way of measuring attitudes. The sociologist, E.S. Bogardus, had come up with the pseudo-metrical notion of 'social distance' that he tried to measure by means of questions about the respondents' willingness or unwillingness to admit members of another group to various degrees of social closeness, e.g. as marriage partners, neighbours or fellow citizens (Bogardus, 1925). In the same year, Floyd Allport had also submitted a claim to have developed a method of measuring attitudes (Allport and Hartman, 1925). He was very clear about the motivation for such an undertaking:

> One of our most important tasks in social psychology is the development of scales and techniques for studying national and racial attitudes, and for measuring allegiance – or hostility – to institutional fictions and stereotypes of nation, race and class. (Allport, 1932: 223)

Such goals did not simply represent the personal ambitions of one or two social scientists, but were part of a widely shared project that provided for the rationalization of educational and administrative programmes by means of precise measurement and calculation of their likely effects. In the US, such programmes have long been seen as part of a 'cult of efficiency' (Callahan, 1962) that began to affect ever larger areas of social life during the first part of the twentieth century. More generally, the phenomenon can be seen as part of a pervasive modern trend that enlists the human sciences in the task of making individuals more predictable, calculable and manageable (Rose, 1988).[5]

An influential text by P.M. Symonds, devoted to the application of psychological knowledge, provides a good example of this trend. Symonds starts with the following proposition:

> Control of nature has been particularly facilitated by the invention of instruments of measurement. Similarly, the control of human conduct and education depends on the development of more exact methods of describing human conduct. The exact description of human conduct can be rendered most efficient when it is reduced to a form of measurement, for then small differences are most accurately portrayed and small differences most accurately noted. (Symonds, 1931: v)

Symonds identifies four areas which present 'the more pressing problems in the control of human relations' (p. 8): crime, insanity, vocational competence, and 'diagnosis of citizenship' (p. 11). The last area is largely concerned with character education and the inculcation of 'certain attitudes towards vital social issues'. From this point of view, Symonds welcomes the development of 'measures' of social attitudes which had just taken place. Such techniques would enable one to ensure that programmes for changing wrong into right attitudes could be monitored to make them more efficient. The big chance to put this into practice did not occur until a decade later, with America's entry into World War II, but the social promise of attitude measurement was apparent from the beginning.

But those who were most convinced of the benefits of attitude measurement on general, ideological, grounds did not necessarily have the technical sophistication to successfully carry through such an undertaking. The person who took the crucial steps in codifying attitude measurement did not at first know what he was doing. This was L.L. Thurstone, an engineer by training, who had made the switch to Psychology early in his career. Teaching psychophysical methods at the University of Chicago, he looked around for applications that might prove more interesting for his students than the classical example of comparing lifted weights. Instead of weights, he presented his students with pairs of offences, asking them to indicate which of the two they regarded as more serious, and pairs of nationalities, where his students had to say which one they would prefer to associate with (Thurstone, 1952: 306–307). He soon realized that he had not been the first to extend psychophysical methods to 'stimuli' that were not physical. J.M. Cattell, one of the pioneers of modern American psychology, had used variants of such procedures to 'measure' the eminence of scientists, and others had attempted measurements of literary merit and of the estimated excellence of children's handwriting and of children's drawings. There was, by this time, nothing startling in extending the idea of measurement from the special area of psychophysics to the much broader realm of social judgement. By his own account, Thurstone was no social psychologist, but when he heard about the social psychological interest in finding a way of measuring attitudes, he seems to have decided that that was what his classroom exercises were:

> Our work on attitudes was started when I had some correspondence with Floyd Allport about the appraisal of political opinions, and there was discussion here at that time about the concept of social distance which had been introduced by Bogardus. It was in such a setting that I speculated about the possible use of the new psychophysical toys. I wrote a paper entitled 'Attitudes can be measured'. (Thurstone, 1952: 310)

How did Thurstone propose to make good on this claim? Certainly not by giving some crudely behaviouristic meaning to the term 'attitude'. No, he was fully committed to the psychological imperative of seeing attitudes as inferred entities that existed within the individual below the surface of observable behaviour. Therefore, he needed to assume a close connection between these invisible entities and some observable signs that would reliably indicate their presence. Potentially, this opened up an enormous range of possibilities. For example, Thomas and Znaniecki (1918), in the work which made 'attitude' a concept in the social sciences, used textual passages in private letters as the empirical basis for inferring attitudes. Others (e.g. Hart, 1933) were using the content of magazine articles as an indication of attitudes. But Thurstone could not even consider such possibilities because they did not lend themselves to the application of his 'psychophysical toys'.

It was Floyd Allport's foray into attitude research that provided Thurstone with the empirical format he needed. In an earlier study, Allport and Hartman (1925) had written out sets of statements that represented various opinions on a number of political issues such as

Prohibition – a hot topic at the time. For example, the statement: 'Prohibition is correct in principle and although it cannot be strictly enforced, should nevertheless be retained', and the statement: 'Though prohibition is good in principle, it cannot be enforced, and therefore is actually doing more harm than good', were both included in a 'scale' of thirteen statements reflecting opinions about Prohibition. This scale was presented to student subjects who had to indicate which one statement most closely represented their own opinion about Prohibition. The technique of obtaining individuals' agreement or disagreement with statements on a list presented to them by a stranger had previously been used on a large scale in marketing research and to some extent in political polling (Converse, 1987). There was no sharp boundary between the practical employment of social judgement methods in advertising research and their use by psychologists like J.M. Cattell (Kuna, 1979). By the late 1920s these procedures had become part of the taken for granted social practices of American social life and the consumer culture. No one would have questioned that it was 'opinions' which these practices revealed.

But the relation of 'attitudes' to opinions uncovered in this way was somewhat more problematical. On the one hand, there was a marked tendency among psychologists to treat attitudes and opinions as synonymous (Bain, 1928). On the other hand, there were those who made a distinction between surface opinions, which had a more specific quality, and underlying attitudes which were of a more general nature. Thurstone sided with the second group. His distinction was between attitude, defined as 'the sum total of a man's inclinations and feelings, prejudice or bias, preconceived notions, ideas, fears, threats, and convictions about any specified topic' (Thurstone, 1928: 531), and opinion, defined as 'a verbal expression of attitude'. He proposed to 'use opinions as the means for measuring attitudes' (p. 532). Two stipulations, basic to the entire project of attitude measurement, appear here. First, that opinions be held to provide an index of intra-individual attributes, called attitudes. This assumption establishes a claim by psychologists to provide a scientific basis for otherwise low level opinion research. Secondly, it is stipulated that attitudes are to be measured by their verbal expression as opinions. This was quite arbitrary, as Thurstone seems to have recognized, for one could just as easily have said that a person's attitudes are revealed only in their actions and not in their merely verbal opinions. However, Thurstone's preference did help to give a scientific aura to the widespread use of the cheap and quick method of collecting responses to opinion statements. Any hope that social psychology would recover from what one reviewer referred to as 'questionnaire disease' (Bain, 1930) was now gone.

But the crucial assumption underlying the notion of attitude measurement is yet to come. As we have seen, Thurstone did not shrink from assigning complexity to attitudes. However, that complexity was far beyond the reach of measurement. A simplification was necessary. So Thurstone introduced a distinction between a person's attitude in the psychological sense and something about that attitude which could be measured. The latter was called the 'attitude variable', for 'the very idea of measurement implies a linear continuum of some sort such as length, price, volume, weight, age' (Thurstone, 1928: 534). The attitude variable had to be described in such a way 'that one can speak of it in terms of "more" and "less"' (p. 536). Measurement, therefore, would substitute for something psychological and complex something else that was defined by its variation along one dimension, usually a position on a scale of being more or less pro or anti a given issue, like Prohibition or immigration restriction.

In the case of more complex issues more than one dimension might have to be invoked, but that would not affect the principle of reducing all forms of qualitative complexity to independently defined linear dimensions. As was recognized quite early, this entailed breaking down a complex state of affairs and measuring it in fragments. In the words of Gordon Allport: 'The price one must pay for bi-polarity and quantification in such cases is, of course, extreme, and often absurd *elementarism*' (Allport, 1935: 820; original italics). Other social psychologists were just as sceptical about the trade-off involved in the technology of attitude measurement. The most important textbook of the 1930s pointed to the danger that attitudes reduced to a linear scale would become 'like the victims of Procrustes' (Murphy et al., 1937: 897); in other words, mutilated to fit into a pre-constructed frame.

This did not stop the onward march of attitude measurement. The coming of the New Deal with its ambitious social programmes had increased the appetite of state agencies for polling techniques that went beyond the requirements of marketing research and election forecasts. Rensis Likert, a student of Thurstone's and employee of the US Department of Agriculture, devised a somewhat simplified version of attitude measurement that was much less cumbersome and time consuming than Thurstone's original methodology. In this form attitude measurement quickly caught on, both in academic and in field settings. Accepted procedure had cemented a conceptual link between underlying attitudes and the expressed opinions by means of which attitudes could be measured. The enormous popular success of opinion polling during the 1930s (Gallup and Rae, 1940) certainly did not hurt the prospects of research into attitudes, because it was easy to see the latter as providing the basic science counterpart to the more practically oriented opinion research.

But what really put attitude research on the map as a significant psychological industry was the practical use to which it was put in World War II. The US War Department established an 'Information and Education Division', staffed to a significant extent by social scientists who already had a commitment to the attitude concept and its practical definition by the current measurement technology. Large scale studies of military morale, as well as the effects of propaganda and of various organizational factors, were conducted by means of this technology, the results being published after the war in the monumental multi-volume *Studies in Social Psychology in World War II* (Stouffer et al., 1949–50). A similar approach was only slightly less pervasive in large scale studies of civilian morale (Allport and Veltfort, 1943; Schmeidler and Allport, 1944) conducted at the time. In the words of one historian: 'the measurement of soldiers' and civilians' attitudes in the Second War corresponded to the measurement of recruits' intelligence in the First War as the consecration under fire of new psychological techniques for handling masses of men' (Fleming, 1967: 345). Just as intelligence testing had become the firmly institutionalized defining practice for the category of intelligence after World War I, so attitude measurement, or scaling, became the institutionalized defining practice for the category of 'attitude' after World War II.

Conceptually, the ground had been prepared for this development by Thurstone's analogy between psychophysical judgement and judgement applied to verbal statements having a social target. In his original argument, Thurstone still relied on an analogy between the comparison of two physical objects on a physical dimension like weight and the comparison of two opinion statements on a dimension of pro or anti some issue like Prohibition. In Likert's simplified method this analogy was no longer needed, as long as the results obtained by this method correlated statistically with the results obtained by Thurstone's method. The assumptions built into the claim that attitudes could be measured by these means thus sank ever further from view. What emerged was a technology to be applied quite unproblematically.

As in the case of intelligence, it was the technology that henceforth defined the practical employment of the concept. There might still be differences among investigators regarding the form of words used to define 'attitude', but these differences were of little importance compared to the emerging consensus about the way in which attitudes were to be investigated in practice. Research on attitudes now meant getting agree/disagree responses, usually from groups of students, to opinion statements that intercorrelated sufficiently to form what was called a 'scale'. The use of several, statistically linked, opinion statements distinguished attitude 'scaling' from opinion polling which generally worked with single questions but took pains to construct really representative samples of some real life population. Academic attitude research never bothered about this kind of sampling, because it was not concerned with the social distribution of opinions but with supposedly universal attributes of the hypothetical entities underlying surface opinions. The distinction between opinions and attitudes came to be based on a conceptual and practical division between the social content of opinion statements and certain formal properties that could be constructed statistically.

That construction, however, depended on yet another implicit assumption, which also went back to Thurstone's original foray into attitude measurement. All measurement, even physical measurement, has to deal with the existence of variability. A few physical observations are routinely discarded as being due to human error. In psychological measurement the problem of variability is more pervasive, so that, from its beginnings, it had to rely on statistical means to extract the 'true' value of a parameter from a distribution of variable judgements (Fechner, 1966). In classical psychophysics such sets of judgements were always drawn from the same individual. However, when Thurstone applied the psychophysical analogy to attitude measurement, he quietly pooled judgements from several individuals, and this procedure became part of the generalized practice of attitude scaling. What was not recognized was that such a procedure produces a construct that is inter-individual, rather than intra-individual. If, like the psychological attitude researchers, one interprets this construct as representing an intra-individual entity, one makes the (implicit) assumption that the individuals whose responses have been pooled share the same cognitive representation of social stimuli (Jaspars and Fraser, 1984), i.e., that opinion statements are as unambiguous and as little in need of interpretation as physical stimuli, for example the heaviness of weights. This assumption is surely quite wrong. Worse still, one cannot assess the degree to which it is wrong without stepping outside the framework of conventional attitude measurement. As long as one remains within this framework, therefore, one can never know to what extent one's data are the result of variable inter-subject agreement on the meaning of the items constituting one's scale.[6]

This was not a significant source of concern for most investigators in the field of attitude research, however, because they were content to live with an 'operational' definition of attitude. Attitudes were whatever it was that attitude scales measured, just as intelligence was whatever intelligence tests measured. The question of the meaning of such measures was not often addressed.

A multiplicity of attitudes vs. an ideology?

It was in the aftermath of World War II that some concern about the meaning of social attitudes did emerge. This was a direct response to the horrors that Nazism had recently visited upon the world, horrors that seemed to be the product of crazed minds. Yet it was known that Nazism had had widespread popular support and might find a fertile soil elsewhere. What kind of mind, what kind of subjectivity, might prove hospitable to this virus?

Social scientists from Germany, who had themselves been targets of Nazi hate, had had to ask this question somewhat earlier in a different context. During the final years of the Weimar Republic in Germany, with the threat of a Nazi takeover on the horizon, associates of the Frankfurt Institute for Social Research had concerned themselves with the social outlook of groups in Germany, particularly workers. Much of this work was theoretical, but at least one major empirical investigation issued from this concern, Erich Fromm's study of *The Working Class in Weimar Germany* (Fromm, 1984). Here, responses to mostly open-ended questions were obtained from a considerable number of subjects and analysed qualitatively as well as quantitatively. In an American context this would have been regarded as a study of social attitudes, but the German investigators thought of it as a contribution to the theory of how objective social conditions, social consciousness and individual character interrelated.

Towards the end of World War II the Frankfurt tradition of social research briefly impinged on American attitude research because of the availability of exiled scholars previously associated with the Frankfurt Institute. The most significant result of this collaboration appeared in 1950 in the form of a lengthy research monograph known as *The Authoritarian Personality* (Adorno et al., 1950), a work which was an extraordinary amalgam of American technology and German theorizing. On the one hand, there was copious use of attitude scales, but on the other hand, some of the questions to which the study addressed itself and some of the interpretive categories with which it operated were European imports. In the present context, the most significant feature of the work is its pervasive reliance on the category of 'ideology'. Two of the five parts of the study are said to be about 'ideology', a concept which was almost unknown in the older American attitude research – and which was to disappear again from American social psychology a few years later.

Whereas the category of 'social attitudes' was a recent American construction, the concept of 'ideology' had a fairly long tradition of European social thought behind it. By 1945, social attitudes had been successfully claimed by the discipline of Psychology as purely individual attributes, whereas 'ideology' remained an essentially socio-political category that applied to individuals only by virtue of their membership of particular social groups. The attempt to marry the two notions was thus problematic from the start.

But the attitude–ideology dissonance involved two further contradictions which are worth mentioning here because of what they tell us about the nature of the attitude concept. First, the most common understanding of 'ideology' was based on a fundamental distinction between forms of social consciousness that were adequate to objective social conditions and forms that were not. The latter usually represented the kind of systematic falsification and distortion of the truth that was referred to by the term 'ideology'. By contrast, the psychological understanding of 'social attitudes' did not involve any reference to their 'truth' in representing social reality. Attitudes were essentially individual valuations, but the valuations were those of the individuals to whom attitudes were attributed, not the valuations of those who did the attributing. Whereas the category 'ideology' carried clear moral connotations and expressed a social commitment on the part of those who employed it, 'social attitudes' had become part of the morally neutral language of a 'behavioural science' that simply registered facts without presuming to take a stand on them. The investigators of *The Authoritarian Personality* were therefore attempting to mix two disparate ways of doing social science, a morally and politically neutral way for which physical science was the model, and a socially engaged way whose commitments were built into its language. This unnatural mixture seems to have been a product of the times and the subject matter of the study: Fascism and virulent racism. These were not 'issues' like Prohibition or 'sexual freedom on campus', but matters of life and death. At that point the morally neutral language of attitudes no longer proved adequate. Later on, as social psychology increasingly turned its back on questions of a deeply political nature, nothing beyond the attitude concept was required to handle its limited range of concerns.

The second aspect of the contrast between attitudes and ideologies relates to a feature of the ideology concept that has not yet been mentioned. In English the term 'ideology' is sometimes used as the equivalent of the German *Weltanschauung*, or world view. Now, while a *Weltanschauung* may be intrinsically political, that is not necessarily the case. One might refer to an aesthetic or artistic world view, for example. What is being highlighted here is not so much the socio-political dimension as the internal coherence, the structural unity, of a set of views. Certainly, when the authors of *The Authoritarian Personality* referred to 'ethnocentric ideology', or 'religious ideology', for example, that is largely what they meant. Here the term 'ideology' is introduced in order to do justice to the observation that various opinions and attitudes typically go together, not only statistically, but also meaningfully. In other words, attitudes on specific issues are seen as having a place and a function in some higher order of subjective life, a world view or 'ideology'. Analysing extreme anti-Semitism, Adorno (Adorno et al., 1950: 619) writes: 'Charging the Jews with all existing evils seems to penetrate the darkness of reality like a searchlight and to allow for quick and all-comprising orientation.' Here anti-Semitism is not just an attitude among other attitudes, it is an essential feature of a world view; it has become an ideology.

This kind of analysis alerts us to the fact that the traditional use of the attitude concept implied a particular way of representing social consciousness. Attitude measurement, as we have seen, involved a layered conception of social consciousness by its distinction between surface opinion, expressed in specific opinion statements, and underlying attitude, measured by a scale composed of such statements. But that is as far as the layering went. There was no layer of social consciousness that was deeper or more comprehensive than the layer made up of specific attitudes. These often correlated statistically, but insofar as that observation was seen as requiring an explanation at all, the explanation was sought in the realm of personal constitution. The concept of ideology, on the other hand, introduced a further layer of social consciousness that accounted for the coherence (and therefore the statistical correlation) among attitudes. On this view, specific social attitudes were not separate entities but intimately and meaningfully interconnected parts of a larger whole, ultimately traceable to certain social conditions.[7] In that case, the attitudes isolated by the common scaling methods would be essentially artefacts that may actually mislead us in our attempt to understand social consciousness. If one pursues this line of analysis, then the deployment of the concept of social attitudes in twentieth-century social psychology can itself be characterized as ideological, and this time in the quasi-political sense of 'ideological'. What would be involved would be a systematic distortion or falsification of the true nature of social consciousness.

However, there is another possibility. Perhaps the model of social consciousness implied by the social psychological attitude concept is peculiarly appropriate under certain historical and social conditions, specifically the conditions in which this concept emerged. If the structure of social consciousness is itself historically variable, then it may not always take on the form of ideology. That there have been times and places marked by an ideological way of relating to the world is surely undeniable. But there may be circumstances which favour a breakdown of ideology and result in less integrated forms of social consciousness. Perhaps then the social psychology of social attitudes is but one aspect of a more pervasive phenomenon akin to what is sometimes referred to as 'the end of ideology' (Bell, 1960). Unfortunately, such a neat explanation has to face the complicating presence of one particular ideology, that of liberal democracy. The political institutions promoted by this ideology actually presuppose that social consciousness takes a form similar to the image underlying the social attitude model. Where people are polarized by deep ideological divisions, conflicts are not decided by majority vote but by more drastic means. The institutions of liberal democracy can only function properly in the hands of individuals who implicitly believe that human minds reflect the pluralism of these institutions. The image of many individuals taking different positions on a multiplicity of attitude scales accords perfectly with an idealized version of the institutions of liberal democracy.

What is presupposed in that version is exactly what was presupposed in the notion that attitudes could be measured, namely, that individuals take positions on the *same* set of attitudinal dimensions. That ultimately reduces all inter-individual differences to quantitative differences, to differences of degree. Politics can then be thought of as a balancing of positions until a (temporary) equilibrium is reached. But if there is disagreement about the very dimensions of disagreement – as happens in cases of ideological conflict – such political mechanisms no longer work. The theory and practice of social psychological attitude scaling has political implications that should not be overlooked. It is hard to accept as purely accidental the extraordinary consonance between the social psychological deployment of the category of 'social attitudes' and the socio-political culture in which this deployment has flourished. What seems more likely is that this category, like other psychological categories, has always been deeply embedded in a very specific historical assembly of cultural understandings and social practices.

Notes

1. *Psychological* social psychology is distinct from *sociological* social psychology, a branch of the discipline of sociology. Between Allport's delineation of the field of social psychology and later American psychological texts there is a continuity which does not exist for earlier attempts, like those of McDougall (1908), or Ross (1908). See also Post (1980).

2. Strictly speaking, this is only true of English-language psychology, and even here there are rare exceptions (e.g. Allport and Vernon, 1933). In Germany, the psychology of expression flourished until the early part of the post-World War II period. English-language references to this curious phenomenon are almost non-existent, but see Asendorpf and Wallbott (1982).

3. Many other examples are to be found in the papers by Messer (1906), and Bühler (1907–8). Quite a detailed and accurate English-language account of these experiments is given in Humphrey (1951). Important parts of Messer's paper, as well as the previously cited paper by Mayer and Orth (1901) are available in English translation in Mandler and Mandler (1964). See also Titchener (1909).

4. Research on this topic provides an excellent illustration of the marked tendency, within twentieth-century Psychology, to treat conceptual questions as though they were empirical questions (see Smedslund, 1991). The nature and degree of relationship between 'attitude' and 'behaviour' will obviously depend on how these categories are defined, and that depends, not on some external given, but on us.

5. Rose (1990) interprets this trend in terms of the Foucauldian category of 'governmentality'.

6. Ranking items on any kind of dimension would not supply this knowledge, because it is possible that several subjects may construct the same rank order, but for different reasons. Thurstone (1959: 237) had been very clear about the foundation of attitude scaling: 'the separations between the statements in the [attitude] scale may be ascertained by psychophysical principles on the common assumption that equally often noticed differences are equal.' At no point did he seem to notice that 'equally often noticed' by many individuals might not permit the same inference as 'equally often noticed' by one individual on different occasions. The unproblematic equation of psychophysical and social judgement was facilitated by seeing both in stimulus–response terms. Judgements were

reduced to automatic and reactive acts of 'noticing'. This excised the meaning-conferring, socially constructive, aspect of the sociological attitude-value scheme of Thomas and Znaniecki (Wiley, 1986).

7. The Gestalt psychological characterization of attitudes as 'forces' in a phenomenal field (Koffka, 1935) also points vaguely in the same direction, though the social dimension was only added later (Asch, 1952).

9
METALANGUAGE: THE TECHNOLOGICAL FRAMEWORK

In the sphere of scientific activity there are profound affinities between language and method. Both are ways of constituting specific fields of investigative and controlling action (Tseëlon, 1991). If it is to qualify as scientific, method must be explicitly described, and this cannot be done without reference to the kinds of things the method is applied to. A scientific method is never just a wordless or signless practice; it is a practice under some description. So the practitioners' understanding of what they are doing is intimately tied up with their understanding of the world in which or to which they are doing it. On the other hand, a language is never just a system of representation; as soon as it is used it becomes a practice. People 'do things with words' (Austin, 1962); in speaking or writing they carry out performances that have significance for their world. So language and method are intimately bound to each other.

That bond may become manifest in a variety of forms. The links between language and method may vary in closeness, and there may be large differences in the relative importance of one or other pole in this relationship. In this chapter I want to explore the historically unique constitution of the language–method bond that occurred during a crucial period in the development of modern Psychology. That involves tracing the most significant steps by which the language of psychological methodology came to provide an overarching categorical framework for representing psychological reality.

Like biology, methodology was the source of a metalanguage applied to already existing psychological categories. A key term in this metalanguage was 'variable'. When they deployed the methodological metalanguage, psychologists were no longer looking at slices of reality called 'motives', 'attitudes' or 'personality' – they were studying 'motivational variables', 'attitudinal variables' or 'personality variables'. The new metalanguage did not replace the older biological framework; it merely added an extra layer of description. That layer, however, came to play a more thoroughly hegemonic role than the older framework ever did. By the 1950s use of the methodological metalanguage had virtually become mandatory in the context of psychological investigation and theorizing.

The significance of stimulus–response psychology

Talk of 'variables', however, represented a later phase in the development of a method-based metalanguage. Some time earlier, the language of stimulus and response had come to assume a similar role. It has often been observed that the agenda of behaviourism essentially amounted to a proposal for translating all the mentalistic concepts of psychology into a physicalistic language. But that was not the only change in psychological language that was associated with the earlier forms of behaviourism. There was also a strong preference for describing all psychological processes in stimulus–response terms. In fact, this second item on the behaviourist agenda was initially more acceptable than the first. The majority of American psychologists were not particularly sympathetic to J.B. Watson's crude and extreme physicalism (Samelson, 1981), but stimulus–response psychology seemed an altogether more reasonable idea, at least in experimental circles. That was because stimulus–response psychology seemed to make practical sense. There were in fact two rather different reasons for advocating stimulus–response psychology in the 1920s: because of a preference for a reductionistic psychology based on a mechanistic biology; and because of a desire to treat the standard method of psychological experimentation as the bedrock that would provide a firm foundation for psychological concepts. If one gave pride of place to the second reason, one could easily be a stimulus–response psychologist without being a card-carrying behaviourist.

The prime example for this second option is the immensely influential Columbia psychologist, R.S. Woodworth, who explicitly advocated stimulus–response psychology, but who, when he asked himself whether he was a behaviourist, essentially decided that he didn't know and didn't much care (Woodworth, 1939). Woodworth's position certainly represented mainstream American experimental psychology much more closely than did Watson's. His general textbook bore the title *Psychology: A Study of Mental Life* when it first appeared in 1921, its subtitle a real snub for the behaviourists. But it became by far the most widely used text of its time (Winston, 1988) and saw several subsequent editions. It was followed in 1938 by the authoritative graduate manual *Experimental Psychology*, popularly known as the 'Columbia Bible'.

Although he was a very successful textbook author, Woodworth was first and foremost an experimentalist, actively engaged in laboratory work throughout his career. He always regarded the laboratory as the fountainhead of solid psychological knowledge, and his advocacy of stimulus–response psychology was closely connected with that conviction. It was because psychological experimentation was essentially concerned with stimulus–response relations that the schema of stimulus and response could and should function as the basis for psychological explanation.

> Whenever we have any human action before us for explanation, we have to ask what the stimulus is that arouses the individual to activity, and how he responds. Stimulus–response psychology is solid, and practical as well; for if it can establish the laws of reaction, so as to predict what responses will be made to a given stimulus, and what stimulus can be depended on to arouse a desired response, it furnishes the 'knowledge that is power'. Perhaps no more suitable motto could be inscribed over the door of a psychological laboratory than these two words, 'Stimulus–Response'. (Woodworth, 1921: 68)

In advocating the practicality of stimulus–response Woodworth was certainly not oblivious to the possibilities of practical psychological applications for purposes of social control. In fact, at the very beginning of his book he tried to sell the discipline of Psychology on the basis of its supposed military usefulness during World War I. But closer attention to the textual context and to his less popular writings shows quite clearly that it was the practicality of the laboratory that was closest to his heart. He immediately proceeds to justify the above passage by pointing out that even 'the modern introspectionist' would 'find a congenial home in a stimulus–response laboratory'. And a few years later he would claim that, while he had no quarrel with 'the concrete experiments' of Gestalt psychology, the empirical facts fitted a linear stimulus–response account much better than they did the Gestalt 'system' (Woodworth, 1927).

Like most American psychologists at the time, Woodworth was preoccupied by and unhappy about the division of Psychology into 'schools'. There seems to have been a strong feeling that this division undermined the discipline's claims to scientific status. Science was supposed to be the source of certain knowledge which was grounded in the laboratory, rather than in mere theory. So if psychologists would just agree to play down their theoretical differences and concentrate on the experimental procedures which they had in common, they would collectively benefit. Like so many of his colleagues, Woodworth was much concerned with what he called 'the solidarity of the psychological group' (1930: 327), and he thought that this could best be achieved 'from below upwards', by appealing to 'the actual research of psychologists' (ibid.), rather than their theoretical predilections. That meant finding the lowest common denominator of experimental practice (which he identified with science in general) and building consensus on that. Now, this basic feature seemed to him to lie in the fact that science 'always deals with systems that are subject to outside influences' (1930: 329). Science devoted itself to the study of these outside influences, which, in Psychology, took the form of stimulus–response relationships.

Woodworth strongly repudiated the suggestion that his proposal did no more than add another variant to the list of psychological schools. Although he never referred to stimulus–response psychology as a language, he used it as such. It provided him with the means for redescribing all substantive psychological terms and categories in a way that immediately characterized them as topics for experimental investigation. Confronted with any psychological phenomenon whatever, the psychologist is to ask, 'what is the stimulus, and what the response?' (Woodworth, 1921: 484). Woodworth shows how this rule can be applied even to such seemingly recalcitrant topics as play, dreams, thought and imagination. Whatever else might be said about these and other psychological phenomena, they must be translated into stimulus–response terms when they enter scientific psychological discourse. One very important effect of this translation is that it gives exemplary, paradigmatic, status to psychological experiments in interpreting psychological events in general. In this way, experiments on delayed reactions in animals can become paradigmatic for the understanding of human purpose, experiments on paired associate learning can elucidate the nature of memory, experiments on muscular fatigue can provide the model for understanding any acquired predisposition, and reaction time experiments can become the basic exemplar for all behaviour. Invariably, translation into the metalanguage of stimulus and response is required for any of these analogies to work.

In the two decades after the first appearance of Woodworth's basic text this language became pervasive in the psychological literature. The committed behaviourists were not likely to find fault with it, but many more American psychologists probably shared Woodworth's profound indifference to the niceties of psychological theory as well as his equally profound respect for experimental methodology. He had indeed been quite sensitive to a fundamental feature of that methodology, as it had come to be used in psychological laboratories. Quite generally, psychological experiments involved exposing their subjects to a specific set of varied external conditions and recording specific aspects of their conduct under these conditions. Broadly speaking, psychological experiments did have a stimulus–response structure, or at least, that was how they were typically described in the psychological literature. Therefore, description of objects of psychological interest in terms of the stimulus–response language always carried the clear implication that the fundamental structure of these objects was entirely congruent with the structure of psychological experiments. As already indicated, this entailed the important corollaries that (a) these objects of psychological interest could most appropriately be investigated in the laboratory, and conversely, (b) that such laboratory investigations were of exemplary significance for the understanding of the objects of interest. It is not surprising that stimulus–response terminology became a popular lingua franca among experimentally oriented psychologists.

Two fundamental features of this terminology have had long term consequences for the discipline. In the first place, psychologists' understanding of their own practice was affected. The language of stimulus and response is an asocial and impersonal language that requires translation of all terms referring to social or specifically human relationships into a terminology that makes no categorical distinction between these and essentially biological categories. This was touched on in previous chapters. Insofar as discourse about psychological practice was couched exclusively in stimulus–response language, blindness to the intrinsically social nature of that practice prevailed. Psychological experiments involving human subjects are of course social situations that require the highly patterned interaction of the participants (Danziger, 1990a). Without the experimenter's authority (an intrinsically social concept), or without verbally transmitted understandings among human agents, there would be no experiment. But in the language of stimulus and response such features became invisible. All that was supposedly going on was that the experimental subject reacted to stimuli. In this way the fiction that there was no essential difference between psychological experiments and experiments in the natural sciences could be maintained and the occasional voice that questioned this (Rosenzweig, 1933) could be ignored. It was not until the 1960s that there was any kind of discussion of the social features of psychological experimentation, but by then the weight of traditional conceptions was too strong to permit any widespread confrontation of the underlying issues (Gadlin and Ingle, 1975).

A second long term consequence involves psychologists' understanding of the relationship between their empirical practice and their theoretical concepts. A fundamental change in that understanding became manifest once American experimentalists had discarded the pre-World War I influence of earlier European models. In the era of Wundt, when psychology was mentalistic, there was an inevitable disjunction between the practice of experimental psychology and the theoretical constructions used to explain the outcome of experiments. Experimental practice was based on something like a stimulus–response schema. Stimuli, like visual distances or auditory intervals, would be presented and then some kind of reaction, a sensory judgement or motor response perhaps, would be obtained from the experimental subject. But the theoretical processes invoked to explain the results of such experiments had an altogether different structure. Here we find concepts like unconscious inference, apperception or creative synthesis which represent integrative cognitive events that transcend the stimulus–response manipulations characteristic of experimental methodology. By 1920, however, such theoretical concepts had been declared unscientific and redundant. In future, all theoretical concepts would have to be translated into stimulus–response terms if they were to pass muster. In other words, the specially created structure of events in the psychological laboratory came to function as a kind of model or template for the theoretical construction of the objects of psychological investigation.

Not all areas of science are characterized by the same relationship between theory and experimental practice (Knorr Cetina, 1992). For example, experiments can be regarded as yielding *signs* that point to an underlying reality, or they can be regarded as an actual *simulation* of the part of reality being investigated. In the history of experimental psychology there seems to have been a change from the first to the second of these conceptions, a change that coincided with the shift of the discipline's centre from Germany to America. Initially, experimental psychology had inherited its object of investigation, the typical adult consciousness, from a particular cultural and philosophical tradition. It merely applied special techniques to the study of this object. But once the disciplinary apparatus of investigation had been institutionalized the possibility emerged of allowing this apparatus, rather than tradition, to define the objects of psychological science. The realization of this possibility was inseparably bound up with an increase in the social influence of the practitioners of psychological science. It was *their* practice which was to play the constituting role in defining the structure of psychological reality. In this sense the discourse of psychology became a discourse of practice, the practice of the experts.

But that development would not have been as successful as it was if the new language of psychology had not had a certain appeal to social interests outside the discipline. By limiting itself to a language that directly reflected the practical manipulations of experts the new psychology pandered to dreams of 'social control' within which most social problems were transformed into individuals' problems that could be solved by applying the appropriate technological fix. For the new psychological discourse that spread so rapidly in North America during the years following World War I psychological reality was defined as the sum of the possibilities of expert psychological manipulation.

Within the discipline, the popularity of the new conception of the relation between experimental and theoretical reality undoubtedly owed something to its compatibility with mechanistic concepts of the reflex that had come down from the nineteenth century. But although the biological background of stimulus–response terminology might have helped to establish it in the first instance, there was always a significant minority of more clinically, or more humanistically, oriented psychologists who were not impressed by this background. As a neutral language that all psychologists might feel comfortable using, stimulus–response had its defects. Starting in the 1930s, we find its place gradually being taken by a substitute that preserved the basic conception of the relationship between experiment and theory but that avoided the mechanistic echoes from the past. This substitute was the language of variables.

Psychologists encounter 'variables'

By the 1950s, most psychologists had adopted the habit of referring to any of the things they investigated as 'variables'. Whether it was a matter of specifying features of the social or physical environment, or a matter of categorizing dispositions, actions or attributes of individuals, psychological theory and research was apt to define them all as 'variables'. This is quite remarkable, in view of the fact that modern psychology flourished for more than half a century before much was heard of 'variables'. There are rare instances where an early psychologist uses the term 'independent variable',[1] but there is not even a hint of widespread or systematic use before the 1930s. As Winston (1988, 1990) has noted, the term begins to crop up at that time in the writings of prominent figures like Tolman (1932), Woodworth (1934) and Boring (1933).

For Woodworth and other stimulus–response psychologists the transition to the language of variables was quite simple. What had previously been referred to as a stimulus was now categorized as an 'independent variable'; similarly, responses became 'dependent variables'. The rather crude elementarism of stimulus–response psychology was not affected by this change of terminology, nor was its simplistic view of causality.[2]

Switching from stimulus–response to variables did have certain tactical advantages. First of all, the historical link with an out-of-date quasi-reflexological schema was finally broken. This gave the language of dependent and independent variables a greater apparent degree of theoretical neutrality than the language of stimuli and responses. It was therefore better suited to become the common language of disciplinary consensus. Different interpretations of what variables represented were permissible, as long as all psychologists agreed that the units of their investigative practice were 'variables'. Secondly, the language of variables could accommodate the practice of psychologists who were engaged in establishing correlations among measures, e.g. personality traits, that had not been experimentally manipulated and hence were not expressible in the language of stimulus and response. The new language was thus broader in scope and more flexible.

The ultimate source of the concept of a variable lies in nineteenth-century mathematics. But how did it find its way into the discipline of Psychology? An important clue is provided by the fact that prior to the 1930s there already existed a special sub-category of psychological literature in which the concept of a variable is present as a matter of course. That special category consists of texts and articles in the area of psychological statistics and the closely related area of educational statistics. In this literature the concept of a variable is employed routinely in the discussion of statistical regression and techniques of correlation. By the 1920s several statistical texts in which the concept appears were not only being used in courses on psychological statistics (e.g. Jones, 1921; Garrett, 1926; Holzinger, 1928) but were also being widely cited in psychological research articles (especially Kelley, 1923). At this time a background in Galtonian statistics was becoming a normal part of training in psychology, and psychological statistics was being given a more important place in the curriculum. From being taught more or less incidentally within other courses, psychological statistics was now promoted to the status of a topic that required a course of its own. By 1925 a survey by the American Statistical Association established the existence of twelve such courses in Departments of Psychology, a figure which was considered to be an underestimation at the time (Walker, 1929).

The conceptual groundwork for these developments had been laid some years earlier by mathematical statisticians like Karl Pearson and G. Udny Yule, whose work forms the link between nineteenth-century mathematical and twentieth-century psychological statistics. The concept of the variable was central to their contributions. Thus, one finds that the middle section of Yule's enormously influential statistical text is entitled 'The theory of variables' (Yule, 1911), and the term is also to be found in the titles of articles in Pearson's journal *Biometrika* (e.g. Harris, 1909; Pearson, 1910). Charles Spearman, who learned about correlational techniques from the Galton–Pearson School, was probably the first to refer to variables in the psychological literature (Spearman, 1904b). However, at this stage, and for almost three decades thereafter, the term was almost always employed in a strictly statistical context, i.e. in the course of discussions of correlational methods. Only occasionally is the term used in a substantive psychological, rather than a statistical, context (e.g. Knight and Remmers, 1923).

The widespread use of the concept of the variable in a purely psychological context during the 1930s and 1940s must be seen against this historical background. When prominent figures like Tolman and Woodworth began to use this concept in constructing a framework for *all* psychological theorizing and experimenting they could count on it being generally familiar to their by now statistically educated colleagues. That is why they never bother to explain what they mean by this key term, even though it plays such an important role in their exposition. In order to become objects for the type of research psychologists were increasingly engaging in, psychological phenomena like retention, task difficulty, situational knowledge, motivation, affect, etc. did indeed have to be reconstructed as statistical variables. It was perhaps only a matter of time before the originally clear distinction between the psychological kernel and its statistical representation would become blurred.[3] But before we trace this process in the empirical literature we must note the remarkable *theoretical* elevation of the category 'variables' that took place during the 1930s.

Variables enter theoretical discourse

The first use of the concept of the variable in a systematic theoretical manner occurs in E.C. Tolman's *Purposive Behavior in Animals and Men*, published in 1932. There Tolman presents his new version of behaviourism, ushering in the era of neo-behaviourism. In the final section of the book, which he entitles 'This system qua system', he steps back and offers a kind of metatheoretical analysis of his own systematic position, and to do this he uses a metalanguage that enables him to compare his own position with others on his own terms. The concept of the variable plays a key role in this analysis. Quite explicitly, he sets out to compare the variables assumed by his own system with those assumed by other systems (p. 395), the other systems being those of Charles Spearman, E.B. Titchener and the Gestaltists.

What is most remarkable about Tolman's procedure here is that variables are given the status of *psychological* constructs. Previously, variables had been part of the *empirical methodology* of psychologists, at least of those psychologists who followed the Galtonian paradigm. Variables were empirical constructions entailed by the application of correlational techniques to psychological data and nothing more. But now variables were beginning to acquire a psychological, and not merely a statistical, existence.

Previously, whenever psychologists had employed the relevant statistical techniques, they had to give their empirical data a variate form, but this had not at first had much impact on the way in which psychologists formulated their theorizing about their subject matter. The distinction between the level of empirical *statistical* technique and theorizing at the level of underlying *psychological* processes remained relatively clear. Even Spearman and the factor analysts maintained a consistent terminological distinction between the *variables* that entered into empirical correlations and the *factors* that were assumed to underlie these correlations. This left room for fundamental disagreements about the nature of the underlying factors, as the controversy between Spearman and G.H. Thomson illustrates (Thomson, 1920).

However, by the time that Tolman was working on his book this distinction was beginning to wear thin. It is noteworthy that he introduces the crucial chapter in which variables are given a *theoretical* status with a footnote in which he expresses his gratitude to his colleague, R.C. Tryon, 'for stimulating much of the present chapter [and] for a number of the ideas incorporated in it' (Tolman, 1932: 395). Now, Tryon was a specialist in the correlational methods which then dominated psychological statistics. In an article published in the *Psychological Review* three years before the appearance of Tolman's book (Tryon, 1929) he had addressed the question of how the existence of a statistical correlation between two variables was to be interpreted. Two features of his approach to the problem are of interest in the present context. First, in his discussion of underlying factors common to the correlated empirical variables he uses the terms 'common factor' and 'common variable' interchangeably. In other words, he no longer considers it necessary to distinguish between the component of a statistical technique and a hypothesized psychological entity. Secondly, Tryon emphasizes a *causal* interpretation of purely functional mathematical relationships between variables, though in this respect he was not without predecessors.

These developments prepared the ground for the position adopted by Tolman, where the remaining link of the concept of the variable to specific statistical techniques is dispensed with altogether. Any and all postulated psychological processes are now categorized as 'variables'. In the case of factors derived from individual differences research, like Spearman's 'mental energy' or 'self control', this hardly goes beyond what Tryon had already implied, but when we find Titchener's 'sensations', 'images' and 'affections' referred to as variables we know that we have entered new territory. And when we encounter Tolman's discussion of Gestalt Psychology in terms of variables identified only as 'Gestalts', it becomes clear that variables are no longer what they used to be. Indeed, Tolman invents a new category of what he calls 'intermediate' or 'intervening' variables which function as 'behavior-determinants' (Tolman, 1932: 412). They include innate, genetic, capacities as well as learned capacities and 'purposive and cognitive determinants' acting within particular stimulus–response sequences. Any hypothetical intra-individual event, force, disposition, process, state, ability, etc. that is assigned a causal role in behaviour is now subsumed under the category of 'intervening variable'. Tolman had introduced the key term for a new metalanguage that would facilitate intra-disciplinary discourse across the deep divisions created by differences in subject matter and theoretical preference.

His innovation proved popular and, within one decade, had come to define the terms of the dominant neo-behaviourist discourse (Bergman and Spence, 1941; Hull, 1943a). That made it legitimate to refer to anything that was the object of psychological investigation as a variable, irrespective of its empirical or theoretical status, or of whether it indeed had a variate structure. By the 1950s, the metalanguage of variables had become the common medium for all branches of the discipline aspiring to the honorific designation, 'science'. At that time, the editor of a multi-volume self-presentation of the discipline, sponsored by the American Psychological Association, advised all contributors to describe the structure of their systems in terms of an 'exhaustive itemization of systematic independent, intervening, and dependent variables' (Koch, 1959: 717). His own discussion of the entire range of contributions began with a section on 'The intervening variable paradigm for theory "construction"' (Koch, 1959: 733). Tolman's example had been extraordinarily effective.

In part, this was probably due to the strong link between the language of variables and the already well established language of stimulus and response. Both implied the same strictly linear conception of psychological causality. Woodworth had formulated this conception in the

form of his S – O – R schema, where O represents events within
the organism. These are conceptualized as hypothetical or invisible
stimulus–response links. In Tolman's version, the place of intra-
organismic events was taken by 'intervening variables'. These were
thought of as forming the links between independent and dependent
variables, much as the O term had linked stimulus and response in the
older scheme. In both cases the representation of situations and actions
in terms of discrete, logically independent elements became the model
for the conceptualization of all psychological reality. Just as behaviour
and its situational setting were represented as composed of a multitude
of distinct stimuli and responses, or independent and dependent
variables, so everything within the individual was now represented in
terms of a multitude of intervening variables. Both Woodworth and
Tolman aimed at providing the means for what they regarded as a
scientific way of describing purposeful activity. Their solutions
resembled one another so strongly that Tolman (1932: 423) considered
them to be 'siblings'.[4]

The metalanguage of stimulus–response and that of variables also
played a similar role sociologically. Both incorporated the principle that
the constructive activity of psychologists in their investigative practice
was to be regarded as the ultimate meaning conferring operation for all
permissible psychological concepts. In the earlier version this was
accomplished by insisting on the reduction of all psychological concepts
to the elements in terms of which psychologists constructed their
experimental investigations. In the later version, the same basic principle
soon began to sail under the flag of 'operational definition'. By 1936,
Tolman (1936/1951) was referring to his approach as 'operational
behaviorism', a term that nicely described much psychological discourse
and practice beyond the confines of dogmatic behaviourism. The idea
that psychological practice was to define the meaning of psychological
concepts was effective, not only because it was an expression of
professional privilege, but also because it erected a sharply defined
boundary between scientific and lay discourse, especially where the
same terms occurred in both. In those large parts of psychology whose
vocabulary depended heavily on everyday language the survival of a
vigorous scientific community could hardly be guaranteed without this
kind of boundary.

Variables in research practice

As we saw earlier, the *technical* term 'variable' became quite well known
to research practitioners in the 1920s through their use of statistical
methods. Around mid-century, however, there occurs a profound
change in the way the term is used in the research literature. If one looks
through empirical research reports published at that time, one finds that

the term is becoming a key component in the metalanguage that investigators use to describe, not just an element of technique, but the real objects of their investigation. For example, researchers increasingly claim to be investigating, not just something called 'personality', but entities called 'personality variables'. Similarly, research on emotion is billed as the investigation of 'emotional variables', and the probing of the subjects' past is discussed in terms of 'past history variables'. More generally, both the objects of investigation and the investigative situation are now described in terms of such categories as 'experimental variables', 'social variables' and 'clinical variables'. One encounters a translation of the diverse features, attributes, components and aspects of the investigated world into a uniform metalanguage that allows for only one kind of interrelationship among them, namely, the additive relationship of variables. Natural language description of situations and events had allowed for the representation of a great variety of elements and of their complex interrelationships. It was however inexact and often ambiguous. The language of variables promised to establish scientific clarity and precision by recognizing only one kind of element and only one kind of interrelationship.

If one examines the empirical articles appearing in prominent psychological journals between 1938 and 1958 (Danziger and Dzinas, 1997), one finds that the proportion referring to variables increased substantially during this twenty-year period. By 1958, three-quarters of the articles in both *The Journal of Abnormal and Social Psychology* and the *Journal of Personality* referred to variables, though in 1938 only a quarter of those in the former journal, and one-eighth of those in the latter, had done so. In two journals representing the 'hard' experimental areas of the discipline, (the *Journal of Experimental Psychology* and *The American Journal of Psychology*), the trend was also present, though not as marked. (For the former, the increase was from 33 per cent to 59 per cent; for the latter from 21 per cent to 39 per cent.) Virtually all the papers examined employed statistical methodology, even in 1938. So the rise in reference to 'variables' cannot be accounted for by a rise in the number of studies making use of variables in a technical sense, because virtually all the studies did so. It is not the need to describe a specific technology which accounts for the increasing talk of 'variables', but a new way of describing the reality investigated.

There were obviously factors at work in the research community which favoured increased reference to variables. However, the influence of the new theoretical metalanguage of 'independent', 'dependent' and 'intervening' variables does not seem to have been among these factors, at least not initially. In 1938 not a single empirical paper in any of the four journals employed these terms, in spite of the fact that they were by then in theoretical use. Even in 1948, only six out of a total of 209 empirical papers in four journals refer to 'independent' and 'dependent' variables, and 'intervening variables' appears in exactly one case. By

1958 the situation is beginning to change, though even now only seven out of 390 papers mention 'intervening variables'. However, 27 per cent of the studies reported in *The Journal of Abnormal and Social Psychology*, and 17 per cent of those in the *Journal of Personality*, now refer to 'independent' and 'dependent' variables. In the journals devoted to the more traditionally experimental areas of Psychology this proportion tends to be somewhat lower, reaching 14 per cent in the *Journal of Experimental Psychology* and only 5 per cent in *The American Journal of Psychology*.

By this time several influential texts for research students had made their appearance which had in common a definition of the experimental method in terms of independent and dependent variables (Festinger, 1953; Underwood, 1949; Woodworth and Schlosberg, 1954). The last of these was actually the second edition of a previously mentioned pre-war text (Woodworth, 1938) that had pioneered this way of conceptualizing psychological experiments. In the words of a historian, it 'encouraged future psychologists to think of their research problems and formulate their research questions in terms of one or two independent variables, and not in terms of a multidimensional space of reciprocally interacting factors' (Winston, 1990: 398). By the 1950s this message had been echoed by other textbook writers, and its effects had become clearly noticeable in the empirical literature of the discipline.

Ironically, the message seems to have been heeded a little more faithfully in the 'softer' areas of the discipline than in the traditionally experimental areas. Our count indicates that in 1958 the overall proportion of papers making explicit reference to independent and dependent variables is more than twice as high in the journals catering to research in social, abnormal, and personality psychology than it is in the traditionally experimental journals. This suggests that among the contributors to the journals with a relatively shallow experimental tradition there may have been a few diligent apprentices, anxious to show off their new skills by an invocation of the buzz words of the now fashionable version of experimentalism. Contributors to those journals that had an old and relatively secure experimental tradition behind them would presumably be able to continue in this tradition without the new experimental rhetoric. That would apply particularly to *The American Journal of Psychology*, the oldest of these journals.

One gains a better perspective on this historical pattern if one extends one's horizon beyond the discipline of Psychology. Variables were also becoming popular in the neighbouring discipline of Sociology. In *The American Journal of Sociology*, for example, there was also a marked and steady increase in references to variables over the twenty-year period – from 10 per cent in 1938 to 58 per cent in 1958. Actually, one school of American sociological thought had attributed a kind of higher meaning to variables some years before psychologists did. A leading representative of that school expressed this meaning as follows:

> One method of obtaining control in the social science laboratory is, first, to determine the significant factors, or variables, which influence behavior, and then to find out for each its quantitative value in extent or degree. In this way, where it is possible, the social sciences obtain what is an approximation of the controlled experiment in the method of the physical sciences. (Burgess, 1929: 47)

Analysis of situations into quantitative variables was considered to be the way in which the social sciences could successfully imitate their admired model, the physical sciences. It is not unlikely that a significant number of psychologists would have cherished similar sentiments at the time. Among other things, the metalanguage of variables seems to have given expression to a swelling tide of 'physics envy' among American social scientists. If one talked, not of personality, but of personality variables, for example, one was talking like a scientist.

One difference between the situation in Sociology and that in Psychology was that, in the case of the latter, the adoption of the language of variables had a more automatic, non-reflective, quality. Such critical voices as existed (e.g. Cantril, 1950) were either marginalized or simply ignored. In Sociology, however, there was quite a powerful alternative tradition – particularly in the form of symbolic interactionism – which provided a basis for a direct attack on the inappropriate application of the concept of the variable. In 1956 Howard Blumer, a figure of considerable influence in American Sociology, launched a highly visible critique of the use of variables in his discipline. That use, he thought, was too often based on the 'basic fallacy' that independent variables exerted their influence 'automatically' without the intervention of interpretive processes among the persons acted upon. Analysis in terms of variables had become a way of eliminating questions of meaning from the explanation of human conduct. A variable constitutes 'a distinct item with a unitary qualitative make-up' (Blumer, 1956: 688), but the items that are important in the meaningful world of human action are neither clearly distinct from one another, nor do they remain qualitatively unchanged, irrespective of context. Blumer's analysis may actually have strengthened the resolve of some of his colleagues to stick to their variables, for the attraction of this style of social scientific practice was precisely that it enabled one to replace the messiness and ambiguity of the 'subjective' analysis of meaning with the investigator's distinct constructs that always remained the same, no matter what the context.

A more detailed textual analysis of empirical papers published in psychological journals during the period under review indicates that talk about variables did indeed have the function of avoiding the issue of meaning. Explanation in terms of the meaning of situations for experimental subjects is consistently eschewed in favour of a model in which persons 'respond' under the 'influence' of 'variables' that have the solidity of physical objects. A typical example is a study of Rorschach responses in relation to depression scores on a widely used personality inventory, the MMPI (Blake and Wilson, 1950). Both measures are of course constructions of scientific psychology which depend on the interpretations that individuals make when placed in certain situations. However, when the study is reported in approved journal form, there is no reference to this. Instead, we get talk of depression as an 'adjust-mental variable [which] directly influences perceptual selectivity' (p. 459). Referring to depression as an 'adjustmental variable' ('operation-ally defined' by MMPI scores) transforms it from a qualitative feature of subjective worlds into an objective entity that varies only in degree and that has causal effects on other objective entities, like 'Rorschach determinants' in our illustrative example. The language of variables was thus the perfect vehicle for an eclectic kind of neo-behaviourism that wished to banish subjective meaning as an explanatory principle without any commitment to *specific* mechanistic alternatives.

All that remained of the mechanistic fantasies, so dear to the card-carrying behaviourists, was a *general* commitment to the explanation of human conduct in terms of the causal efficacy of 'operationally defined' (but objectively existing) variables, additively interacting. Two inter-related conceptual moves were necessary in order to accomplish the construction of this position. Both depended on fudging the existential status of the variables employed in psychological research. In the empirical literature of the time we find a widespread tendency to slide between the use of 'variable' as a label for a statistical construct and as a description of an objective natural force with causal efficacy. Thus, the variable 'depressive tendency' in our illustrative article refers both to MMPI scores and to something that has a distinct, causally active, existence in human individuals. Now, about the existence of MMPI scores as variables there can be no doubt, because these are artefacts that we have constructed along the lines prescribed by a particular statistical model. But in themselves such variables are not very interesting. What makes them psychologically interesting is the imputation that they are identical, or at least closely related, to other variables that operate out there in the real world without our intervention. The step from variables in the modest statistical sense to variables in the grand ontological sense is a huge one, yet, in writing up their research, psychological investi-gators were constantly taking it, apparently without a moment's reflection.

This is not to say that, in the psychological literature of the time, one cannot find examples of careful distinctions between hypothetical causal determinants and their empirical referents, but these remained largely limited to theoretical texts. Very few empirical research papers bothered with such niceties, and, judging by the published products, neither did journal editors or reviewers. In transposing the category of 'variables' from a statistical to an ontological context psychologists had committed themselves to a nebulous language whose ambiguities often proved convenient. Empirical reports usually did not limit themselves to modest statements about the contribution of specific variables to statistical variance but talked in terms of the 'influence', the 'direct influence', the 'effect', of particular variables. In the published journal texts the variables that investigators had constructed by means of their measuring instruments often appear as causal agents, variously described as 'determinative factors', 'influencing variables', 'determining variables', which 'affect' psychological processes, 'produce' effects, and play a 'determinative' role. This could just be taken as a loose way of referring to observed statistical relationships, but the context makes it quite clear that ontological claims were being made, and that the reader was being invited to think in terms of causal forces at work in real individuals.

The evidence of the journal literature suggests that this aspect of the language of variables was developing in a practical research context without any explicit reference to the contemporaneous theoretical discourse about 'intervening variables'. Yet there was a remarkable symmetry between the two. The theoretical discourse of neo-behaviourism, focusing on the status of hypothetical entities, tended to reduce them to observed relationships among empirical variables (sometimes adding a meaning that was characteristically designated as 'surplus'). At the same time, research investigators, who were constructing these empirical variables in their daily practice, were endowing them with theoretical meaning by using a language which blurred the distinction between hypothetical and empirical elements. The starting points and the directions of theoretical and empirical discourse were different, but the products were very similar. Theoretical discourse started with theoretical terms and moved in the direction of giving them the strongest possible link to empirical variables. Empirical discourse started with the latter and moved in the direction of equating them with their theoretical counterparts. The two levels of discourse converged in producing a version of psychological reality that amounted to a reification of psychological research practice.

Variables as lingua franca

Earlier in this chapter it was suggested that the language of stimulus–response provided a kind of lingua franca which made it possible for experimental psychologists to communicate with each other in spite of the theoretical differences that existed between them. There is evidence that the language of variables functioned in a similar way for psychologists in the areas of clinical and personality research.

We have already seen that, contrary to what one might have expected, it was not the journals covering the 'harder', more experimental, parts of the discipline that led the way in adopting the language of variables. In the post-World War II period it was first of all the *Journal of Personality* and then also *The Journal of Abnormal and Social Psychology* that showed a massive increase in the proportion of articles referring to variables. The meteoric rise of the 'variable' was first signalled by the *Journal of Personality*, which has the lowest proportion of articles using the term in 1938 but by far the highest proportion in 1948. Ten years later, three-quarters of its articles were employing the term. Moreover, when one examines the textual context of 'variable', one finds that the commonest pairing in *all* the journals is with 'personality'. During this twenty-year period, the term 'personality variables' changes from a rarely used form to a ubiquitous phrase in the psychological literature. What was behind this surge?

In 1938 the area of personality psychology had just entered a phase of consolidation in which a common model of empirical research provided a link between previously incommensurable theoretical orientations. Until the late 1930s personality psychology had been essentially an arena for competing schools, but at that point the three virtually simultaneous texts by Gordon Allport, Ross Stagner, and Henry Murray established an eclectic position that privileged empirical research over theoretical principles and thus founded the field as it still exists today. Although the Allport text came to enjoy a certain didactic pre-eminence, it was the Murray text that appears to have been the most significant from the point of view of day to day research practice. It was certainly the one most likely to be cited in research papers.

For the fate of the 'variable' in personality psychology Murray's *Explorations in Personality* was of prophetic significance. Published in 1938, at a time when the use of the term 'variable' in the relevant journal literature can only be described as sporadic, this comprehensive research monograph was remarkable for its ubiquitous use of the term. Indeed, it contains a hundred-page chapter entitled 'Variables of personality'. It is hardly surprising that it is frequently cited in journal articles that participate in the rapidly expanding usage of the term during the next decade. But what accounts for the sudden prominence of 'personality variables' in this 1938 text? It certainly had nothing to do with its author's own theoretical predilections. Henry Murray was perhaps the last person one would have expected to encourage the use of such terminology. His background was in Jungian psychology, and he was regarded with great suspicion by his more conventional, scientifically inclined colleagues in the Harvard Psychology Department (Triplet, 1992).

However, the most striking feature of *Explorations in Personality* is that it was a collaborative product rather than the expression of the views of a single author. Although Henry Murray was its chief architect, a dozen psychologists and another dozen graduate research assistants are listed as collaborators. These were all individuals who participated in the research of the Harvard Psychological Clinic, generously funded by the Rockefeller Foundation. They were quite a motley crew, described by

Henry Murray as 'a group composed of poets, physicists, sociologists, anthropologists, criminologists, physicians; of democrats, fascists, communists, anarchists; of Jews, Protestants, Agnostics, Atheists; of pluralists, monists, solipsists; of Freudians, Jungians, Rankians, Adlerians, Lewinians, and Allportians' (Murray, 1938: xi).

Although their spokesman bravely declared that they 'did not wish to succumb to the great American compulsion to co-operate' (ibid.), co-operate they did. The relative coherence of their 700-page research monograph is evidence of that. How did they achieve such a feat? By building on the one thing they had in common: some measure of faith in the appropriateness of the empirical techniques then in vogue for providing significant knowledge about human individuals. These techniques included the familiar statistical methods for estimating the degree of relationship among variables. This meant that whatever their theoretical and ideological differences they agreed that in practice the things they were trying to investigate had to be treated as variables. And with that agreement they had provided themselves with an escape from their Tower of Babel. They had found an apparently neutral language that made a modicum of communication possible, a language that actually enabled them to formulate a common research objective in spite of the profound disagreements that otherwise divided them. Murray, their spokesman, states this objective very succinctly when introducing the report on their labours: 'What are the fundamental variables in terms of which a personality may be comprehensively and adequately described?' (ibid.: x). The participants in this collaborative research endeavour could continue to hold whatever pet theories they liked, as long as they agreed to define their research objectives in the language of variables. This was the basis on which personality psychology could surmount its fractionation into feuding schools and construct something that came to resemble what Thomas Kuhn would later characterize as 'normal science'.

Using the language of variables at the Harvard Clinic also proved convenient for another, related, reason. As so often happens in a clinical institutional context, there were the conflicting pulls of practical clinical work and research work to contend with. The Clinic's 'diagnostic council', a group that was at the core of its collaborative endeavour, had to try to reconcile these demands. Not surprisingly, theoretical development was an early casualty of the compromises that had to be made: 'Time constraints meant that the diagnostic council decisions were almost always based on statistical averages of ratings rather than on discussion, and the whole enterprise was oriented toward achieving practical results rather than developing theory' (McLeod, 1992: 10). In such a situation, the language of variables would provide an apparently innocent, yet convenient, medium for achieving a culturally sanctioned compromise. The elaboration of 'personality variables' and their intercorrelations would provide an actuarial basis for practical diagnostic

decisions and also a way of conducting quantitative studies that qualified as research. Discussion of the meaning of such variables would even
provide an acceptable substitute for theorizing about hypothetical
structures and processes in the old style inspired by psychoanalysis.

For psychologists faced with problems similar to those of the Harvard
group the new language of variables had obvious attractions. Just as this
language had provided the basis for a necessary minimum of understanding among the members of the Harvard group it came to provide
the common language in which personality psychologists beyond this
group were able to communicate with each other in spite of their often
considerable theoretical differences. Over a longer period of time this
arrangement had the effect of making these theoretical differences seem
less important. Eventually, the old theories became irrelevant in a
research context and were replaced by other kinds of theory that were
essentially a reflection of methodological and practical commitments.

The situation that led to the widespread adoption of the language of
variables at the Harvard Psychological Clinic, and then in personality
psychology generally, was essentially duplicated in other parts of the
discipline, notably in abnormal and social psychology. In the 1940s these
areas were hardly less marked by deep theoretical and ideological
divisions than the area of personality psychology. One need only think
of the profound ideological conflicts that received their expression in the
formation and early days of the Society for the Psychological Study of
Social Issues and the innumerable schools of thought about how best to
explain psychological disorder. Here too, the language of variables made
it possible at least to communicate on one level and thereby to satisfy an
important condition for the formation of something like a scientific
community. At the same time, it provided a discursive framework for a
kind of research that was compatible with an institutional practice based
on the normative use of interpersonal variance for diagnostic purposes.
Many individuals who were active in the area of personality psychology
were also involved in either abnormal or social psychology, so the
spontaneous transfer of such a convenient medium from one area to
another would have been relatively easy.

Theoretical reflections

It is time for some critical reflections on the implications of the historical
analysis presented in this chapter. It has been suggested that psychological investigators were ready to accept their own quantitative
research technology as the one philosophically unproblematic component of their discipline. Whatever suspicion there might be of mentalistic
concepts, and however inconclusive the theoretical debates among the
psychological schools, a common statistical research technology would
form the solid rock on which a scientific psychology could be built.

No doubt, the language of variables proved so seductive at the time because it was tied to apparently neutral statistical techniques that a great many psychologists were using in any case. And this apparent neutrality extended to the term 'variable', even when it was no longer used in a strictly statistical context. But of course the neutrality was only apparent, because the description of personality and of social situations as constituted by sets of distinct variables was in fact theory laden. Recognition of this was hindered by the seldom questioned assumption that the step from methods of investigation to independently existing objects of investigation could be executed quite unproblematically. Yet, in the war against metaphysics the innocent-seeming technology of analysing variables played the role of a Trojan Horse. For if one proceeded as though such an analysis provided a *direct reflection* of psychological reality one was, in effect, making a metaphysical choice. One was now committed to a particular model of psychological reality as composed of a certain kind of element and a certain kind of relationship. In this model there could only be elements that retained their identity irrespective of the relationships into which they entered, all elements being logically independent. Such elements would vary only quantitatively, not qualitatively, between individuals and between situations, and the relationship between them would be essentially additive (cf. Runkel, 1990: ch. 8).

Such a model certainly had its uses for purposes of making practical predictions within a limiting framework of conditions. If one's goals were essentially economic, and one had no mandate or interest in changing existing social arrangements or values, an analysis in terms of variables would often be perfectly adequate. Thus, if one accepted a particular criterion of success and failure (prescribed by prevailing values), one could calculate the relative efficiency of investing fixed resources in one direction rather than another. For instance, a given overall level of educational success can be more efficiently achieved by investing in the education of individuals with high rather than low scores on certain tests. For this purpose it is unnecessary to develop any kind of psychological theory about the nature of mental ability – an analysis of statistical relationships among empirical variables is all that is required. Of course, if social criteria of success or the distribution of social resources were to be questioned, some sort of psychological theory would probably be invoked, both by the advocates of change and by the defenders of the status quo. At that point, psychological engineering would no longer provide an adequate model.

In promoting the language of variables to the status of a metalanguage, psychologists had adopted the language of psychological engineering as a universal medium for theoretical exposition. In other words, they had conflated conceptual control and instrumental control. Philosophers of science have pointed out that scientists 'may achieve remarkable instrumental control without correctly understanding their instruments' (Nickles, 1989: 311; also Hacking, 1983), a situation common in the field of engineering. Theoretical understanding and the technical production of particular effects are quite different in principle, though historically various links between them may develop (Manicas, 1987: ch. 13). In the present case, the prescriptive equation of conceptual control with instrumental control imposed severe limitations on what was admissible as psychological theory. Causality was reduced to a crude concatenation of antecedents and consequents, while complex systems and meaningful patterns were replaced by statistical relationships among a never ending list of elements that always remained logically independent of one another. Of course, the restrictions imposed by this language were broken on numerous occasions, not least by Tolman himself, and then variables became mere *indices* or signs that pointed to a different kind of reality. But such moves were generally made apologetically, because they were perceived as running counter to the norms of real science. By the 1950s the language of variables had taken over the scientific high ground. Those who limited themselves to it never had to answer for themselves, while those who went beyond it were obliged to offer excuses.

Ironically, the way in which variable research was deployed in social scientific practice constituted one of the fundamental differences between it and the common practices of physical science (Winston and Blais, 1996). In the social sciences the command to look for variables was taken to mean that phenomena ought to be investigated in terms of their variation – in Psychology, typically, inter-individual variation. Had physicists proceeded like this they would have attempted to study the *differences* among a variety of falling bodies, or the differences among a variety of warm bodies. Fortunately, this was not their approach, for had it been, it is highly improbable that they would ever have arrived at the law of gravity or the principles of thermodynamics. At least in the modern period, it was clearly understood that the explanation of physical phenomena was one thing and the explanation of their variation quite another. Had it not been for the lack of this basic insight in large segments of the social sciences, it is unlikely that the analysis of variation would have achieved the pre-eminent position it did.[5]

The present chapter has been devoted to an exploration of the ways in which the disciplinary language of Psychology was shaped by the nature of its investigative practice, and more particularly, by the way in which that practice was understood within the discipline. What emerged historically was a kind of isomorphism between the structure of investigative practice and the structure of the objects of investigation. Before they could become objects for scientific psychology, terms referring to psychological objects had to be translated into the terms that were appropriate within the framework of psychological research. Thus, social action, for example, had to be translated into responses to social stimuli, and personality had to be translated into personality variables.

This replaced categories taken from everyday discourse with new categories that were based on a reification of the terms imposed by particular forms of investigative practice.

This historical process represents only one aspect of the complex and intimate relationships that developed between psychological practice and psychological theory. Another aspect, analysed by Gigerenzer (1991), involves the function of methodological tools, e.g. inferential statistics, as sources of theoretical metaphors and concepts. It is becoming more and more apparent that the technology of psychological research – once regarded as a neutral and passive tool – has played, and continues to play, a vitally important determining role in the history of the discipline and of the discursive objects it constructs. There is a whole family of interrelationships between concepts and practices that has not yet been fully explored or even named. In the meantime, perhaps one should update what William James famously referred to as 'The Psychologist's Fallacy'. He defined this as 'the confusion of his own standpoint with that of the mental fact about which he is making his report' (James, 1890, I: 196). In the twentieth century one would want to substitute the more noncommittal 'psychological' for 'mental'; but above all, one would want to be clear about the fact that psychologists' 'own standpoint' has been decisively shaped by their methodological commitments. These commitments have been a mixed blessing at best. On the one hand, they have been a source of productive heuristics and have allowed something like Kuhn's 'normal science' to go ahead. On the other hand, they have blinkered the discipline conceptually and taken it down some very long blind alleys.

Notes

1. William James, for instance, employs the term once in his *Principles of Psychology* (1890, I: 59) and again in a discussion of Dewey's ideas published in 1904. (I am indebted to Paul Ballantyne for finding the relevant passages.)

2. That view can be summarized in terms of the following assumptions, common to the stimulus–response scheme and analysis in terms of variables: '1. Cause comes before effect. As a corollary, cause and effect are separate, non-overlapping events. 2. Cause and effect appear in local, distinguishable episodes having a beginning and an ending. . . . As a corollary, the beginning and the end are recognizable. 3. The laws of nature are everywhere the same . . . if a law holds at one place or time, it will hold in every place and time' (Runkel, 1990: 78).

3. Jerome Kagan (1989: 130), for example, seems to be suggesting this when he writes: 'During this century the disciplines that study behavior, thought, and affect have favored continua over categories and linear over non-linear relations. These presuppositions . . . dominate the modern psychological laboratory, partly as a consequence of the dissemination of statistical procedures in the interval between the two World Wars. . . . Investigators who ignored statistical analyses were regarded as less competent.'

4. My focus here (as elsewhere) is purely on Tolman as a voice in the public discourse of a discipline, not on the intellectual biography of an individual. From the latter point of view, there was clearly a considerable distance between where Tolman started and where

he ended up. He began his career in the mixed empiricist-phenomenological tradition of James, Holt and Perry, but, as Still (1987) has suggested, his absorption in the language and the experimental practices of Psychology pointed him in a different direction. He may have started with insights into the direct perception of purpose, but, 'given his audience, there was an inevitability in the progression of his thought' so that 'he was eventually obliged to express them [his insights] in a language akin to that of the more mechanistic psychology that became dominant during the 1930s' (Still, 1987: 181).

5. Kurt Lewin and B.F. Skinner were two major figures who did recognize the importance of this distinction quite explicitly. Many other European psychologists, e.g. Sigmund Freud and Jean Piaget, recognized it implicitly, which is why they had no use for 'variables'. On Lewin, see Danziger (1992a); more generally, see Lewontin (1985), and Lieberson (1985).

10

THE NATURE OF
PSYCHOLOGICAL KINDS

Historical roots of psychological categories

Traditional prescriptions for the practice of a scientific psychology seem to imply an image of the psychologist as a sort of visitor from outer space (Ingleby, 1990), unaffected by local cultural traditions or the preconceptions embedded in human language. Right at the beginning of this book that image was rejected in favour of one that depicts psychology as a cultural construction with specific historical roots. The body of the book was devoted to an exploration of some of these roots. In light of this exploration, what can we say about the sources of psychological categories? Obviously, these categories all depend on certain semantic traditions and a historically emerging usage. Is it possible to go beyond such general statements by identifying some of the major factors in the historical formation of psychological categories?

I propose to answer this question positively by first recalling the various layers of discourse that have been examined in the preceding pages. At each of these levels a particular set of conceptual distinctions emerges so as to form a specific network of interconnected categories that enables a certain kind of understanding of human subjects.

At a relatively deep level there are broad distinctions that have pervasive effects. In this book we have concentrated on the distinctions introduced by a certain kind of moral discourse that first became fully articulate in eighteenth-century Britain. Aiding both self-understanding and self-justification under new social and economic circumstances, this discourse was based on a fundamental sense of separation between human individuals as well as between individual agents and their actions. In Chapter 3 we saw how this manifested itself in the emergence of a network of categories with modern meanings, such as self, consciousness and motive. The new moral sensibility also involved revolutionary changes in the understanding of ancient categories like reason and passion without which modern conceptions of intelligence and emotion would have remained literally unthinkable.

Had there been no further developments psychology would have remained simply a part of moral discourse. In part, it has indeed remained so, but of course the special authority of modern Psychology derives, not from its moral implications, but from its scientific pretensions. These latter depend on its methodology and on its use of categories that carry a special scientific aura. Twentieth-century Psychology talks not only of motives and emotions but also of stimuli and organisms. Such categories have their origin in biology, not in moral philosophy. They constitute a different layer of historical development. Their psychological use is predicated upon the emergence of a distinction between a physiological and a psychological domain and upon the troubled history of that distinction. This was explored in Chapter 4. But beyond that, the biological heritage weighs heavily on pervasive categories of twentieth-century Psychology, like behaviour and learning, as well as more specific categories like intelligence (Chapters 5 and 6). In all these cases, an essentially biological understanding of human action and human capability was built into the categories used for their depiction.

A third layer of psychological discourse was added with the professionalization of psychology and its institutionalization as a discipline. These developments entailed the creation of a class of psychological specialists whose very existence imposed new functions on psychological language. Previously, psychological distinctions and psychological terms had been everyone's property, and psychological usage had become widely diffused in philosophical, medical, educational and literary texts. This diffusion did not end in the twentieth century – quite the contrary. But there now emerged an ever growing army of experts whose pronouncements on matters psychological were of a special kind, because they were supposedly founded on the indisputable authority of science. These experts claimed to have a superior kind of access to psychological knowledge that was not available to those outside the fold of science. In due course, the activities of members of this new class led to the formation of a new layer of psychological language, partly for internal use among themselves and partly for use in their dealings with the lay public or with other groups of specialists. In part, this new layer was composed of a myriad of technical terms, each relevant to a relatively limited domain. In this book, however, the focus has not been on that aspect of the new psychological language but on the more subtle adaptation of existing terms to describe major domains reshaped by the activity of the new professionals.

The establishment of a recognized class of psychological specialists always depended on their maintaining a delicate balance between the ideal of a universalistic and uninvolved science and accommodation to the requirements of local sectoral interests. Without the former, no special authority claims could be upheld in the long run; without the latter, there was no employment and scant social support, material and otherwise. This balancing act was reflected in many of the general categories around which the new specialists organized their work.

Among the examples discussed in this book the categories of intelligence, learning and motivation show this most clearly. In each of these there was a melding of a putatively biological category with categories derived from specific social practices, i.e. social selection in the case of intelligence, educational practices in the case of learning, and management practices in the case of motivation. That made it possible to provide a whole array of local social practices with an apparently scientific justification, a function at which the new professionals excelled.

If the new Psychology was to be a science relevant to life outside the laboratory its categories had to suit the practical contexts in which it was beginning to be applied. As a result, psychological language became enriched by an array of terms that had already achieved some currency in those contexts. A few of these terms – such as the ones examined in this book – came to define categories of psychological phenomena to which a fundamental significance was attached. They served as a focus for psychological research and differentiated the domains of psychological knowledge. Why did they, and not others, achieve this status? As I have already suggested, that depended on the ease with which they could be assimilated to quasi-biological categories of apparently universal validity.

The combination of a universal biological meaning with a local social meaning was mediated by the development of specific technologies. Certain investigative practices, certain methods of psychological research and assessment – intelligence and personality testing, techniques for measuring the strength of attitudes and motives, standard learning situations, and so on, provided the basis for constituting classes of scientifically validated phenomena that could be produced in a variety of practical settings. In the course of time, the role of such technologies in establishing the meaning of psychological categories became ever more decisive.

With the growth of a professional community of psychologists the meaning of psychological categories also began to be affected by the role they played in the life of this community of experts. The categories in question were involved, not only in the interaction of experts with their lay public, but also in the internal communication on which the cohesion of the scientific community depended. This factor emerges particularly strongly in the development of a kind of metalanguage – as described in Chapter 9 – which functions as a lingua franca among members of the discipline. Here too, the role of certain technologies is critical. Another aspect of the life of the disciplinary community that may have effects on the meaning of categories is its relationship to neighbouring communities of experts. Professional rivalries and attempts at maintaining or extending disciplinary boundaries play a role here. One example of such effects was noted in Chapter 8 in connection with the history of the category 'social attitude' which was more or less annexed by Psychology, only to be given an essentially asocial meaning.

The intervention of a third layer of effects through the emergence of disciplinary communities by no means abolishes the other two layers. Scientific psychological categories still have to be consonant with culturally sanctioned assumptions about humans and their relationship to the world, and they also continue to be shaped by established scientific traditions. Disciplinary communities have only a limited space within which to reshape categories in accordance with their own requirements. Their members remain bound by philosophies that have come to be taken for granted in their culture as well as by traditional interpretations of the meaning of their own practices (MacIntyre, 1984: 221).

The politics of psychological language

Whether it was a matter of providing a framework for a moral philosophy appropriate to social relations based on contract and exchange, whether it was a matter of rationalizing particular scientific procedures and ideologies, or whether the interests of professionalizing groups of experts were at stake, the categories constituted in psychological language were intimately linked to particular social practices. Although it was always claimed to be simply a reflection of some objectively existing psychological reality, the meaning of these categories always depended on the use to which they were put in specific social contexts. Psychological classificatory terms established a framework for communicating about certain aspects of human life and experience, and such communication was never entirely disinterested, uninvolved or innocent. Historical actors operated within and upon this framework in order to accomplish certain ends, to produce certain effects and prevent others. When the constraints of received categories no longer suited current actors, they began using them in ways that altered their meaning. They also invented new categories, often by emphasizing distinctions that had not seemed important before, or by grouping together things that had previously seemed to be quite different.

It hardly needs pointing out that the phenomena involved here are strictly *public* phenomena. The texts that make use of and convey the meaning of psychological categories exist in a domain of public discourse where they may have effects on the way readers pursue their own work, and on their understanding of their own actions, even their feelings and hopes. The authors of such texts are well aware of this and aim to *do* something with their words (Skinner, 1988b), though what they accomplish may not be what they had hoped for. In other words, the texts constitute a public domain to which individuals may sometimes contribute as innovators but which also constrains and affects their thoughts and actions. Whatever personal significance authors' contributions may have had for them may be of biographical interest but is not germane to an analysis of the historical development of public discourse. Once in the public domain these contributions mingle with the effects of countless other contributions and become part of a discursive formation that must be analysed on its own terms.

It would be a mistake to pursue this analysis in terms of distinctions derived from traditional accounts of the activity of isolated knowers. Such accounts usually distinguish between *concepts* assumed to exist inside an individual mind and the *language* that an individual uses to label and describe these concepts. This distinction does not apply at the level of public discourse. Here there is only a language and the manner of its deployment by certain users. The life of concepts is studied as part of this context, not as the content of private minds. Hence the distinction between a concept that is essentially private and a language that is essentially public becomes inapplicable. In this book, as the reader may have noticed, such a distinction is not made. Nor are concepts attributed with a power and an essence of their own, as used to be the fashion in the quaint idealist historiography of old. Language only acts as the carrier of concepts insofar as it is deployed by its users in specific discursive contexts.

At this level, psychological language must be studied as part of social life and that means taking account of its political role. Common ways of describing the character of human actions, the constitution of human individuals, the contours of human experience, always have social consequences and are unlikely to be politically innocent (Deetz, 1994). The categories of such descriptions often provide a resource for justifying particular social arrangements and legitimizing social practices by establishing a taken for granted discursive framework. Political changes are usually implicated in conceptual transformation, and vice versa (Farr, 1989).

Psychological categories have a political dimension because they are not purely descriptive but also normative. Adopting a particular classification of psychological phenomena, and implicitly rejecting a myriad possible alternative classifications, means establishing a certain form for the recognition of human conduct and human individuality. Whatever people are, whatever they do, will be recognized only in the forms prescribed by some system of classification. For instance, in the prevailing Western system everyone is expected to have private motives, everyone is expected to have social attitudes, everyone is expected to fall somewhere in the distribution of intelligence. In principle, individuals could claim that these categories misrepresented their own experience, but the social and scientific pressures are such that virtually no one does. For most persons the prevailing discursive system becomes inescapable and motives, attitudes, intelligence and so on are the forms in which they experience their own subjectivity.[1] The discursive resources that might enable people to experience themselves and others differently are generally not available.

It is not only in this sense that prevailing psychological categories are normative. These categories invariably function as conduits for the transmission of social evaluation. Thus, intelligence, even test intelligence, constitutes a criterion for judging people; the concept of attitude establishes a focus for the expression of encouragement or discouragement; and the reification of motives provides a whole vocabulary for expressing approval or disapproval of particular courses of action.

While psychological categories had long functioned in this way in the informal situations of everyday life, psychological science gradually achieved a privileged position with regard to their use in more formal settings. When educationists decided on a child's life chances, when the military designed programmes to boost morale, when advertisers looked for ways of influencing consumers, they were likely to make use of the categories of intelligence, attitude and motivation, respectively. But they used them in a rationalized context where some means of demonstrating and comparing the effectiveness of their actions was required (cf. Porter, 1995). Psychological science could supply these means through the standardized techniques of measurement which it had developed. In this way the categories of psychological investigation, defined by these techniques, were transformed into categories of institutional practice. Concomitantly, disciplinary power was extended from phenomena produced under laboratory-like conditions to phenomena that formed part of life outside the laboratory. Such political consequences were not necessarily intended by anyone, but, given the appropriate cultural context, they tended to follow from the anchoring of category meaning in a technology designed for that purpose by specialists with a particular professional identity.

The reference of psychological categories

It may well be that the categories of scientific psychology have political effects but nevertheless represent natural divisions among objective features of the world that exist independently of the efforts of psychologists. This is certainly how most psychologists think of the categories they employ in their work. They tend to use them as though they referred to 'natural kinds', groups of naturally occurring phenomena that inherently resemble each other and differ crucially from other phenomena. Is there any validity to this view?

To answer this question it is necessary, first, to remind oneself that the categories one meets in psychological texts are discursive categories, forms of words, not the things themselves. There is a distinction, often ignored by practitioners, between the language used to describe a particular set of phenomena and the phenomena themselves (Gergen, 1982, 1985). We can read the descriptive text, but what exactly is the relationship between it and whatever it is that it refers to? Psychological categories are discursive objects that supposedly refer to something outside discourse (Danziger, 1993). But how do they refer? Are they a mirror held up to the world that reflects the divisions to be found there?

This image may be appropriate for the relationship an isolated individual might have with a natural world lacking all human qualities. In this model the individual forms some kind of mental representation of objects that are out there and learns to apply verbal labels to them. The objects carry on with their existence irrespective of this process. They don't care what they are called or if they are called anything at all, and their natural existence in no way depends on how they are represented by any human individual. But as soon as we substitute artificial for natural objects – that is, objects created by humans – the situation changes. Now, the existence of the object, perhaps an axe or a god, does depend in some way on how it is represented by its creator – had it been represented in some other way it would have been created differently. In other words, the relationship between verbal labels or mental images and their objective reference has ceased to be *merely* representational and has become at least partly *constitutional*. The way the object is constituted now depends on its human creator and the relationship between the object's existence and its representation has become quite intimate. A plan for a building, for example, is not simply a representation of something that would exist without such a plan, it is something that imposes a particular form on what it depicts.

The conduct of scientific investigations has much in common with the design of buildings. This is partly recognized when we use the same word, design, in reference to the planning of buildings and the planning of experiments. But it goes further than that. The experimental outcome would not exist had the experimenters not intervened in the natural course of events. Experimental outcomes are artefacts, not natural phenomena. At the very least, they are co-constituted by human agents. Of course this also applies to the phenomena produced through the administration of psychological tests, questionnaires, rating scales, or any other instrument of investigation.

Among the instruments of investigation the most basic one is often overlooked. It is language. Without language the other instruments could not be constructed, the results of investigations could not be described, hypotheses could not be formulated, and investigators could not arrive at a common understanding of what they were doing. No wonder that the role of language is so often overlooked in texts dealing with the technique of investigation. It is a case of the fish being the last animal to discover water. The entire investigative enterprise is so immersed in language that it is simply taken for granted and its role becomes invisible. Language, however, is not a neutral medium; it is crucial for the constitution of the phenomena under investigation. Nothing ever becomes an object of investigation without being categorized in some way, even if the classification changes in the course of the investigation. This categorization gives the object its identity and enables investigators to have a particular understanding of what they are doing.

Investigators, like everyone else, live in a world that has already been classified. The best scientific work may lead to a questioning of an existing category, but much of the time research proceeds within a framework of established categories. Even when the meaning of a category is questioned, it is unlikely to be one of the fundamental categories that define the field. It is only in exceptional circumstances, as when a new discipline is created or redefined, that the work of category construction is displayed openly on a large scale. This book has examined such a case. The period that has provided its major focus, the early part of this century, was a period during which the discipline of Psychology was remaking itself, particularly in the US, and the construction of new categories as well as the reworking of old ones was very much part of this process.

Quite clearly, the display of new phenomena was part of this. I say 'display', and not 'discovery', because the nature of the process by which new phenomena entered the discourse of the discipline is precisely what is at issue here. To say that these phenomena were 'discovered' is to prejudge the issue in favour of the much criticized mirror model of classification. According to the classical version of this model, individuals first find new features in the world and then alter their concepts and categories to get a better reflection of a world that now includes the new features. However, the process may be the reverse of this. New features may emerge as a result of a different way of classifying and conceptualizing; it may then be more appropriate to speak of a process of construction rather than discovery.[2] But perhaps that implies a degree of freedom that the investigator does not have. So let us simply say that the new features are displayed.

Displayed to whom? Not simply to a solitary investigator, surely, for we are not dealing with a secret art like alchemy but with science, which is a form of public knowledge. For public display some conventions of representation are necessary, and these always rely on a language, artificial or natural. Even a graph or a table of figures must be verbally labelled, that is interpreted, to convey its proper meaning. A scientific fact is always a fact under some description. The discursive framework within which factual description takes place is as much part of science as its hardware and its techniques of measurement. To be effective, such a framework must be shared – an idiosyncratic description of a fact will not be accepted as a scientific statement. In other words, the work of reference is not a solitary labour but a social activity. Any reference to the 'facts of the world' has to rely on some discursive framework in use among a particular group of people at a particular time. Facts are there to be displayed, but they can only be displayed within a certain discursive structure.[3] Changes in these structures present opportunities for the display of different facts.

As we have seen, the categories of psychological discourse have changed quite considerably in the course of time. This was a change that was closely connected with broad social changes as well as with the concerns, material, ideological and professional, of emerging groups of specialists. Psychological categories were always relevant to the lives of those who used them, whether they were ordinary people or experts. Changes in these lives were accompanied by changes in psychological categories. Although it is difficult to say that these categories represent *natural* kinds, what one can say is that they represent *relevant* kinds.[4] They are relevant to the people who use them, relevant to their concerns, their interrelationships with each other, their possibilities of action. There are factors in their lives which lead them to make and to emphasize certain distinctions and to ignore any number of others. That is reflected in the changes in psychological categories that we have traced in this book.

Natural kinds or human kinds?

Should one regard psychological categories as natural kinds? Initially, I mentioned two criteria for the existence of a natural kind: that it be independent of the efforts of investigators, in this case psychologists, and that there be some inherent resemblance among the phenomena belonging to a kind. In light of the foregoing discussion and the historical material considered in the preceding chapters there seem to be no grounds for accepting the 'naturalness' of psychological categories on the basis of the first criterion. The second criterion requires a little further consideration.

Even if one grants that systems of classification depend on the people doing the classifying, one could still maintain that a particular system provides the most accurate, the most veridical, representation of the natural resemblances that exist in the objective world. The underlying idea would be that natural divisions are of a kind that permits only one true representation, all other versions being departures from this one truth. What is wrong with this idea is its attribution to some world outside our experience of features that are specifically features of shared experienced worlds. In particular, the existence of defined objects distinguished from each other by certain patterns of resemblance is as much a feature of shared experienced worlds as is the existence of schemes of classification (Putnam, 1981). The two go hand in hand. Strictly speaking, there are no 'raw' data in science. Whatever forms the subject of scientifically informed perception is already classified in some way. This does not mean that such perceptions depend on nothing but discourse; what it means is that scientific discourse is only able to represent objects as they have been constituted by the categories of that discourse.[5]

Furthermore, the very notion of natural kinds may be peculiarly inappropriate for psychology. A defining characteristic of natural objects that I have already referred to is their indifference to the descriptions applied to them. If we change our identification of a chemical compound as a result of advances in techniques of analysis, this changes our knowledge of the compound but the compound itself remains the same compound it always was. But the objects represented in psychological language are generally not like that. A person who learns not to think of his or her actions as greedy or avaricious but as motivated by a need for achievement or self-realization has changed as a person. Students who learn to classify things they see under a microscope no longer have the same perceptual experience they had during their initial encounter with microscopic preparations. The sorts of things that psychology takes as its objects, people's actions, experiences and dispositions, are not independent of their categorization.

There are two reasons for this. First, the individuals who are the carriers of psychological objects are able to represent these objects to themselves in a self-referential fashion. Unless one joins the behaviourists in assigning a purely epiphenomenal status to such representations, it is apparent that their existence introduces a profound distinction between psychological objects and natural objects that have no capacity for self-reference. The manner of their articulation in language becomes a constituent part of psychological objects so that their identity changes with changes in psychological language (Taylor, 1985).

Secondly, psychological properties are intelligible features of the world only by virtue of their display within a discursive context. They do not exist preformed in some private realm before they enter into social life. Whatever forms they assume are due to their embeddedness in particular discursive practices. The conception of psychological entities as natural objects is often grounded in a naive belief in the existence of a private world of psychological essences. However, distinctions that constitute emotions as emotions, motives as motives, cognitions as cognitions, and so on, do not exist in some sealed private box *before* they are so labelled in public.[6] Identifying experiences, actions and dispositions is not like sticking labels on fully formed specimens in a museum. Psychological objects assume their identity in the course of discursive interaction among individuals.

Distinguishing among kinds of actions and kinds of people is part of human interaction everywhere. Psychology attempts to offer causal explanations of the domains created by these distinctions, using empirical investigation and theoretical hypotheses. The extent to which these attempts act back on the distinctions themselves depends on the authority commanded by psychological expertise in a particular culture. It also depends on the way in which psychological work relates to existing needs and interests. If the work is truly innovative and threatens established preconceptions and relationships it will meet a great deal of resistance. But the great bulk of psychological work has never been in any danger of this fate. Both in its inspiration and in its effects it has been profoundly conservative. Except on a very superficial level, it has shared the prevailing preconceptions of its culture and arranged its investigations in such a way that no knowledge with revolutionary implications could possibly emerge from them. In assessing the effect of psychological science on psychological kinds it is easy to overlook the biggest effect of all, namely, the reinforcement of existing culturally embedded preconceptions and distinctions.[7]

This cultural embeddedness accounts for the taken for granted quality that so many psychological categories possess. It is a quality that makes them appear 'natural' to the members of a particular speech community sharing a certain tradition of language usage. However, this sense of 'natural' is not to be confused with the concept of natural kinds that has featured in the present discussion. Natural kinds have nothing to do with culture, whereas the natural-appearing kinds of psychology have everything to do with it. We need a term for the latter that will recognize this distinction. The term 'human kind', introduced by Ian Hacking (1992), is useful here. Hacking's main interest is in categories that define kinds of people, like homosexual or multiple personality disorder, but, in principle, kinds of human activity are covered too. The difference between natural and human kinds rests on the distinctions I have already mentioned, that is, whether the kind is self-referring and whether it is intrinsically part of social practice. The categories discussed in this book are all human kinds rather than natural kinds.

One consequence of the distinguishing features of human kinds is that their relationship to the reality they refer to is different from that of natural kinds. The latter refer to something that would be the case, whether any particular act of reference had occurred or not. Human kinds, on the other hand, affect that which they refer to. Historically, 'the category and the people in it emerged hand in hand' (Hacking, 1986: 229). The way humans categorize themselves and their activities is not independent of their actual conduct, because, as we have noted, such categorization is part of human conduct and therefore not a matter of indifference to the people concerned. This leads to what Hacking (1994) has described as 'looping effects', the reaction of people to the classes to which they and their activities are consigned. This reaction may range all the way from passive acceptance to militant refusal. In other words, the meaning of human kinds develops and changes in the course of interactions among those affected. (This interaction has sometimes been described as a process of 'negotiation', though that implies a more deliberate and more articulate process than is often the case.) Human kinds of the sort discussed in this book are not natural kinds, but neither are they mere legends. They do refer to features that

are real. But it is a reality in which they are themselves heavily implicated, a reality of which they are a part.

The reality to which human kinds refer is a cultural reality, and that
in several senses: first, because the phenomena depicted are ones which
exist only in some cultural context; secondly, because these phenomena
commonly depend on a certain social technology for their visibility and
their production; thirdly – and this is the aspect that has been the focus
here – because the categories used in their representation are culturally
grounded. What implications does this grounding have for Psychology's
scientific project?

The categories of scientific Psychology are partly derived from certain
taken for granted, but historically formed, distinctions and partly reflect
the requirements of a scientific community in the making. Much of the
time there is little or no conflict between these factors. This is not
surprising, because the society that generated the first modern
psychological categories was the same society that gave rise to the
normative order of empirical science. However, this society was never a
monolith. Although it was marked by certain pervasive features, its
numerous divisions also created much dissonance. One source of
dissonance was the division between lay knowledge and scientific
knowledge. In the case of psychology the division was particularly
troublesome because human action is action under some description, so
that, if Psychology was to study this topic, the choice between accepting
the lay description and imposing its own description was ever present.
Popular relevance meant respecting lay categories, but the project of
building a scientific community required a different kind of language.
Where lay usage depended on innumerable local contexts and subtle
distinctions, scientific usage demanded abstract categories and precise,
not subtle, distinctions.

The more uncompromising psychologists became in their exclusive
commitment to the requirements of scientific language the more
impoverished their descriptions became, at least from the point of
view of ordinary usage. But this was hardly seen as a sacrifice by many
practitioners who valued the pursuit of universality and accuracy above
all else. The successful development of a methodologically based metalanguage, as described in Chapter 9, was the fruit of this pursuit.
However, it was a dry, shrivelled fruit that provided limited sustenance
for those who wanted to see a unification of the discipline on the basis
of scientific theory. What was commonly overlooked was that the
culturally rather narrow foundations of the discipline already provided
it with a kind of unity. After the first third of the twentieth century
Psychology became essentially an American discipline. This was not
only because, for a while, the scale of its practice in the rest of the world
paled into insignificance compared to its exuberant growth in the United
States. More significantly, it was imported, and sometimes reimported,
by the rest of the world as part and parcel of its importation of

American values, American educational and business practices, American media, American advertising, American conceptions of mental health, and so on. For this reason, if for no other, an exploration of the historical foundations of American psychology has international significance.

This study is incomplete in a number of respects. For one thing, the categories selected for attention form but a part of even the most general categories of American-style Psychology, let alone its more specific categories. Hopefully, others will be examined in due course, especially categories that have achieved prominence more recently, like cognition. Our focus on a limited time period eliminated many potential candidates. Equally important is the recognition that there have been many alternative ways of categorizing psychological phenomena that do not form part of the main course taken by American Psychology. This does not mean that they belong in the dustbin of psychology's history. Quite the contrary.

There are only two things we can be sure of in speculating about future developments. One is that this is not the end of history; in other words, that the categories of psychology will continue to change. In this process old categories will acquire new meaning and some will be discarded altogether. New categories will take their place, and some of these may represent traditions that were in eclipse for much of the twentieth century. The second belief which may be asserted with some confidence is that changes in psychological categories will continue to be heavily dependent on changes in the societies within which these categories have a role. Their meaning will continue to be negotiated and contested among the groups to whom they matter. As the identity of these groups changes, both nationally and globally, the kinds that seem so natural today will become tomorrow's legends.

Notes

1. This emphasis on the normative significance of psychological categories owes much to the work of Foucault, especially Foucault (1977). This aspect of Foucault's work has been further developed by a number of authors (see especially Rose, 1996). Commenting on the implications of Foucault's analysis, Joseph Rouse (1987: 217) writes: 'Classifications provide intelligible ways for people to understand themselves (and the things around them) and to act. The imposition of new categories that come to figure in our various configurations of possible action constrains people in significant ways and even produces different kinds of people. *Classification is an important form of power*' (italics added).

2. This problematic began to have an influence on psychological research some years ago, see e.g. Medin (1989); Nelson (1991).

3. The philosopher Hilary Putnam has frequently emphasized this point: 'We can and should insist that some facts are there to be discovered and not legislated by us. But this is something to be said when one has adopted a way of speaking, a language, a 'conceptual scheme'. To talk of 'facts' without specifying the language to be used is to talk of nothing' (Putnam, 1991: 114).

4. The notion of 'relevant kinds' was introduced by the philosopher Nelson Goodman in the course of his demonstration that any process of induction depends on taking certain classes as relevant and others as irrelevant. Relevance is a matter of emphasizing certain distinctions and de-emphasizing others, and this can account for differences between one constructed world and another: 'Some relevant kinds of the one world, rather than being absent from the other, are present as irrelevant kinds; some differences among worlds are not so much in entities comprised as in emphasis or accent, and these differences are no less consequential. Just as to stress all syllables is to stress none, so to take all classes as relevant kinds is to take none as such' (Goodman, 1978: 11).

5. One of the very few attempts by a psychologist to address the problem of natural kinds pins its hopes on so-called 'micropsychology', operating with units that simply involve 'a change of behavior, e.g. a change in the direction of gaze' (Fiske, 1991). The advantages of operating at this level would however be purely technical (e.g. clearer category boundaries); the basic dependence of data on classificatory schemes remains unaffected. The choice of such categories as 'behaviour' and 'gaze', for example, is driven by certain historical traditions, not by anything in the 'nature' of the case, and the observations reported within this framework are just that: observations made possible by adopting this framework rather than another.

6. These considerations ultimately derive from Wittgenstein's (1953) strictures on private language. The psychological implications of Wittgenstein's insights have been extensively developed by a number of authors, Bloor (1983), Coulter (1989), and Harré and Gillett (1994) among others. For anthropological perspectives on the discursive formation of psychological objects, see Lutz and Abu-Lughod (1990).

7. This tendency can lend credibility to a sharp juxtaposition of social constructionism and realism, as in Greenwood (1994).

REFERENCES

Where later editions, reprints or translations are cited an original publication date is provided. This refers to the *Work*, not to the edition or translation cited.

Adorno, T.W., Frenkel-Brunswik, E., Levinson, D.J. and Sanford, R.N. (1950) *The Authoritarian Personality*. New York: Harper.

Allport, F.H. (1924) *Social Psychology*. Boston: Houghton Mifflin.

Allport, F.H. (1932) 'Psychology in relation to social and political problems', in P.S. Achilles (ed.), *Psychology at Work*. New York: McGraw-Hill. pp. 199–252.

Allport, F.H. (1933) *Institutional Behavior*. Chapel Hill: University of North Carolina Press.

Allport, F.H. and Hartman, D.A. (1925) 'Measurement and motivation of atypical opinion in a certain group', *American Political Science Review*, 19: 735–760.

Allport, G.W. (1927) 'Concepts of trait and personality', *Psychological Bulletin*, 24: 284–293.

Allport, G.W. (1929) 'The composition of political attitudes', *American Journal of Sociology*, 35: 220–238.

Allport, G.W. (1935) 'Attitudes', in C. Murchison (ed.), *A Handbook of Social Psychology*. New York: Russell and Russell. pp. 798–844.

Allport, G.W. (1937) *Personality: A Psychological Interpretation*. New York: Holt.

Allport, G.W. and Veltfort, H.R. (1943) 'Social psychology and the civilian war effort', *Journal of Social Psychology*, 18: 165–233.

Allport, G.W. and Vernon, P.E. (1933) *Studies in Expressive Movement*. New York: Macmillan.

Ammacher, P. (1965) *Freud's Neurological Education and its Influence on Psychoanalytic Theory*. New York: International Universities Press.

Andersen, M.L. (1994) 'The many varied social constructions of intelligence', in T.R. Sarbin and J.I. Kitsuse (eds), *Constructing the Social*. London: Sage. pp. 119–138.

Angell, J.R. (1904) *Psychology*. New York: Henry Holt.

Angell, J.R. (1907) 'The province of functional psychology', *Psychological Review*, 14: 61–91.

Angell, J.R. (1913) 'Behavior as a category in psychology', *Psychological Review*, 20: 255–270.

Annas, J. (1992) *Hellenistic Philosophy of Mind*. Berkeley: University of California Press.

Aquinas, St Thomas (1947) *Summa Theologica*, vol. 1. New York: Benziger Bros.

Ardal, P.S. (1966) *Passion and Value in Hume's Treatise*. Edinburgh: Edinburgh University Press.

Aristotle (1962) *Nicomachean Ethics*, trans. M. Ostwald. Indianapolis: Bobbs-Merrill.

Aristotle (1984) *The Complete Works of Aristotle*, 2 vols, ed. J. Barnes. Princeton, NJ: Princeton University Press.

Asch, S.E. (1952) *Social Psychology*. New York: Prentice-Hall.

Asendorpf, J. and Wallbott, H. (1982) 'Contribution of the German "expression psychology" to nonverbal communication research', *Journal of Non-Verbal Behavior*, 6: 135–147.

Ashton, R. (1991) *G.H. Lewes: A Life*. Oxford: Clarendon Press.

Austin, J.L. (1962) *How to Do Things with Words*. Cambridge, MA: Harvard University Press.

Averill, J.R. (1985) 'The social construction of emotion: with special reference to love', in K.J. Gergen and K.E. Davis (eds), *The Social Construction of the Person*. New York: Springer-Verlag. pp. 89–109.

Bain, A. (1868) *Mental Science: A Compendium of Psychology and the History of Philosophy*. New York: Appleton.

Bain, A. (1977) *The Senses and the Intellect* and *The Emotions and the Will*. ed. D.N. Robinson. Washington, DC: University Publications of America. (Originals published in 1855 and 1859.)

Bain, R. (1928) 'An attitude on attitude research', *American Journal of Sociology*, 33: 940–957.

Bain, R. (1930) 'Theory and measurement of attitudes and opinions', *Psychological Bulletin*, 27: 357–379.

Baker, G.P. and Hacker, P.M.S. (1984) *Language, Sense and Nonsense*. Oxford: Blackwell.

Baldwin, J.M. (1894) *Mental Development in the Child and the Race*. New York: Macmillan.

Baldwin, J.M. (ed.) (1901) *Dictionary of Philosophy and Psychology*. New York: Macmillan.

Barrett, E.B. (1911) *Motive-Force and Motivation Tracks: A Research in Will Psychology*. London: Longmans, Green.

Beer, T., Bethe, A. and von Uexküll, I. (1899) 'Vorschläge zu einer objektivierenden Nomenklatur in der Physiologie des Nervensystems', *Biologisches Zentralblatt*, 19: 517–521.

Bell, D. (1960) *The End of Ideology: On the Exhaustion of Political Ideas in the Fifties*. Glencoe, IL: Free Press.

Bentham, J. (1969) 'A table of the Springs of Action', in P. McReynolds (ed.), *Four Early Works on Motivation*. Gainesville, FL: Scholars' Facsimiles. (Originally published 1815.)

Benton, E. (1974) 'Vitalism in nineteenth century scientific thought: a typology and reassessment', *Studies in History and Philosophy of Science*, 5: 17–48.

Bergman, G. and Spence, K.W. (1941) 'Operationism and theory in psychology', *Psychological Review*, 48: 1–14.

Bindra, D. (1985) 'Motivation, the brain, and psychological theory', in S. Koch and D.E. Leary (eds), *A Century of Psychology as Science*. New York: McGraw-Hill. pp. 338–363. (Reissued, American Psychological Association, 1992.)

Binet, A. (1903) *L'Étude expérimentale de l'intelligence*. Paris: Schleicher.

Binet, A. and Henri, V. (1895) 'La psychologie individuelle', *L'Année Psychologique*, 2: 411–465.

Binet, A. and Simon, T. (1916) *The Development of Intelligence in Children*, trans. E.S. Kite. Baltimore: Williams & Wilkins. (French original published 1905).

Birnbaum, L.T. (1965) 'Behaviorism: John Broadus Watson and American social thought'. PhD thesis, University of California, Berkeley.

Blake, R.R. and Wilson, G.P. (1950) 'Perceptual selectivity in Rorschach determinants as a function of depressive tendencies', *Journal of Abnormal and Social Psychology*, 45: 459–472.

Bloor, D. (1983) *Wittgenstein: A Social Theory of Knowledge*. New York: Columbia University Press.

Blumer, H. (1956) 'Sociological analysis and the "variable"', *American Sociological Review*, 21: 683–690.

Bogardus, E.S. (1925) 'Measuring social distance', *Journal of Applied Sociology*, 9: 299–308.

Boring, E.G. (1933) *The Physical Dimensions of Consciousness*. New York: Century.

Boring, E.G. (1942) *Sensation and Perception in the History of Experimental Psychology*. New York: Appleton Century Crofts.

Brock, A. (1994) 'Whatever happened to Karl Bühler?', *Canadian Psychology*, 35: 319–329.

Brooks, G.P. and Aalto, S.K. (1981) 'The rise and fall of moral algebra: Francis Hutcheson and the mathematization of psychology', *Journal of the History of the Behavioral Sciences*, 17: 343–356.

Brown, J. (1992) *The Definition of a Profession: The Authority of Metaphor in the History of Intelligence Testing 1890–1930*. Princeton, NJ: Princeton University Press.

Brown, T. (1831) *Lectures on the Philosophy of the Human Mind*, 2 vols. Hallowell: Glazier, Masters & Co. (Originally published 1820.)

Bryan, W.L. and Harter, N. (1899) 'Studies on the telegraphic language. The acquisition of a hierarchy of habits', *Psychological Review*, 6: 345–375.

Bühler, K. (1907–8) 'Tatsachen und Probleme zu einer Psychologie der Denkvorgänge', *Archiv für die gesamte Psychologie*, 9: 297–365; 12: 1–92.

Bühler, K. (1927) *Die Krise in der Psychologie*. Jena: Fischer.

Bühler, K. (1990) *Theory of Language: The Representational Function of Language*. Amsterdam/Philadelphia: John Benjamins. (German original published 1934.)

Burdach, K.F. (1826) *Die Physiologie als Erfahrungswissenschaft*. Leipzig: Voss.

Burgess, E.W. (1929) 'Basic social data', in T.V. Smith and L.D. White (eds), *Chicago: An Experiment in Social Science Research*. Chicago: University of Chicago Press. pp. 47–66. As cited in Lieberson (1985).

Butler, J. (1950) *Five Sermons Preached at the Rolls Chapel and a Dissertation upon the Nature of Virtue*. Indianapolis: Bobbs-Merrill. (Originally published 1726.)

Calhoun, D. (1973) *The Intelligence of a People*. Princeton, NJ: Princeton University Press.

Callahan, R.E. (1962) *The Cult of Efficiency*. Chicago: University of Chicago Press.

Canguilhem, G. (1955) *La Formation du concept de réflexe aux 17e et 18e siècles*. Paris: Presses Universitaires de France.

Canguilhem, G. (1988) *Ideology and Rationality in the History of the Life Sciences*. Cambridge, MA: MIT Press.

Canguilhem, G. (1989) *The Normal and the Pathological*. New York: Zone Books.

Cannon, W.B. (1929) *Bodily Changes in Pain, Hunger, Fear and Rage*. New York: Appleton-Century.

Cantril, H. (1950) 'An inquiry concerning the nature of man', *Journal of Abnormal and Social Psychology*, 45: 490–503.

Carpenter, W.B. (1857) 'The phasis of force', *National Review*, 4: 359–394.

Carpenter, W.B. (1874) *Principles of Mental Physiology with their Applications to the Training and Discipline of the Mind and the Study of its Morbid Conditions*. London: King.

Carson, J. (1993) 'Army alpha, army brass, and the search for army intelligence', *Isis*, 84: 278–309.

Carson, J. (1994) 'Intelligence and the construction of human difference in France and America'. PhD dissertation, Princeton University.

Carugati, F.F. (1990) 'Everyday ideas, theoretical models and social representations: the case of intelligence and its development', in G.R. Semin and K.J. Gergen (eds), *Everyday Understanding: Social and Scientific Implications*. London: Sage. pp. 130–150.

Cattell, J. McK. (1890) 'Mental tests and measurements', *Mind*, 15: 373–381.

Cattell, J. McK. (1904) 'The conceptions and methods of psychology', *Popular Science Monthly*, 66: 176–186. (Reprinted in A.T. Poffenberger (ed.) *James McKeen Cattell: Man of Science*, Lancaster, PA: Science Press, 1947.)

Cattell, R.B. (1943) 'The description of personality: basic traits resolved into clusters', *Journal of Abnormal and Social Psychology*, 38: 476–506.

Chen, W.K.C. (1933) 'The influence of oral propaganda material on students' attitudes', *Archives of Psychology*, 23(150): 1–43.

Claparède, E. (1903) 'The consciousness of animals', *International Quarterly*, 8: 296–315. (French original published 1901.)

Cohen, S. (1983) 'The mental hygiene movement, the development of personality and the school: the medicalization of American education', *History of Education Quarterly*, 23: 123–149.

Collins, S. (1985) 'Categories, concepts or predicaments?: remarks on Mauss's use of philosophical terminology', in M. Carrithers, S. Collins and S. Lukes (eds), *The Category of the Person: Anthropology, Philosophy, History*. Cambridge: Cambridge University Press. pp. 46–82.

Colvin, S.S. (1911) *The Learning Process*. New York: Macmillan.

Converse, J.M. (1987) *Survey Research in the United States: Roots and Emergence 1890–1960*. Berkeley: University of California Press.

Coulter, J. (1989) *Mind in Action*. Atlantic Highlands, NJ: Humanities Press.

Crapanzano, V. (1990) 'On self characterization', in J.W. Stigler, R.A. Shweder and G. Herdt (eds), *Cultural Psychology: Essays on Comparative Human Development*. Cambridge: Cambridge University Press. pp. 401–423.

Cravens, H. (1978) *The Triumph of Evolution: American Scientists and the Heredity-Environment Controversy 1900–1941*. Philadelphia, PA: University of Pennsylvania Press.

Cravens, H. (1985) 'The wandering IQ: American culture and mental testing', *Human Development*, 28: 113–130.

Danziger, K. (1982) 'Mid-nineteenth century British psycho-physiology: a neglected chapter in the history of psychology', in W.R. Woodward and M.G. Ash (eds), *The Problematic Science: Psychology in Nineteenth Century Thought*. New York: Praeger. pp. 119–146.

Danziger, K. (1983) 'Origins of the schema of stimulated motion: towards a pre-history of modern psychology', *History of Science*, 21: 183–210.

Danziger, K. (1990a) *Constructing the Subject: Historical Origins of Psychological Research*. Cambridge: Cambridge University Press.

Danziger, K. (1990b) 'Generative metaphor and the history of psychological discourse', in D.E. Leary (ed.), *Metaphors in the History of Psychology*. New York: Cambridge University Press. pp. 331–356.

Danziger, K. (1992a) 'The project of an experimental social psychology: historical perspectives', *Science in Context*, 5: 309–328.

Danziger, K. (1992b) 'Reiz und Reaktion', *Historisches Wörterbuch der Philosophie*, 8: 554–567. Basel: Schwabe.

Danziger, K. (1993) 'Psychological objects, practice, and history', *Annals of Theoretical Psychology*, 8: 15–47.

Danziger, K. (1997) 'The historical formation of selves', in R.D. Ashmore and L. Jussim (eds), *Rutgers Series on Self and Social Identity*, vol. 1: *Self and Identity: Fundamental Issues*. New York: Oxford University Press.

Danziger, K. and Dzinas, K. (1997) 'How psychology got its variables', *Canadian Psychology*.

Darwin, C. (1872) *The Expression of the Emotions in Man and Animals*. London: Murray.

Darwin, C. (1981) *The Descent of Man and Selection in Relation to Sex*. Princeton, NJ: Princeton University Press. (Originally published 1871.)

Darwin, E. (1794–96) *Zoonomia*. London: Johnson.

Dashiell, J.F. (1925) 'A quantitative demonstration of animal drive', *Journal of Comparative Psychology*, 5: 205–208.

Dashiell, J.F. (1928) *Fundamentals of Objective Psychology*. Boston: Houghton Mifflin.

Daston, L. (1992) 'The naturalized female intellect', *Science in Context*, 5: 209–235.

Deetz, S. (1994) 'The new politics of the workplace: ideology and other unobtrusive controls', in H.W. Simons and M. Billig (eds), *After Postmodernism: Reconstructing Ideology Critique*. London: Sage. pp. 172–199.

Descartes, R. (1931) 'The passions of the soul', in E.S. Haldane and G.R.T. Ross (trans.), *The Philosophical Works of Descartes*, vol. 1. Cambridge: Cambridge University Press. pp. 331–427.

Dessoir, M. (1902) *Geschichte der neueren deutschen Psychologie: von Leibniz bis Kant*. 2nd edn. Berlin: Duncker.

Dewey, J. (1894) 'The theory of emotion I. Emotional attitudes', *Psychological Review*, 1: 553–569.

Dewey, J. (1896) 'The reflex arc concept in psychology', *Psychological Review*, 3: 357–370.

Dewey, J. (1922) *Human Nature and Conduct*. New York: Henry Holt.

Dewey, J. (1930) *The Quest for Certainty*. London: Allen & Unwin.

Droba, D.D. (1933) 'The nature of attitude', *Journal of Social Psychology*, 4: 444–463.

Dumont, L. (1977) *From Mandeville to Marx: The Genesis and Triumph of Economic Ideology*. Chicago: University of Chicago Press.

Dzendolet, E. (1967) 'Behaviorism and sensation in the paper by Beer, Bethe, and von Uexküll (1899)', *Journal of the History of the Behavioral Sciences*, 3: 256–261.

Ebbinghaus, H. (1885) *Ueber das Gedächtnis: Untersuchungen zur experimentellen Psychologie*. Leipzig: Duncker & Humblot.

Ellenberger, H.F. (1970) *The Discovery of the Unconscious*. New York: Basic Books.

English, H.B. (1928) *A Student's Dictionary of Psychology*. 3rd edn. Yellow Springs: Antioch Press; New York: Harper & Bros.

Everson, S. (ed.) (1991) *Companions to Ancient Thought, 2: Psychology*. Cambridge: Cambridge University Press.

Fancher, R.E. (1985) *The Intelligence Men: Makers of the IQ Controversy*. New York: Norton.

Fancher, R.E. (1990) *Pioneers of Psychology*. 2nd edn. New York: Norton.

Faris, E. (1928) 'Attitudes and behavior', *American Journal of Sociology*, 34: 271–281.

Farr, J. (1989) 'Understanding conceptual change politically', in T. Ball, J. Farr and R.L. Hanson (eds), *Political Innovation and Conceptual Change*. Cambridge: Cambridge University Press. pp. 24–49.

Fechner, G. (1966) *Elements of Psychophysics*, vol. 1, trans. H.E. Adler. New York: Holt, Rinehart & Winston. (Originally published 1860.)

Ferrier, D. (1876) *The Functions of the Brain*. London: Smith, Elder.

Festinger, L. (1953) 'Laboratory experiments', in L. Festinger and D. Katz (eds), *Research Methods in the Behavioral Sciences*. New York: Holt, Rinehart & Winston. pp. 136–172.

Figlio, K. (1977) 'The historiography of scientific medicine: an invitation to the human sciences', *Comparative Studies in Society and History*, 19: 262–286.

Fiske, D.W. (1991) 'Macropsychology and micropsychology: natural categories and natural kinds', in R.E. Snow and D.E. Wiley (eds), *Improving Inquiry in Social Science*. Hillsdale, NJ: Erlbaum. pp. 61–74.

Fleming, D. (1967) 'Attitude: the history of a concept', *Perspectives in American History*, 1: 287–365.

Folsom, J.K. (1917) 'What can the psychology of interests, motives, and character contribute to vocational guidance?', *Journal of Applied Psychology*, 1: 253–264.

Foucault, M. (1977) *Discipline and Punish*. New York: Random House.

Foucault, M. (1986) *The Care of the Self: The History of Sexuality, Vol. 3*. New York: Pantheon.

Foucault, M. (1988) *Technologies of the Self*. Boston: University of Massachusetts Press.

Fox, C. (1988) *Locke and the Scribblerians: Identity and Consciousness in Early Eighteenth Century Britain*. Berkeley: University of California Press.

Freud, S. (1954) 'Project for a scientific psychology', in S. Freud, *The Origins of Psychoanalysis: Letters to Wilhelm Fliess, Drafts and Notes*. New York: Basic Books. pp. 347–445. (Original drafted 1895.)

Fromm, E. (1984) *The Working Class in Weimar Germany: A Social Psychological Study*. Cambridge, MA: Harvard University Press.

Frost, E. (1920) 'What industry wants and does not want from the psychologist', *Journal of Applied Psychology*, 4: 18–24.

Gadlin, H. and Ingle, G. (1975) 'Through the one-way mirror: the limits of experimental self-reflection', *American Psychologist*, 30: 1003–1009.

Gallup, G. and Rae, S.F. (1940) *The Pulse of Democracy*. New York: Simon & Schuster.

Galton, F. (1962) *Hereditary Genius*, 2nd edn. Cleveland: World Publishing. (Originally published London: Macmillan, 1869.)

Gardiner, H.M., Metcalf, R.C. and Beebe-Center, J.G. (1970) *Feeling and Emotion: A History of Theories*. Westport, CT: Greenwood Press. (Originally published 1937.)

Garrett, H.E. (1926) *Statistics in Psychology and Education*. New York: Longmans, Green.

Gergen, K.J. (1982) *Toward Transformation in Social Knowledge*. New York: Springer-Verlag.

Gergen, K.J. (1985) 'Social pragmatics and the origins of psychological discourse', in K.J. Gergen and K.E. Davis (eds), *The Social Construction of the Person*. New York: Springer. pp. 111–127.

Geuter, U. (1992) *The Professionalization of Psychology in Nazi Germany*. Cambridge: Cambridge University Press.

Gigerenzer, G. (1991) 'From tools to theories: a heuristic of discovery in cognitive psychology', *Psychological Review*, 98: 254–267.

Golinski, J.V. (1990) 'Language, discourse and science', in R.C. Olby, G.N. Cantor, J.R.R. Christie and M.J.S. Hodge (eds), *Companion to the History of Modern Science*. London: Routledge. pp. 110–123.

Goodman, N. (1978) *Ways of Worldmaking*. Indianapolis: Hackett.

Goodnow, J.J. (1984) 'On being judged "intelligent"', in P.S. Fry (ed.), *Changing Conceptions of Intelligence and Intellectual Functioning*. New York: North Holland. pp. 91–106.

Gould, S.J. (1981) *The Mismeasure of Man*. New York: Norton.

Gowin, E.B. (1917) *The Executive and his Control of Men: A Study of Personal Efficiency*. New York: Macmillan.

Graumann, C.F. (1986) 'The individualization of the social and the desocialization of the individual: Floyd H. Allport's contribution to social psychology', in C.F. Graumann and S. Moscovici (eds), *Challenging Conceptions of Crowd Mind and Behavior*. New York: Springer. pp. 97–116.

Gray, P.H. (1967) 'Spalding and his influence on research in developmental behavior', *Journal of the History of the Behavioral Sciences*, 3: 168–179.

Gray, P.H. (1968) 'Prerequisite to an analysis of behaviorism: the conscious automaton theory from Spalding to William James', *Journal of the History of the Behavioral Sciences*, 4: 365–376.

Greenwood, J.D. (1994) *Realism, Identity and Emotion*. London: Sage.

Gutting, G. (1990) 'Continental philosophy and the history of science', in R.C. Olby, G.N. Cantor, J.R.R. Christie and M.J.S. Hodge (eds), *Companion to the History of Modern Science*. London: Routledge. pp. 127–147.

Hacking, I. (1983) *Representing and Intervening*. New York: Cambridge University Press.

Hacking, I. (1986) 'Making up people', in T.C. Heller, M. Sosna and D.E. Wellerby (eds), *Reconstructing Individualism: Autonomy, Individuality, and the Self in Western Thought*. Stanford, CA: Stanford University Press. pp. 222–236.

Hacking, I. (1992) 'World-making by kind-making: child abuse for example', in M. Douglas and D. Hull (eds), *How Classification Works: Nelson Goodman among the Social Sciences*. Edinburgh: Edinburgh University Press. pp. 180–238.

Hacking, I. (1994) 'The looping effects of human kinds', in D. Sperber, D. Premack and A.J. Premack (eds), *Causal Cognition: A Multi-Disciplinary Approach*. Oxford: Clarendon Press. pp. 351–383.

Hacking, I. (1995) *Rewriting the Soul: Multiple Personality and the Sciences of Memory*. Princeton, NJ: Princeton University Press.

Haggerty, M.E. (1913) 'The laws of learning', *Psychological Review*, 20: 411–422.

Hall, M. (1836) *Lectures on the Nervous System and its Diseases*. London: Sherwood, Gilbert & Piper.

Hallam, J.R. (1994) 'Some constructionist observations on "anxiety" and its history', in T.R. Sarbin and J.I. Kitsuse (eds), *Constructing the Social*. London: Sage. pp. 139–156.

Haller, A. (1922) *Von den empfindlichen und reizbaren Teilen des Körpers*, ed. K. Sudhoff. Leipzig: J.A. Barth. (Originally published 1753.)

Haller, A. (1966) *First Lines of Physiology*, ed. L.S. King. New York: Johnson Reprint. (Originally published 1757–66.)

Hamilton, W. (1863) *Lectures on Metaphysics*. 2nd edn. Boston: Gould & Lincoln.

Hanson, F.A. (1993) *Testing Testing*. Berkeley: University of California Press.

Harré, R. and Gillett, G. (1994) *The Discursive Mind*. London: Sage.

Harris, J.A. (1909) 'The correlation of a variable and the deviation of a dependent variable from its probable value', *Biometrika*, 6: 438–443.

Hart, H. (1933) 'Changing social attitudes and interests', in *Recent Social Trends in the United States: Report of the President's Research Committee on Social Trends*, vol. 1. New York: McGraw-Hill. pp. 382–442.

Hartley, D. (1749) *Observations on Man, His Frame, His Duty, and His Expectations*. London.

(Reprinted Scholars' Facsimiles, Gainesville FL, 1966; and Georg Olms, Hildesheim, 1967.)

Harwood, J. (1983) 'The IQ in history', *Social Studies of Science*, 13: 465–477.

Hebb, D.O. (1949) *The Organization of Behavior*. New York: Wiley.

Heelas, P. (1986) 'Emotion talk across cultures', in R. Harré (ed.), *The Social Construction of Emotions*. Oxford: Blackwell. pp. 234–266.

Herder, J.G. (1778) 'Vom Erkennen und Empfinden der menschlichen Seele', in B. Suphan (ed.), *Herder's Sämtliche Werke*, vol. 8. Hildesheim: Olms, 1967.

Hirschman, A.O. (1977) *The Passions and the Interests: Political Arguments for Capitalism before its Triumph*. Princeton, NJ: Princeton University Press.

Hoff, T. (1990) 'Theories of body expression in their historical relationship to psychological concepts', PhD dissertation, York University, Toronto.

Holland, H. (1852) *Chapters on Mental Physiology*. London: Longman, Brown, Green & Longman.

Hollingworth, H.L. (1928) *Psychology, its Facts and Principles*. New York: Appleton.

Holt, E.B. (1915) *The Freudian Wish and its Place in Ethics*. New York: Henry Holt.

Holzinger, K.J. (1928) *Statistical Methods for Students in Education*. Boston: Ginn.

Horkheimer, M. (1947) *The Eclipse of Reason*. New York: Oxford University Press.

Hübner, K. (1983) *Critique of Scientific Reason*. Chicago: University of Chicago Press.

Hull, C.L. (1943a) 'The problem of intervening variables in molar behavior theory', *Psychological Review*, 50: 273–291.

Hull, C.L. (1943b) *Principles of Behavior*. New York: Appleton-Century.

Hume, D. (1978) *A Treatise of Human Nature*, ed. L.A. Selby-Bigge, 2nd edn, revised by P.H. Nidditch. Oxford: Clarendon Press. (Originally published 1739.)

Humphrey, G. (1951) *Thinking*. London; Methuen.

Hutcheson, F. (1969) *An Essay on the Nature and Conduct of the Passions and Affections with Illustrations on the Moral Sense*. Gainesville, FL: Scholars' Facsimiles. (Originally published 1728.)

Huxley, T.H. (1874) 'On the hypothesis that animals are automata, and its history', *Fortnightly Review*, 22: 555–580.

Ingleby, D. (1990) 'Problems in the study of the interplay between science and culture', in F.J.R. van de Vijver and G.J.M. Hutschemaekers (eds), *The Investigation of Culture: Current Issues in Cultural Psychology*. Tilburg: Tilburg University Press. pp. 59–73.

Jackson, J.H. (1931) *Selected Writings of Hughlings Jackson*, vol. 1, ed. J. Taylor. London: Staples.

James, W. (1890) *Principles of Psychology*, 2 vols. New York: Henry Holt.

James, W. (1904) 'The Chicago School', *Psychological Bulletin*, 1: 1–5.

James, W. (1911) *On Vital Reserves*. New York: Henry Holt.

James, W. (1983) 'Person and personality', in F. Burckhardt (ed.), *Essays in Psychology: William James*. Cambridge, MA: Harvard University Press. pp. 315–321. (Originally published 1895.)

Jaspars, J. and Fraser, C. (1984) 'Attitudes and social representations', in R.M. Farr and S. Moscovici (eds), *Social Representations*. Cambridge: Cambridge University Press. pp. 101–123.

Jaynes, J. (1976) *The Origins of Consciousness in the Breakdown of the Bicameral Mind*. Boston: Houghton Mifflin.

Jennings, H.S. (1899) 'The psychology of a protozoan', *American Journal of Psychology*, 10: 503–515.

Jennings, H.S. (1904) 'The behavior of Paramecium', *Journal of Comparative Neurology and Psychology*, 14: 441–510.

Jennings, H.S. (1906) *Behavior of the Lower Organisms*. New York: Columbia University Press. (Reprinted Indiana University Press, 1962.)

Jones, D.C. (1921) *First Course in Statistics*. London: Bell.

Jowett, B. (1892) *The Dialogues of Plato*, vol. 2, 3rd edn. London: Oxford University Press.

Kagan, J. (1988) 'The meaning of personality predicates', *American Psychologist*, 43: 614–620.

Kagan, J. (1989) *Unstable Ideas: Temperament, Cognition, and Self.* Cambridge, MA: Harvard University Press.

Kames, Lord (1970) *Elements of Criticism.* New York: Georg Olms. (Originally published 1762.)

Katz, D. and Braly, K. (1933) 'Racial stereotypes of one hundred college students', *Journal of Abnormal and Social Psychology*, 28: 280–290.

Kaye, F.B. (ed.) (1924) *The Fable of the Bees: or Private Vices, Publick Benefits by Bernard Mandeville*, 2 vols. Oxford: Clarendon Press.

Kelley, T.L. (1923) *Statistical Method.* New York: Macmillan.

Kevles, D.J. (1968) 'Testing the army's intelligence: psychologists and the military in World War I', *Journal of American History*, 55: 565–581.

Kirkpatrick, J.T. (1985) 'Some Marquesan understandings of action and identity', in G.M. White and J. Kirkpatrick (eds), *Person, Self, and Experience: Exploring Pacific Ethnopsychologies.* Berkeley: University of California Press. pp. 80–120.

Kitayama, S. and Markus, H.R. (1994) 'The cultural construction of self and emotion: implications for social behavior', in S. Kitayama and H.R. Markus (eds), *Emotion and Culture: Empirical Studies of Mutual Influence.* Washington, DC: American Psychological Association. pp. 89–130.

Kitchener, R.F. (1977) 'Behavior and behaviorism', *Behaviorism*, 5: 11–71.

Knight, F.B. and Remmers, H.H. (1923) 'Fluctuations in mental production when motivation is the only variable', *Journal of Applied Psychology*, 7: 209–223.

Knorr Cetina, K. (1992) 'The couch, the cathedral, and the laboratory: on the relationship between experiment and laboratory science', in A. Pickering (ed.), *Science as Practice and Culture.* Chicago: University of Chicago Press. pp. 113–138.

Koch, S. (1951) 'The current status of motivational psychology', *Psychological Review*, 58: 147–154.

Koch, S. (1956) 'Behavior as "intrinsically" regulated: work notes towards a pre-theory of phenomena called "motivational"', in M.R. Jones (ed.), *Nebraska Symposium on Motivation 1956.* Lincoln: University of Nebraska Press. pp. 42–86.

Koch, S. (1959) 'Suggested discussion topics for contributors of systematic analyses' and 'Epilogue', in S. Koch (ed.), *Psychology: A Study of a Science*, vol. 3. New York: McGraw-Hill. pp. 713–723 and 729–788.

Koffka, K. (1935) *Principles of Gestalt Psychology.* New York: Harcourt Brace.

Köhler, W. (1925) *The Mentality of Apes*, 2nd edn. New York: Harcourt Brace.

Krantz, D.L. and Allen, D. (1967) 'The rise and fall of McDougall's instinct doctrine', *Journal of the History of the Behavioral Sciences*, 3: 326–338.

Kraus, S.J. (1995) 'Attitudes and the prediction of behavior: a meta-analysis of the empirical literature', *Personality and Social Psychology Bulletin*, 21: 58–75.

Kugelmann, R. (1992) *Stress: The Nature and History of Engineered Grief.* Westport: Praeger.

Kuna, D. (1979) 'Early advertising applications of the Gale-Cattell order-of-merit method', *Journal of the History of the Behavioral Sciences*, 15: 36–46.

Lakoff, G. (1987) *Women, Fire, and Dangerous Things: What Categories Reveal about the Mind.* Chicago: University of Chicago Press.

Lapointe, F.H. (1972) 'Who originated the term "psychology"?' *Journal of the History of the Behavioral Sciences*, 8: 328–335.

Laycock, T. (1845) 'On the reflex functions of the brain', *British and Foreign Medical Review*, 19: 298–311.

Laycock, T. (1860) *Mind and Brain.* Edinburgh: Sutherland & Knox.

Leary, D.E. (1990) 'William James on self and personality', in M.G. Johnson and T.B. Henley (eds), *Reflections on The Principles of Psychology: William James after a Century.* Hillsdale, NJ: Erlbaum. pp. 101–137.

Lee, V.L. (1983) 'Behavior as a constituent of conduct', *Behaviorism*, 11: 199–224.

Lewes, G.H. (1877) *The Physical Basis of Mind.* Boston: Osgood.

Lewontin, R.C. (1975) 'Genetic aspects of intelligence', *Annual Review of Genetics*: 387–405.

Lewontin, R.C. (1985) 'The analysis of variance and the analysis of causes', in R. Levins and R. Lewontin, *The Dialectical Biologist.* Cambridge, MA: Harvard University Press. pp. 109–122.

Leys, R. (1990a) *From Sympathy to Reflex: Marshall Hall and his Opponents.* New York: Garland.

Leys, R. (1990b) 'Adolph Meyer: a biographical note', in R. Leys and R.B. Evans (eds), *Defining American Psychology: The Correspondence between Adolf Meyer and Edward Bradford Titchener.* Baltimore, MD: Johns Hopkins University Press. pp. 39–57.

Lieberson, S. (1985) *Making it Count: The Improvement of Social Research and Theory.* Berkeley: University of California Press.

Lippmann, W. (1922) *Public Opinion.* New York: Macmillan.

Lloyd, G.E.R. (1992) 'Methods and problems in the history of ancient science', *Isis,* 83: 564–577.

Locke, J. (1959) *An Essay concerning Human Understanding,* ed. A.C. Fraser. New York: Dover. (Originally published 1690–1700.)

Locke, J. (1980) *Second Treatise of Government,* ed. C.B. Macpherson. Indianapolis: Hackett. (Originally published 1690.)

Lotze, R.H. (1853) 'Pflüger's Die sensoriellen Functionen etc.', *Göttinger gelehrte Anzeigen,* 3: 1737–1776.

Lutz, C.A. (1988) *Unnatural Emotions: Everyday Sentiments on a Micronesian Atoll and their Challenge to Western Theory.* Chicago: University of Chicago Press.

Lutz, C.A. and Abu-Lughod, L. (eds) (1990) *Language and the Politics of Emotion.* Cambridge: Cambridge University Press.

McClelland, D.C., Atkinson, J.W., Clark, R.A. and Lowell, E.L. (1953) *The Achievement Motive.* New York: Appleton-Century-Crofts.

McDougall, W. (1908) *An Introduction to Social Psychology.* London: Methuen.

McDougall, W. (1912) *Psychology: The Study of Behaviour.* London: Williams & Norgate.

McDougall, W. (1932) 'On the words character and personality', *Character and Personality,* 1: 3–16.

McDougall, W. (1933) *The Energies of Men.* London: Methuen.

MacIntyre, A. (1984) *After Virtue,* 2nd edn. Notre Dame, IN: University of Notre Dame Press.

Mackenzie, B.D. (1977) *Behaviourism and the Limits of Scientific Method.* London: Routledge & Kegan Paul.

McLeod, J. (1992) 'The story of Henry Murray's diagnostic council: a case study in the demise of a scientific method', *Clinical Psychology Forum,* 44: 6–12.

MacLeod, R.B. (1975) *The Persistent Problems of Psychology.* Pittsburgh: Duquesne University Press.

Malebranche, N. (1980) *The Search after Truth.* Trans. T.H. Lennon and P.J. Olscamp. Columbus, OH: Ohio State University Press. (Originally published 1674.)

Mandler, J.M. and Mandler, G. (1964) *Thinking: from Association to Gestalt.* New York: Wiley.

Manicas, P.T. (1987) *A History and Philosophy of the Social Sciences.* Oxford: Blackwell.

Marcuse, H. (1956) *Eros and Civilization.* London: Routledge & Kegan Paul.

Markus, G. (1987) 'Why is there no hermeneutics of natural sciences? Some preliminary theses', *Science in Context,* 1: 5–51.

Markus, H.R. and Kitayama, S. (1991) 'Culture and the self: implications for cognition, emotion, and motivation', *Psychological Review,* 98: 224–253.

Maslow, A.H. (1954) *Motivation and Personality.* New York: Harper & Row.

Mayer, A. and Orth, J. (1901) 'Zur qualitativen Untersuchung der Association', *Zeitschrift für Psychologie,* 26: 1–13.

Mayrhauser, R.T. von (1987) 'The manager, the medic, and the mediator: the clash of professional psychological styles and the wartime origins of group mental testing', in M.M. Sokal (ed.), *Psychological Testing and American Society 1890–1930.* New Brunswick, NJ: Rutgers University Press. pp. 128–157.

Mayrhauser, R.T. von (1991) 'The practical language of American intellect', *History of the Human Sciences*, 4: 371–393.

Mayrhauser, R.T. von (1992) 'The mental testing community and validity', *American Psychologist*, 47: 224–253.

Mead, G.H. (1912) 'The mechanism of social consciousness', *Journal of Philosophy, Psychology, and Scientific Method*, 9: 401–406 (Reprinted in A.J. Reck, ed., 1964, *Selected Writings: George Herbert Mead*. Chicago: University of Chicago Press. pp. 134–141.)

Mead, G.H. (1924/25) 'The genesis of the self and social control', *International Journal of Ethics*, 35: 251–277. (Reprinted in A.J. Reck, ed., 1964, *Selected Writings: George Herbert Mead*. Chicago: University of Chicago Press. pp. 267–293.)

Mead, G.H. (1934) *Mind, Self, and Society from the Standpoint of a Social Behaviorist*. Chicago: University of Chicago Press.

Medin, D.L. (1989) 'Concepts and conceptual structure', *American Psychologist*, 44: 1469–1481.

Messer, A. (1906) 'Experimentell-psychologische Untersuchungen über das Denken', *Archiv für die gesamte Psychologie*, 8: 1–224.

Meumann, E. (1908) *Oekonomie und Technik des Gedächtnisses: Experimentelle Untersuchungen über das Merken und Behalten*. 2nd edn. Leipzig: Klinkhardt.

Meumann, E. (1913) *The Psychology of Learning: An Experimental Investigation of the Economy and Technique of Memory*. New York: Appleton.

Meyer, M.F. (1911) *The Fundamental Laws of Human Behavior*. Boston: Badger.

Miller, E.F. (1971) 'Hume's contribution to behavioral science', *Journal of the History of the Behavioral Sciences*, 7: 154–168.

Mills, J.A. (1997) *Hard Nosed Psychologists: A History of Behaviorism*. New York: New York University Press.

Möller, H.-J. (1975) *Die Begriffe 'Reizbarkeit' und 'Reiz'*. Stuttgart: G. Fischer.

Morgan, C.L. (1886) 'On the study of animal intelligence', *Mind*, 11: 174–185.

Morgan, C.L. (1891) *Animal Life and Intelligence*. Boston: Ginn.

Morgan, C.L. (1892) 'The limits of animal intelligence', *Nature*, 46: 417.

Morgan, C.L. (1894) *An Introduction to Comparative Psychology*. London: Walter Scott.

Morgan, C.L. (1898) 'Instinct and intelligence in animals', *Nature*, 57: 326–330.

Morgan, C.L. (1900) *Animal Behavior*. London: Arnold.

Morgan, C.L. (1930) *The Animal Mind*. New York: Longmans, Green.

Moss, F.A. (1924) 'Study of animal drives', *Journal of Experimental Psychology*, 7: 165–185.

Müller, J. (1826) *Zur vergleichenden Physiologie des Gesichtssinnes des Menschen und der Thiere*. Leipzig: C. Cnobloch.

Müller, J. (1838–42) *Elements of Physiology*, trans. W. Baly. London: Taylor & Walton. (Originally published 1833.)

Murphy, G., Murphy, L.B. and Newcomb, T.M. (1937) *Experimental Social Psychology*. New York: Harper.

Murray, H.A. (1938) *Explorations in Personality*. New York: Oxford University Press.

Myers, C.S., Carr, H.W., Morgan, C.L. and McDougall, W. (1910) 'Instinct and intelligence', *British Journal of Psychology*, 3: 209–270.

Nelson, E. (1939) 'Attitudes', *Journal of General Psychology*, 21: 367–399, 401–416.

Nelson, K. (1991) 'Concept development in the perspective of the recent history of developmental psychology', in F.S. Kessel, M.H. Bornstein and A.J. Sameroff (eds), *Contemporary Constructions of the Child*. Hillsdale, NJ: Erlbaum. pp. 93–109.

Nicholson, I. (1996) 'Moral projects and disciplinary practices: Gordon Allport and the development of American personality psychology'. PhD dissertation, York University, Toronto.

Nickles, T. (1989) 'Justification and experiment', in D. Gooding, T. Pinch and S. Schaffer (eds), *The Uses of Experiment: Studies in the Natural Sciences*. Cambridge: Cambridge University Press. pp. 299–333.

Nissen, H.W. (1954) 'The nature of the drive as innate determinant of behavioral organization', in M.R. Jones (ed.), *Nebraska Symposium on Motivation 1954*. Lincoln: University of Nebraska Press. pp. 281–321.

O'Donnell, J.M. (1985) *The Origins of Behaviorism: American Psychology, 1870–1920*. New York: New York University Press.

Overstreet, H.A. (1925) *Influencing Human Behavior*. New York: Norton.

Oxford English Dictionary (1989) 2nd edn. London: Oxford University Press.

Paicheler, G. (1988) *The Psychology of Social Influence*. Cambridge: Cambridge University Press.

Parker, J.D.A. (1991) 'In search of the person: the historical development of American personality psychology'. PhD dissertation, York University, Toronto.

Parmelee, M. (1911) *The Science of Human Behavior: Biological and Psychological Foundations*. New York: Macmillan.

Pauly, P.J. (1987) *Controlling Life: Jacques Loeb and the Engineering Ideal in Biology*. New York: Oxford University Press.

Pavlov, I.P. (1932) 'Reply of a physiologist to psychologists', *Psychological Review*, 39: 91–127.

Pearson, K. (1904) 'On the laws of inheritance in man. II. On the inheritance of the mental and moral characters and its comparison with the inheritance of the physical characters', *Biometrika*, 3: 131–190.

Pearson, K. (1906) 'On the relationship of intelligence to size and shape of head and to other physical and mental characters', *Biometrika*, 5: 105–146.

Pearson, K. (1910) 'On a new method of determining correlation, when one variable is given by alternative and the other by multiple categories', *Biometrika*, 7: 248–257.

Pechstein, L.A. (1917) 'Whole vs. part methods in motor learning', *Psychological Monographs*, 23(2): 1–80.

Perrin, F.A.C. (1923) 'The psychology of motivation', *Psychological Review*, 30: 176–191.

Perrin, F.A.C. (1932) *Psychology, its Methods and Principles*. New York: Holt.

Peters, R.S. (1958) *The Concept of Motivation*. London: Routledge & Kegan Paul.

Pflüger, E. (1853) *Die sensorischen Functionen des Rückenmarks der Wirbelthiere nebst einer neuen Lehre über die Leitungsgesetze der Reflexionen*. Berlin: A. Hirschwald.

Piaget, J. (1950) *The Psychology of Intelligence*. London: Routledge & Kegan Paul.

Pillsbury, W.B. (1911) *The Essentials of Psychology*. New York: Macmillan.

Pillsbury, W.B. (1921) *The Essentials of Psychology*, 2nd edn. New York: Macmillan.

Pingree, D. (1992) 'Hellenophilia versus the history of science', *Isis*, 83: 554–563.

Poffenberger, A.T. (1927) *Applied Psychology: Its Principles and Methods*. New York: Appleton.

Pongratz, L.J. (1967) *Problemgeschichte der Psychologie*. Bern: Francke.

Porter, T.M. (1995) *Trust in Numbers: The Pursuit of Objectivity in Science and Public Life*. Princeton, NJ: Princeton University Press.

Post, D.L. (1980) 'Floyd L. Allport and the launching of modern social psychology', *Journal of the History of the Behavioral Sciences*, 16: 369–376.

Prince, M. (1905) *The Dissociation of a Personality: A Biographical Study in Abnormal Psychology*. New York: Longmans, Green.

Putnam, H. (1981) *Reason, Truth and History*. Cambridge: Cambridge University Press.

Putnam, H. (1991) *Representation and Reality*. Cambridge, MA: MIT Press.

Reeve, C.D.C. (1992) *Practices of Reason*. Oxford: Clarendon Press.

Reil, J.C. (1910) *Von der Lebenskraft*. Leipzig: J.A. Barth. (Originally published 1795.)

Ribot, T. (1885) *Les Maladies de la personalité*. Paris: Alcan.

Richards, G.D. (1987) 'Of what is the history of psychology a history?', *British Journal for the History of Science*, 20: 201–211.

Richards, G.D. (1989) *On Psychological Language*. London: Routledge.

Richards, G.D. (1992) *Mental Machinery. I: The Origins and Consequences of Psychological Ideas from 1600 to 1850*. London: Athlone Press.

Richards, I.A. (1932) *Mencius on the Mind: Experiments in Multiple Definition*. London: Routledge & Kegan Paul.

Richards, R.J. (1987) *Darwin and the Emergence of Evolutionary Theories of Mind and Behavior*. Chicago: University of Chicago Press.

Richardson, R.F. (1912) 'The learning process in the acquisition of skill', *Pedagogical Seminary*, 19: 376–394.

Richter, C.P. (1927) 'Animal behavior and internal drives', *Quarterly Review of Biology*, 2: 307–343.

Ringer, F. (1990) 'The intellectual field, intellectual history, and the sociology of knowledge', *Theory and Society*, 19: 269–294.

Ritter, J. and Gründer, K. (eds) (1989) *Historisches Wörterbuch der Philosophie*, vol. 7. Basel: Schwabe.

Roback, A.A. (1927) *The Psychology of Character*. New York: Harcourt, Brace.

Romanes, G.J. (1882) *Animal Intelligence*. London; Kegan Paul, Trench.

Romanes, G.J. (1884) *Mental Evolution in Animals*. New York: Appleton.

Rosaldo, M. (1980) *Knowledge and Passion: Ilongot Notions of Self and Social Life*. Cambridge: Cambridge University Press.

Rose, N. (1985) *The Psychological Complex: Psychology, Politics and Society in England 1869–1939*. London: Routledge & Kegan Paul.

Rose, N. (1988) 'Calculable minds and manageable individuals', *History of the Human Sciences*, 1: 179–200.

Rose, N. (1990) *Governing the Soul: The Shaping of the Private Self*. London: Routledge.

Rose, N. (1996) *Inventing Our Selves: Psychology, Power and Personhood*. Cambridge: Cambridge University Press.

Rosenzweig, S. (1933) 'The experimental situation as a psychological problem', *Psychological Review*, 40: 337–354.

Ross, D. (1991) *The Origins of American Social Science*. New York: Cambridge University Press.

Ross, E.A. (1908) *Social Psychology: An Outline and Source-Book*. New York; Macmillan.

Rouse, J. (1987) *Knowledge and Power: Toward a Political Philosophy of Science*. Ithaca, NY: Cornell University Press.

Rudolphi, K.A. (1821–23) *Grundriss der Physiologie*. Berlin: F. Dümmler.

Runkel, P.J. (1990) *Casting Nets and Testing Specimens: Two Grand Methods of Psychology*. New York: Praeger.

Russell, J.A. (1991) 'Culture and the categorization of emotions', *Psychological Bulletin*, 110: 426–450.

Samelson, F. (1975) 'On the science and politics of the IQ', *Social Research*, 42: 467–488.

Samelson, F. (1979) 'Putting psychology on the map: ideology and intelligence testing', in A.R. Buss (ed.), *Psychology in Social Context*. New York: Irvington. pp. 103–168.

Samelson, F. (1981) 'Struggle for scientific authority: the reception of Watson's behaviorism, 1913–1920', *Journal of the History of the Behavioral Sciences*, 17: 399–425.

Samelson, F. (1985) 'Organization for the kingdom of behavior: academic battles and organizational policies in the twenties', *Journal of the History of the Behavioral Sciences*, 21: 33–47.

Scheerer, E. (1989) 'Psychologie', *Historisches Wörterbuch der Philosophie*, 7: 1599–1653.

Schiff, M. and Lewontin, R.C. (1986) *Education and Class: The Irrelevance of IQ Genetic Studies*. Oxford: Clarendon Press.

Schmeidler, G.R. and Allport, G.W. (1944) 'Social psychology and the civilian war effort', *Journal of Social Psychology*, 20: 145–180.

Schneider, W.H. (1992) 'After Binet: French intelligence testing, 1900–1950', *Journal of the History of the Behavioral Sciences*, 28: 111–132.

Sechenov, I.M. (1965) *Reflexes of the Brain*, trans. S. Belsky. Cambridge, MA: MIT Press. (Originally published 1863.)

Semin, G.R. (1990) 'Everyday assumptions, language and personality', in K.J. Gergen and G.R. Semin (eds), *Everyday Understandings: Social and Scientific Implications*. London: Sage. pp. 151–175.

Senn, P.R. (1966) 'What is "behavioral science"? – notes towards a history', *Journal of the History of the Behavioral Sciences*, 2: 107–122.

Sharp, S.E. (1899) 'Individual psychology: a study in psychological method', *American Journal of Psychology*, 10: 329–391.

Shea, C.M. (1980) 'The ideology of mental health and the emergence of the therapeutic liberal state: the American Mental Hygiene Movement, 1900–1930'. PhD dissertation, University of Illinois, Urbana-Champaign.

Sherman, M. (1932) 'Theories and measurement of attitudes', *Child Development*, 3: 15–28.

Sherrington, C.S. (1961) *The Integrative Action of the Nervous System*. New Haven: Yale University Press. (Originally published 1906.)

Shotter, J. (1990) *Knowing of the Third Kind: Selected Writings on Psychology, Rhetoric, and the Culture of Everyday Social Life*. Utrecht: ISOR.

Shweder, R.A. and Bourne, E.J. (1984) 'Does the concept of the person vary cross-culturally?', in R.A. Shweder and R.A. LeVine (eds), *Culture Theory: Essays on Mind, Self and Emotion*. Cambridge: Cambridge University Press. pp. 158–199.

Simmons, R. (1924) 'Relative effectiveness of certain incentives in animal learning', *Comparative Psychology Monographs*, 2(7): 1–79.

Singer, E.A. (1912) 'On mind as an observable object', *Journal of Philosophy, Psychology and Scientific Method*, 9: 206–214.

Skinner, Q. (1988a) 'Meaning and understanding in the history of ideas', in J. Tully (ed.), *Meaning and Context: Quentin Skinner and his Critics*. Princeton, NJ: Princeton University Press. pp. 29–67.

Skinner, Q. (1988b) 'Language and social change', in J. Tully (ed.), *Meaning and Context: Quentin Skinner and his Critics*. Princeton, NJ: Princeton University Press. pp. 119–132.

Smedslund, J. (1984) 'What is necessarily true in psychology?', *Annals of Theoretical Psychology*, 2: 241–303.

Smedslund, J. (1991) 'The pseudoempirical in Psychology and the case for Psychologic', *Psychological Inquiry*, 2: 325–338.

Smith, J. (1981) 'Self and experience in Maori culture', in P. Heelas and A. Lock (eds), *Indigenous Psychologies: The Anthropology of the Self*. London: Academic Press. pp. 145–159.

Smith, K. (1984) '"Drive": in defense of a concept', *Behaviorism*, 12: 71–114.

Smith, R. (1988) 'Does the history of psychology have a subject?', *History of the Human Sciences*, 1: 147–177.

Smith, R. (1992) *Inhibition: History and Meaning in the Sciences of Mind and Brain*. London: Free Association Books.

Snell, B. (1953) *The Discovery of the Mind: The Greek Origins of European Thought*. Cambridge, MA: Harvard University Press.

Solomon, R. (1976) *The Passions*. New York: Anchor/Doubleday.

Sommer, R. (1892) *Grundzüge einer Geschichte der deutschen Psychologie und Aesthetik*. Würzburg: Stahel.

Sorabji, R. (1979) 'Body and soul in Aristotle', in J. Barnes, M. Schofield and R. Sorabji (eds), *Articles on Aristotle*. London; Duckworth. pp. 42–64.

Sorabji, R. (1993) *Animal Minds and Human Morals: The Origins of the Western Debate*. Ithaca, NY: Cornell University Press.

Sparshott, F. (1994) *Taking Life Seriously*. Toronto: University of Toronto Press.

Spearman, C. (1904a) '"General intelligence", objectively determined and measured', *American Journal of Psychology*, 15: 202–293.

Spearman, C. (1904b) 'The proof and measurement of association between two things', *American Journal of Psychology*, 15: 72–101.

Spearman, C. (1923) *The Nature of Intelligence and the Principles of Cognition*. London: Macmillan.

Spearman, C. (1937) *Psychology down the Ages*. London: Macmillan.

Spencer, H. (1871) *The Principles of Psychology*, 2nd edn. London: Williams & Norgate.

Stagner, R. (1937) *Psychology of Personality*. New York: McGraw-Hill.

Stearns, C.Z. and Stearns, P.N. (eds) (1988) *Emotions and Social Change: Toward a New Psychohistory*. New York and London: Holmes & Meier.

Still, A. (1987) 'Tolman's perception', in A. Costall and A. Still (eds), *Cognitive Psychology in Question*. Brighton: Harvester Press. pp. 176–193.

Stouffer, S.A. et al. (1949–50) *Studies in Social Psychology in World War II*. Princeton, NJ: Princeton University Press.

Strong, E.K. (1918) 'The learning process', *Psychological Bulletin*, 15: 328–343.

Strong, E.K. Jr. (1925) *The Psychology of Selling and Advertising*. New York: McGraw-Hill.

Strong, E.K. Jr. and Loveless, J.E. (1926) '"Want" and "solution" advertisements', *Journal of Applied Psychology*, 10: 346–366.

Sullivan, S. Darcus (1988) *Psychological Activity in Homer: A Study of Phren*. Ottawa: Carleton University Press.

Susman, W.I. (1979) '"Personality" and the making of twentieth century culture', in J. Higham and P.K. Conkin (eds), *New Directions in American Intellectual History*. Baltimore, MD: Johns Hopkins University Press. pp. 212–226.

Swift, E.J. (1903) 'Studies in the psychology and physiology of learning', *American Journal of Psychology*, 14: 201–251.

Swift, E.J. (1904) 'The acquisition of skill in typewriting: a contribution to the psychology of learning', *Psychological Bulletin*, 1: 295–305.

Swift, E.J. and Schuyler, W. (1907) 'The learning process', *Psychological Bulletin*, 4: 307–310.

Symonds, P.M. (1927) 'What is an attitude?', *Psychological Bulletin*, 24: 200–201.

Symonds, P.M. (1931) *Diagnosing Personality and Conduct*. New York: Century.

Taine, H.A. (1872) *On Intelligence*. New York: Holt & Williams. (French original published 1870.)

Taylor, C. (1985) *Human Agency and Language*. Cambridge: Cambridge University Press.

Taylor, C. (1989) *Sources of the Self: The Making of the Modern Identity*. Cambridge, MA: Harvard University Press.

Thomas, W.I. and Znaniecki, F. (1918) *The Polish Peasant in Europe and America*. Boston: Badger.

Thomson, G.H. (1920) 'General versus group factors in mental activities', *Psychological Review*, 27: 173–190.

Thomson, J. (1832) *An Account of the Life, Lectures and Writings of William Cullen, M.D.* Edinburgh: W. Blackwood.

Thomson, M.K. (1927) *The Springs of Human Action: A Psychological Study of the Sources, Mechanisms, and Principles of Motivation in Human Behavior*. New York: Appleton.

Thorndike, E.L. (1902) *The Human Nature Club*. New York: Longmans, Green.

Thorndike, E.L. (1911) *Animal Intelligence*. New York: Macmillan.

Thorndike, E.L. (1913) *Educational Psychology*, vol. 2: *The Psychology of Learning*. New York: Teachers College, Columbia University.

Thorndike, E.L. et al. (1921) 'Intelligence and its measurement: a symposium', *Journal of Educational Psychology*, 12: 121–272.

Thurstone, L.L. (1928) 'Attitudes can be measured', *American Journal of Psychology*, 33: 529–554.

Thurstone, L.L. (1930) 'A scale for measuring attitude toward the movies', *Journal of Educational Research*, 22: 89–94.

Thurstone, L.L. (1952) 'Autobiography', in E.G. Boring, H.S. Langfeld, H. Werner and R.M. Yerkes (eds), *A History of Psychology in Autobiography*, vol. 4. New York: Russell & Russell. pp. 295–321.

Thurstone, L.L. (1959) *The Measurement of Values*. Chicago: University of Chicago Press.

Titchener, E.B. (1909) *Lectures on the Experimental Psychology of the Thought Processes*. New York: Macmillan.

Tolman, E.C. (1932) *Purposive Behavior in Animals and Men*. New York: Century.

Tolman, E.C. (1951) 'Operational behaviorism and current trends in psychology', in E.C. Tolman, *Behavior and Psychological Man*. Berkeley: University of California Press. pp. 115–129. (Originally published 1936.)

Toulmin, S. (1977) 'Self-knowledge and knowledge of the "self"', in T. Mischel (ed.), *The Self: Psychological and Philosophical Issues.* Oxford: Blackwell. pp. 291–317.

Treviranus, G.R. (1822) *Biologie, oder Philosophie der lebenden Natur für Naturforscher und Aerzte,* vol. 6. Göttingen: J.F. Röwer.

Triplet, R.G. (1992) 'Henry A. Murray: the making of a psychologist', *American Psychologist,* 47: 299–307.

Troland, L.T. (1928) *The Fundamentals of Human Motivation.* New York: Van Nostrand. (Reprinted Hafner, New York, 1967.)

Tryon, R.C. (1929) 'The interpretation of the correlation coefficient', *Psychological Review,* 36: 419–445.

Tseëlon, E. (1991) 'The method is the message: on the meaning of methods as ideologies', *Theory and Psychology,* 1: 299–316.

Tufts, J.H. (1904) 'The individual and his relation to society as reflected in the British ethics of the eighteenth century', *Psychological Review Monographs,* 6(25).

Uhrbrock, R.S. (1933) 'Measuring attitudes of 4,500 factory workers', *Psychological Bulletin,* 30: 733–734.

Underwood, B.J. (1949) *Experimental Psychology.* New York: Appleton-Century-Crofts.

van der Veer, R. and Valsiner, J. (1991) *Understanding Vygotsky: A Quest for Synthesis.* Oxford and Cambridge, MA: Blackwell.

Vernon, P.E. (1933) 'The American v. the German methods of approach to the study of temperament and personality', *British Journal of Psychology,* 24: 156–177.

Verwey, G. (1985) *Psychiatry in an Anthropological and Biomedical Context.* Dordrecht: D. Reidel.

Vetter, G.B. (1930) 'The study of social and political opinions', *Journal of Abnormal and Social Psychology,* 25: 26–39.

von Staden, H. (1992) 'Affinities and elisions: Helen and Hellenocentrism', *Isis,* 83: 578–595.

Wahlsten, D. (1994) 'The intelligence of heritability', *Canadian Psychology,* 35: 244–260.

Walker, H.M. (1929) *Studies in the History of Statistical Method.* Baltimore, MD: Williams and Wilkins.

Warden, C.J. (1931) *Animal Motivation: Experimental Studies on the Albino Rat.* New York: Columbia University Press.

Warren, H.C. (1922) *Elements of Human Psychology.* Boston: Houghton Mifflin.

Washburn, M.F. (1916) *Movement and Mental Imagery.* Boston: Houghton Mifflin.

Washburn, M.F. (1936) *The Animal Mind: A Textbook of Comparative Psychology.* 4th edn. New York: Macmillan.

Wasmann, E. (1897) *Instinkt und Intelligenz im Thierreich: Ein kritischer Beitrag zur modernen Thierpsychologie.* Freiburg: Herder.

Watson, J.B. (1913) 'Psychology as the behaviorist views it', *Psychological Review,* 20: 158–177.

Watson, J.B. (1914) *Behavior: An Introduction to Comparative Psychology.* New York: Henry Holt.

Watson, J.B. (1919) *Psychology from the Standpoint of a Behaviorist.* Philadelphia: Lippincott.

Watson, R.I. (1971) 'Prescriptions as operative in the history of psychology', *Journal of the History of the Behavioral Sciences,* 7: 311–322.

Webb, L.W. (1917) 'Transfer of training and retroaction', *Psychological Monographs,* 23(3): 1–90.

Weimer, W.B. (1974) 'The history of psychology and its retrieval from historiography: I. The problematic nature of history', *Science Studies,* 4: 235–258.

Weiner, B. (1992) *Human Motivation: Metaphors, Theories and Research.* Newbury Park, CA: Sage.

Weintraub, K.J. (1978) *The Value of the Individual: Self and Circumstance in Autobiography.* Chicago: University of Chicago Press.

Wertheimer, M. (1945) *Productive Thinking.* New York: Harper.

Wertsch, J.V. (1985) *Vygotsky and the Social Formation of Mind.* Cambridge, MA: Harvard University Press.

White, G.M. (1985) 'Premises and purposes in a Solomon Islands ethnopsychology', in G.M. White and J. Kirkpatrick (eds), *Person, Self, and Experience: Exploring Pacific Ethnopsychologies*. Berkeley: University of California Press. pp. 328–366.

White, G.M. (1992) 'Ethnopsychology', in T. Schwartz, G.M. White and C.A. Lutz (eds), *New Directions in Psychological Anthropology*. Cambridge: Cambridge University Press. pp. 21–46.

White, G.M. (1994) 'Affecting culture: emotion and morality in everyday life', in S. Kitayama and H.R. Markus (eds), *Emotion and Culture: Empirical Studies of Mutual Influence*. Washington, DC: American Psychological Association. pp. 219–239.

Whytt, R. (1768) *Works*. Edinburgh: Balfour. (Originally published 1751.)

Wierzbicka, A. (1995) 'Emotion and facial expression: a semantic perspective', *Culture and Psychology*, 1: 227–258.

Wiley, N. (1986) 'Early American sociology and the *Polish Peasant*', *Sociological Theory*, 4: 20–40.

Wilkes, K.V. (1988) *Real People: Personal Identity without Thought Experiments*. Oxford: Clarendon Press.

Williams, R. (1976) *Keywords: A Vocabulary of Culture and Society*. London: Fontana/Croom Helm.

Wilson, H.B. and Wilson, G.M. (1916) *The Motivation of School Work*. Boston: Houghton Mifflin.

Winston, A.S. (1988) '*Cause* and *Experiment* in Introductory Psychology: an analysis of R.S. Woodworth's textbooks', *Teaching of Psychology*, 15: 79–83.

Winston, A.S. (1990) 'Robert Sessions Woodworth and the "Columbia Bible": how the psychological experiment was redefined', *American Journal of Psychology*, 103: 391–401.

Winston, A.S. and Blais, D.J. (1996) 'What counts as an experiment?: A trans-disciplinary analysis of textbooks, 1930–1970', *American Journal of Psychology*, 109: 599–616.

Wittgenstein, L. (1953) *Philosophical Investigations*. Oxford: Blackwell.

Wober, M. (1974) 'Towards an understanding of the Kiganda concept of intelligence', in J.W. Berry and P.R. Dasen (eds), *Culture and Cognition: Readings in Cross-Cultural Psychology*. London: Methuen. pp. 261–280.

Wolf, T.H. (1973) *Alfred Binet*. Chicago: University of Chicago Press.

Woodworth, R.S. (1918) *Dynamic Psychology*. New York: Columbia University Press.

Woodworth, R.S. (1921) *Psychology: A Study of Mental Life*. New York: Henry Holt.

Woodworth, R.S. (1924) 'Four varieties of behaviorism', *Psychological Review*, 31: 257–264.

Woodworth, R.S. (1927) 'Gestalt psychology and the concept of reaction stages', *American Journal of Psychology*, 39: 62–69.

Woodworth, R.S. (1930) 'Dynamic psychology', in C. Murchison (ed.), *Psychologies of 1930*. Worcester, MA: Clark University Press. pp. 327–336.

Woodworth, R.S. (1934) *Psychology*. 3rd edn. New York: Henry Holt.

Woodworth, R.S. (1938) *Experimental Psychology*. New York: Holt, Rinehart & Winston.

Woodworth, R.S. (1939) *Psychological Issues: Selected Papers of Robert S. Woodworth*. New York: Columbia University Press.

Woodworth, R.S. (1961) 'R.S. Woodworth', in C. Murchison (ed.), *A History of Psychology in Autobiography*. New York: Russell & Russell. pp. 359–380.

Woodworth, R.S. and Schlosberg, H. (1954) *Experimental Psychology*, revised edn. New York: Holt, Rinehart & Winston.

Wundt, W. (1874) *Grundzüge der physiologischen Psychologie*. Leipzig: Engelmann.

Wundt, W. (1894) *Lectures on Human and Animal Psychology*, 2nd edn. New York: Macmillan. (German original published 1892.)

Young, K. (ed.) (1931) *Social Attitudes*. New York: Henry Holt.

Young, P.T. (1936) *Motivation of Behavior: The Fundamental Determinants of Human and Animal Activity*. New York: Wiley.

Young, R.M. (1966) 'Scholarship and the history of the behavioural sciences', *History of Science*, 5: 1–51.

Young, R.M. (1970) *Mind, Brain, and Adaptation in the Nineteenth Century*. Oxford: Clarendon Press.

Yule, G. Udny (1911) *An Introduction to the Theory of Statistics*. London: Griffin.

Zenderland, L. (1987) 'The debate over diagnosis: Henry Herbert Goddard and the medical acceptance of intelligence testing', in M. Sokal (ed.), *Psychological Testing and American Society 1890–1930*. New Brunswick, NJ: Rutgers University Press. pp. 46–74.

INDEX

Lightning Source UK Ltd.
Milton Keynes UK
08 March 2010

151091UK00001B/33/A